THE BUILDING E

CONNEC

D1324918

Ah Lek

2

Alan J. Brookes

Chris Grech

WITHDRAWN

Architectural Press

Architectural Press
An imprint of Butterworth-Heinemann
Linacre House, Jordan Hill, Oxford OX2 8DP
A division of Reed Educational and Professional Publishing Ltd

$\mathcal{R}$ A member of the Reed Elsevier plc group

OXFORD   BOSTON   JOHANNESBURG
MELBOURNE   NEW DELHI   SINGAPORE

First published separately as *The Building Envelope* 1990
and *Connections* 1992
Combined edition 1996

British Library Cataloguing in Publication Data

A catalogue record for this title is available from the British Library

ISBN 0 7506 3096 5

Printed and bound in Great Britain by The Bath Press, Bath

Contents: The Building Envelope

1   **The Bandstand at Haarlem**   2
Wiek Roling with Mick Eekhout

2   **Benthem and Crouwel's House at Almere**   5
Benthem & Crouwel

3   **The Burrell Gallery, Glasgow**   10
Barry Gasson

4   **Boyatt Wood Hostel for the Disabled**   13
Hampshire County Council Architects'
Department

5   **Clarke Ascot House, Brisbane**   19
Chris Clarke

6   **Conservatory at Kew**   22
Property Services Agency

7   **Cribbs Causeway Warehouses, Bristol**   26
Building Design Partnership

8   **The Customs House, Hazeldonk**   31
Benthem & Crouwel

9   **Darling Harbour Exhibition Centre**   34
Philip Cox and Partners

10   **The Devonshire Building, Boston, Mass.**   39
Steffian & Bradley Associates

11   **1 Finsbury Avenue, London (Phase 1)**   41
Arup Associates

12   **IBM Travelling Technology Exhibition**   46
Renzo Piano

13   **Johnson and Johnson World Headquarters,
New Brunswick, New Jersey**   50
I.M. Pei & Partners

14   **Lloyds of London: Atrium**   54
Richard Rogers Partnership

15   **Locomotive Shed, Preston Dock**   58
Brock Carmichael Associates

16   **The Menil Museum, Houston, Texas**   61
Renzo Piano

17   **Museum at Kempsey, New South Wales**   64
Glenn Murcutt

18   **Oculenti Contact Lens Factory, Holland**   66
Thijs Asselbergs

19   **Operations Center for Philip Morris (USA)**   71
Davis Brody & Associates

20   **Parc de la Villette, Paris**   74
Adrien Fainsilber and Rice, Francis and Ritchie

21   **Parsons House, London**   78
Peter Bell & Partners

22   **Patscenter, Princeton, New Jersey**   81
Richard Rogers Partnership

23   **The Richard J. Hughes Justice Complex,
Trenton, New Jersey**   85
Grad/Hillier

24   **Sainsbury's Supermarket at Canterbury**   89
Ahrends Burton & Koralek

25   **Schlumberger Cambridge Research Centre**   72
Michael Hopkins & Partners

26   **Sorting Office, Hemel Hempstead**   97
Aldington, Craig & Collinge

27   **Stansted Airport Terminal Building, Essex**   101
Foster Associates

28   **Swindon Leisure Centre**   107
Borough of Thamesdown Architects'
Department

29   **The Trading Building, Haarlem**   109
Cepezed

30   **'Yacht House' System, Woodgreen**   112
Richard Horden Associates

31   **Victoria Plaza Canopy, London**   116
Heery Architects & Engineers Ltd

32   **Hongkong and Shanghai Bank, Hong Kong**   122
Foster Associates

33   **New Studios and Galleries, Liverpool**   127
Lloyd King & Rod McAllister

Acknowledgements   133

Contents: Connections

1 **Bari Football Stadium** 136
Renzo Piano Building Workshop

2 **Bercy Charenton Shopping Centre, Paris** 140
Renzo Piano Building Workshop

3 **Billingsgate Market Refurbishment, London** 144
Richard Rogers Partnership

4 **Bracken House, London** 149
Michael Hopkins and Partners

5 **Church at Buseno, Switzerland** 154
Mario Campi and Franco Pessina

6 **Crescent Wing, Norwich** 158
Foster Associates

7 **David Mellor Cutlery Factory, Sheffield** 163
Michael Hopkins and Partners

8 **East Croydon Station** 168
Brookes Stacey Randall Fursdon

9 **338 Euston Road, London** 172
Sheppard Robson

10 **Financial Times Building, London** 176
Nicholas Grimshaw and Partners

11 **Finland Lion Lighthouse, Baltic Sea** 180
Esko Lehesmaa

12 **Glass Music Hall, Amsterdam** 184
Pieter Zaanen in association with Mick Eekhout

13 **Hotel Saint James, Bordeaux** 188
Jean Nouvel

14 **Imagination, London** 191
Herron Associates

15 **Interflora Pavilion, Genoa** 196
Alessandro Savioli and Valeria Lelli

16 **Kindergarten, Lausanne** 200
Rodolphe Luscher

17 **Museum of Local History, Hamburg** 204
Von Gerkan, Marg and Partner

18 **Music School, Karlsruhe** 208
Staatliches Hochbauamt I Karlsruhe

19 **One-family House, Lyons** 212
Jourda et Perraudin

20 **Reina Sofia Museum of Modern Art, Madrid** 215
Ian Ritchie Architects in association with Iñiguez & Vazquez

21 **Rover Building, Tokyo** 220
Richard Rogers Partnership

22 **Royal Life, Peterborough** 226
Arup Associates

23 **School of Architecture, Lyons** 230
Jourda et Perraudin

24 **School of Woodland Industry, Dorset** 235
Ahrends, Burton and Koralek

25 **Sculpture Pavilion, Sonsbeek, The Netherlands** 239
Benthem Crouwel Architekten

26 **Sterling Hotel, Heathrow Airport** 243
Manser Associates

27 **Sydney Football Stadium** 247
Phillip Cox, Richardson, Taylor and Partners Pty Ltd

28 **Tent, Hans Road, London** 252
Whitby & Bird Engineers

29 **Tent for the 700th Anniversary of the Swiss Confederation** 255
Mario Botta

30 **Visitors' Centre, Cardiff Bay** 259
Alsop Störmer

Acknowledgements 262

Preface

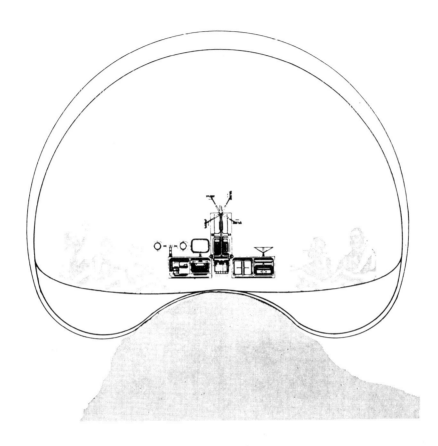

1

*Modern architecture is a progressive force formed
by the conditions of modern life.*[1]

This collection of case studies combines the highly
acclaimed volumes, *The Building Envelope* and *Connections*, placing the details of good modern buildings in
context with each other and explaining the relationship
between them. Thus the authors provide an essential
database for designers working in the field of large-scale
construction.

We have frequently found that many architects and
architectural students are hungry for knowledge of the
new techniques of building. It is surprising how quickly a
detail published in an architectural magazine can enter
the student repertoire; details published one week in the
Architects' Journal or *Architectural Review* will turn up on
a students' scheme the next week, often quoted out of
context.

Architectural criticism of buildings frequently deals
only with their spatial aspects. One possible explanation
for this is that the critics themselves may lack the
necessary information required to make a technical
appraisal. Thus it was easy for Martin Pawley[1] to claim
that 'architecture is an occult workload of ignorance and

obsolete mystery shot through with individual acts of
achievement'.

The process of building can be extremely complicated. Not only are contractual procedures different
due to the emergence of Management Contracts and
Performance Specifications, but the sourcing of the
component parts of a modern building can also be very
complex. Seldom are components processed at a single
source. Thus the aluminium reflectors at the Crescent
Wing of the Sainsbury Centre UEA were spun in
Newcastle, hand polished in Thetford, electroplated in
Birmingham, anodized in Scotland and assembled in
Norwich. In a similar way the superform aluminium
panels for Gatwick Airport North Piers were formed to
shape in Worcester, painted in France, returned to
Birmingham for lamination and erected in Gatwick.
Architects are often unaware that the components are
being multisourced and have difficulty in controlling the
quality of the supplied components. The contractor may
also lack the understanding for the processes involved
and the resulting standards that can be reasonably
expected from his subcontractors.

Students of architecture, although often familiar with
the images of Modern Architecture, are rarely aware of

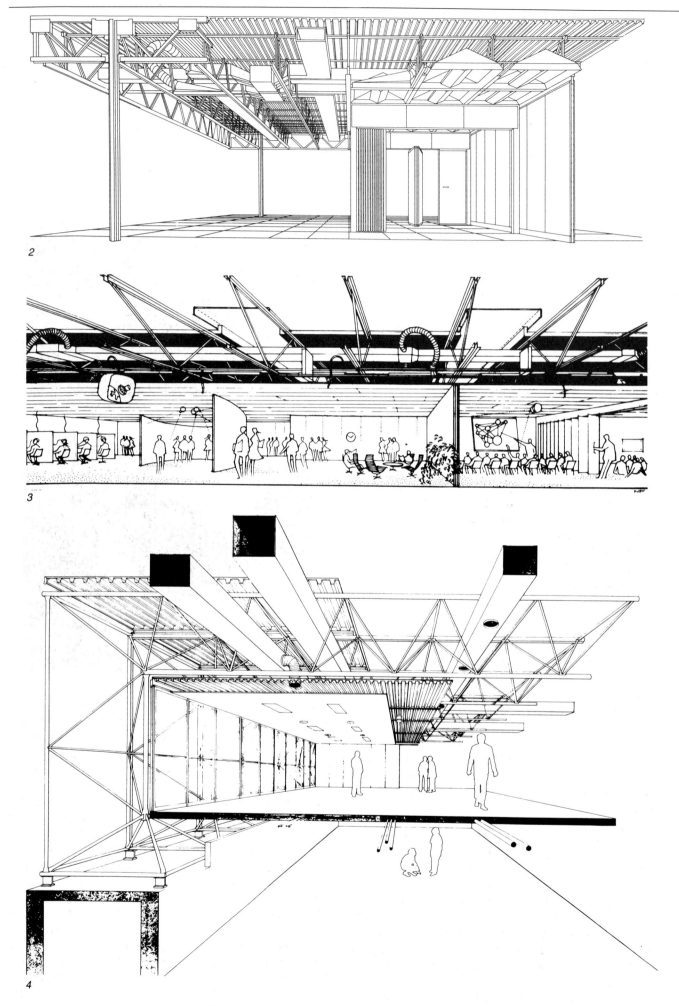

2

3

4

1
*François Dallegret's
environmental bubble*

2
*School Construction Systems
Development, commenced
1961*

3
*Newport Comprehensive
School Competition
submission, Foster
Associates, 1967*

4
*B+B Italia, Como, Piano
Rogers, 1973*

5
*Lloyds Building, London,
Richard Rogers Partnership
with Ove Arup and Partners.
Precast concrete atrium
double bracket*

6
*Bracken House London,
Michael Hopkins and
Partners with Ove Arup and
Partners. Soffit of precast
concrete beam at column
node*

the demands of specification on which the details are based. For this reason details are often used out of their proper context or even without reference to their cost implications. In this book we cannot hope to cover the complexity of the process but can only warn against the assumption that all details have a common derivation or purpose and the particular reasons which led to their use should always be questioned.

It is also our intention to highlight the craft of modern design and the possibilities that new materials present in generating spaces, their means of environmental control and general influence on the form of buildings. The specialist subcontractor responding to a Performance Specification set by the architect is the new craftsman of current construction. At East Croydon Station the extruded aluminium masts with cast stainless steel fittings represent a high degree of design, engineering and craftsmanship. This all adds to the appearance of the overall design in the same way that a Georgian window frame responded to the environmental requirements and techniques of production of its own time.

This concern for detailing the appropriate means to address production and quality control demands a new role and level of responsibility for architects. Modern building design and construction relies on close co-operation from clients, architects, engineers, quantity surveyors, contractors, subcontractors and material suppliers. To be effective each needs the means of conducting a satisfactory dialogue. Precedent studies are a useful means in encouraging a greater understanding of each other's needs.

In 1957, Konrad Wachsmann[2] wrote: 'Human and aesthetic ideas will receive new impulses through the uncompromising application of contemporary knowledge and ability . . . The machine is the tool of our age. It is the cause of those effects through which social order manifests itself'.

Although the language may have changed, construction has not become post-industrial. Building is now the collation of factory-made items bounded by *in-situ* construction. The machine has moved from the building site to the factory. The modern architect thus needs to know the parameters of the manufacturing process and its related quality-control procedures in the same way that he or she was traditionally involved in the site process.

The architect must also communicate with, and gain the trust of, those involved in the manufacturing process who maintain these specialist skills. No book on construction or case studies of cladding systems can replace the accumulated knowledge of staff in these firms of manufacturers, architects and engineers. They

5

6

can, however, give an introduction to the state of the art by showing a precedent, and thus imbue confidence in architects so that they can approach a manufacturer with a reasonable working knowledge of what is feasible. This book is therefore meant as a contribution to that debate.

Practising architects often compare notes on the selection of manufacturers who have the specialist knowledge and the management skills necessary to carry out their intended form of assembly. Architects will often have their own list of persons or companies most knowledgeable in a certain area. Technical consultants assisting the Project Team to source the manufacturers and assist in interpreting the performance requirements of a particular project will take with them knowledge of detailing from one job to another. In this way, for example, the use of precast concrete beams and their overlapping *in situ* cast connections at Bracken House by John Thornton at Ove Arup and Partners, was derived from his previous experience of designing similar connections for the Lloyds Building, originally conceived as a steel framed building. Working closely with the con-

We agreed then on the good things we have in Common. On the advantage of being able to test yourself, not depending on others in the test, reflecting yourself in your work. On the pleasure of seeing your creature grow, beam after beam, bolt after bolt, solid, necessary, symmetrical, suited to its purpose and when it's finished you look at it and you think that perhaps it will live longer than you, and perhaps it will be of use to someone you don't know, who doesn't know you. Maybe, as an old man, you'll be able to come back and look at it, and it will seem beautiful, and it doesn't really matter so much that it will seem beautiful only to you, and you can say to yourself 'maybe another man wouldn't have brought it off'.[4]

crete subcontractor, the consultant engineers developed an integral structural form using their accumulated knowledge base.

Students, as part of their practical training, often associate themselves with the better informed practices where the experience gained from the building process is conveyed to other members of that office formally or by word of mouth. Most of the larger practices have specialized Research and Development units to assist in collating experience from a project basis. In the same way that ideas and techniques were conveyed to apprentices in the Italian Renaissance Master's workshop, similar knowledge of modern techniques is being passed around the profession by key individuals who may be architects, engineers, contractors or manufacturers' representatives. Connections can often be identified between different projects due to the individuals involved. The expressed air handling at the IBM Travelling Exhibition can be compared with those of the Lloyds Building and it may be no accident that the authors of both schemes worked together on the Pompidou Centre when such ideas may have been formed. Individuals moving from one practice to another often take with them a design vocabulary or knowledge of the building process. Such cross-fertilization frequently produces similar hybrid solutions.

'High Tech' is a misnomer. It is not a style of architecture as such, but more of an attitude towards design, taking account of and being involved in the process of construction. Technology-led architecture can be seen as a natural development for the Modern Movement in architecture allowing the use of appropriate technology to inform the designer's intentions. Some authors have identified a thread through Paxton, Prouvé, Gropius, Waschmann, Ehrencrantz, Foster and so on. Certainly Foster Associates' 1967 entry for the Newport comprehensive School Competition translated the California School Construction Systems Development (SCSD) concepts to the UK, which in turn became a forerunner for their IBM building. There is also a remarkable similarity between the perspective defining the four main elements of the SCSD system, roof, deck, services and partitions, and that of a similar view of the B+B Italia Office building in Como, Italy by Piano Rogers produced 10 years later.

There is continued debate on how education/practice can improve the architect's skill. Some in education praise those architecture schools which concentrate on concepts, metaphors and images in design, while others argue that, as well as offering ingredients of vision, we must also embrace the more objective issues of the process of building. In these circumstances, there is a pressing need for teachers to be able to give tutorial advice and then make an informed assessment of the content of the student's submission.

We are not arguing the case for a mystique of construction; quite the reverse. Students should be encouraged to relax into the production of precise constructional information, and be given the confidence to provide a further level of definition to their designs. It is the rigour with which they question current detailing and innovation which will be the foundation stone for their time in practice.

The essential issues of cost and specification are as yet under-described in the educational process. Nor is the process of collaboration necessary within a complete design team well communicated, or modelled, in schools of architecture. Too often the architect is still described in terms of a lone hero.

Whatever criticisms we may receive from outside or within the building industry, it cannot be denied that design transforms circumstance. The creative contribution of architects can be the prime stimulus to the construction process and the motivation of the project team. A well-considered design can save on the overall time and cost of the building. Time in the design development stage can be repaid tenfold by enabling the efficiency of the site process.

Mies van der Rohe[3] said: 'Some people are convinced that architecture will be outmoded and replaced by technology. Such conviction is not based on clear thinking. The opposite happens. Wherever technology reaches its real fulfillment it transcends into architecture'. This philosophy allows the design team to offer not just technology but also a previously unimaginable consideration of space, form and architecture. Innovation can be a route to certainty; if specifications are highly controlled and suitable testing undertaken, this can be a way to achieve robust architecture, not a source of risk.

There is, or ought to be, a clear connection between design and construction in architecture. The understanding of construction should be a joy which informs design ideas. This book is intended in its small way to give at least some inspiration to designers wishing to improve their technical understanding of the newer building processes with which they are now involved and have the information available if they care to seek it.

References

References

1. Pawley, M., 'Technology Transfer,' *Architectural Review*, No. 1087, September 1987, pp. 31–39.
2. Wachsmann, K., *The Turning Point of Building*, Reinhold, New York, 1961.
3. Mies van der Rohe, L., *Speech to Institute of Technology*, Chicago, 1950.
4. Levi, P., *The Wrench*, Sphere Books, 1990

Further reading

Klotz, H., *Vision der Moderns*, Prestel Verlag, Munich, 1986.

Russel, B., *Building Systems, Industrialisation and Architecture*, John Wiley, Chichester, 1981.

Ackermann, K., Industriebau, Deutsche Verlas-Anstalt, Stuttgart, 1984.

Buckminster Fuller, R., *Inventions – the Patented Works of R. Buckminster Fuller*, St Martin's Press, New York, 1983.

Griffoen, A., *Techniek in Bouw en Industrie*, Stichting Bouwresearch, Rotterdam, 1984.

Ogg, A., *Architecture in Steel – the Australian Context*, Royal Australian Institute of Architects, 1987.

Huber, B. and Steiegger, J. C., *Jean Prouvé*, Les Editions d'Architecture Artemis, Zurich, 1971.

Sebastyen, G., *Lightweight Building Construction*, George Godwin, London, 1977.

THE BUILDING ENVELOPE
Applications of New Technology Cladding

1

The Bandstand at Haarlem
Architect
Wiek Roling with Mick Eekhout

1.1.

1.1.
General view of bandstand

1.2.
Basic Tuball node without glazing. 1 Special aluminium casting of main body of node; 2 aluminium casting of top of node bolted down to main body; 3 tubular member with end plate drilled and threaded to fit onto bolt projecting from node

1.3.
Bruno Taut's 1914 Glass House

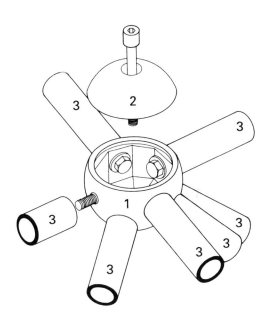

1.2.

1.3.

General

This small music pavilion at Haarlem in Holland (Figure 1.1), which was the winner of a limited competition, has been included here not only for its elegant design, standing on ten fixed pillars on a podium, but also because it demonstrates clearly how a glazed panel can be fitted to a space frame construction. This is a detail requirement which often puzzles students of architecture attempting to fix external panels to a space frame where the nodes clearly are required to project above and below the tubular space-frame connectors.

The other factor to note in this case is the detail of the node itself, with no bolts or nuts to distract the eye. The only visible elements are spherical cast aluminium nodes and extruded aluminium tubular bars, all painted in white, with the glazing between (Figure 1.2).

Inevitably, some comparison must be made with Bruno Taut's Glass House for the Werkbund Exhibition at Cologne of 1914 (Figure 1.3), possibly because of the proportions of the columns to dome or the relationship of the diamond-shaped glass panels. In the case of the Bandstand, however, these diamond shapes are produced with two sheets of triangular glazing with a round rather than pointed dome. It is here that the similarities of construction end. The intention, however, in both cases was to achieve a building with standardized components, and the Bandstand can be seen as a modern example of the latest glazing techniques in the same way that Taut's Glass House promoted the use of glass and therefore the German glass industries that paid for it.

Structure

The structure comprises 10 steel columns with fixed connections to a tubular steel perimeter member serrated to form a semi-hexagonal edge (Figure 1.4) on which the Tuball-type space frame by Octatube is supported. This space frame comprises an extruded aluminium bar which also acts to support the glazing above. This is cunningly cut back at its connection with the nodes (formed by using aluminium castings) so that the form of the castings become visually apparent to the observer (Figure 1.5). The triangular glazed sections (originally designed as polycarbonate) are fixed to the glazing member by an aluminium plate with external bolt connections (Figure 1.6).

It is perhaps unfortunate that the glazing has suffered so much from vandalism, and therefore subsequent ro sealing of this plating member has led to a more untidy condition of the corner plate connections than had no re-sealing been necessary.

References

Eekhout, M., 'An architectural generation of space structures', Paper, First Internat. Conf. on Lightweight Structures in Architecture, Sydney, Australia, August 1986, published by Unisearch Ltd, University of NSW (August 1986), pp. 96–103.

Eekhout, M., 'Het vormgeven van aluminium tot ruimtelijke contructies', Alutech Conf., Utrecht, Feb. 1988.

Eekhout, M., 'Architecture in space structures', PhD thesis, Delft, 1989.

1.4.
Tubular steel columns supporting a serrated périmeter edge beam

1.5.
Tuball glazed space frame node. 1 Spherical aluminium casting; 2 aluminium struts extruded with flange to take glazing assembly, cut away at node; 3 glazing; 4 cover plate

1.6.
Aluminium cover plates with external bolt fixings

1.4.

1.6.

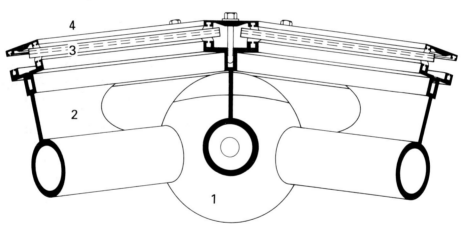
1.5.

Benthem and Crouwel's House at Almere
Architects
Benthem and Crouwel

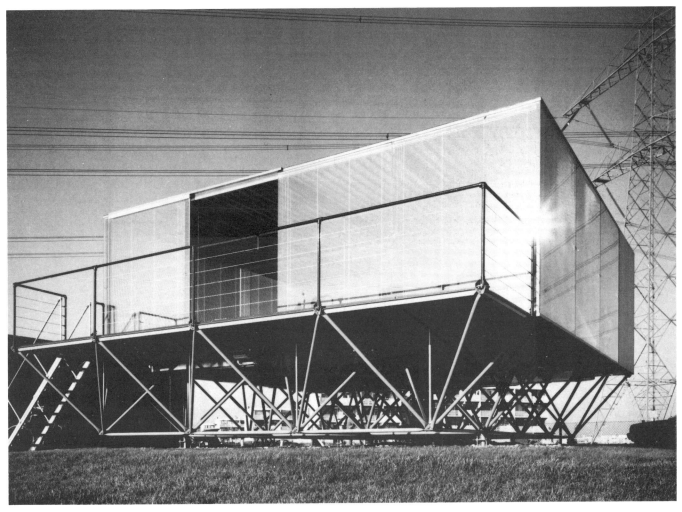

2.1. General view

General

Built on a site in Almere, a new town near Amsterdam, Holland, this design was one of 10 prizewinning entries for a 1982 open-brief competition requiring a structure capable of being dismantled and removed from the site after five years. The prize won the use of the site within that time (Figure 2.1).

Benthem and Crouwel's design attempts to disturb the site as little as possible by resting the modular house on a proprietary steel space frame which is supported at four points on precast concrete industrial flooring slabs. The house is designed to minimal space standards and is planned on a 2 m grid derived from the length (2 m) of a bunk bed (Figure 2.2). Two bedrooms are arranged either side of the kitchen and bathroom, all grouped along one wall of the building. These form the 'solid' part of the walls, while remaining space is taken by the entirely glazed living space with a balcony leading from it.

The glazing is structural, supporting the roof which is flat. The brief of the competition required only structural stability and fire regulations to be adhered to. Benthem and Crouwel decided to use lightweight, low-cost, high-performance materials to enable the building to be demountable and relocated.

The space frame

The space frame is a proprietary steel frame by Octatube (Delft) with octagonal connectors at 2 m centres (Figure 2.3). The struts of the frame are 50 mm diameter tubular steel with flattened ends bolted to connecting plate formed by a 5 mm thick octagonal steel plate. The space frame is connected to four precast concrete industrial flooring slabs, 2 m square, 160 mm deep, placed directly on the ground. In order to allow levelling and for settlement adjustment the fixing plates are connected with thick steel plates, with a sleeved joint which prevents

2.2.
(a) Plan. 1 Bedroom; 2 kitchen; 3
bathroom; 4 living room; 5 heat
exchanger; 6 underfloor heating
ducts; 7 balcony; 8 sliding door.
(b) Section. 1 Living room ; 2
bathroom; 3 heat exchanger; 4
insulated supply ducts to
perimeter grilles; 5 services entry
point

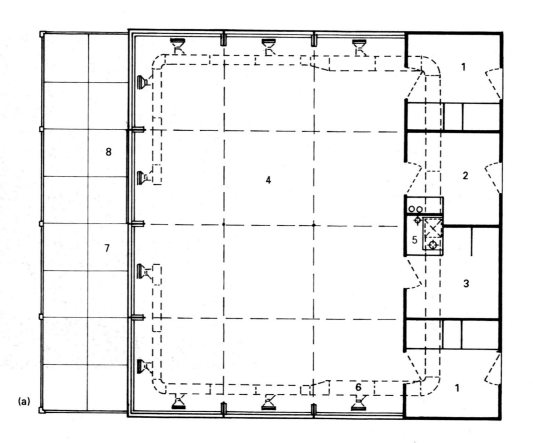

(a)

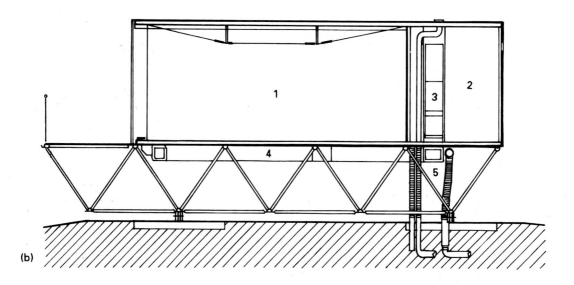

2.2.   (b)

6

2.3.
Octagonal space frame
connectors

2.4.
Sleeved space frame support
detail. 1 Precast concrete base; 2
levelling bolts; 3 sleeved circular
hollow sections; 4 octagonal
space frame connector; 5
flattened tube struts

lateral movement but allows vertical adjustment using
four bolts fixed to the slabs with chemical anchors
(Figure 2.4).

The floor

The floor decking consists of a sandwich panel of 5 mm
plywood on a 30 mm high-density polyurethane foam
core bolted directly to the space-frame substructures.
The upper chord members of the space frame are
omitted, the sandwich floor acting as an upper chord
allowing the integration of bending and compression
forces. To prevent sagging of the floor above the space
frame, 37 × 67 mm timber battens were bonded to the
upper face of the panels at 400 mm centres and a further
skin of 18 mm plywood screwed to them (total thickness,
95 mm). The balcony was made from steel industrial floor
gratings, bolted directly to the space frame.

2.3.

Solid wall panels

The solid panels forming bedroom, bathroom and kitch-
en walls are made of a sandwich of 5 mm skins of
plywood either side of a 30 mm core of high-density
polyurethane foam (Figure 2.9).

Glazed walls

The walls of the main living space are made of 12 mm
thick toughened glass with 15 mm thick glass-stabilizing
fins which prevents the glass from bending under wind
pressure and also restrains the perimeter of the roof. The
interesting feature of this particular construction is the
use of silicone glazing joints and fixing cleats between
the sheets of glass, producing an elegant detail without
the use of window framing.

The glass fins were restrained by aluminium brackets
screwed to the floor and the roof was fixed to the fins by
the same means, using M10 bolts in nylon bushes. In
addition, aluminium corner brackets (functional for 4
days only until the silicone corner joints cure and
become structural) were fitted between the fins and the
glass walls (Figure 2.5). (This technique was later
developed by Benthem and Crouwel for the exhibition
building at Sonsbeek, Arnhem, in 1986 (Figure 2.7),
where neither intermediate nor corner cleats were used.)

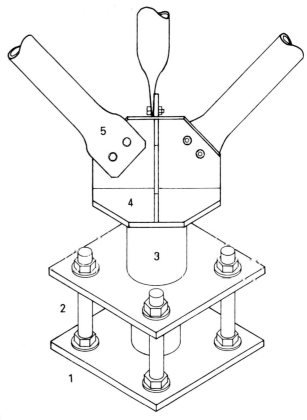

2.4.

2.5.
Details of glass-stabilizing fins. 1
12 mm thick toughened glass
sheets; 2 15 mm thick toughened
glass fins; 3 aluminium brackets
bolted down to floor (three M10
bolts secure the glass fin); 4 glass
sheet slotted into 30 × 20 mm
steel channel and sealed with
silicone sealant; 5 glass
countersunk to take countersunk
bolts fixed to intermediate
aluminium corner cleats; 6

aluminium bracket bolted to roof
deck, restraining head of fin

2.6.
Underfloor ductwork and flexible
drainage hoses

2.7.
Oblique view of sculpture
pavilion, Arnhem

2.7.

The roof

The roof deck is 0.75 mm thick corrugated steel sheet, waterproofed by a 1 mm thick EPDM membrane loose laid without falls in a single piece with interim fixing clips (Figure 2.8) on 50 mm 'Styrofoam' insulation board. The roof deck was reinforced by trusses formed from perforated mild steel angles with 8 mm diameter stainless steel tensioning wires (Figure 2.2). In addition, because the roof was so lightweight it was necessary to tie it down to the floor deck with two stainless steel tensioning wires inside the building. At the perimeter the trusses are bolted to the glass-stabilizing fins and are thus restrained at their edges.

Sequence of assembly

Thus the overall sequence of assembly as shown in Figure 2.10 was:

1. Place foundation slabs;
2. Fix space frame to slabs;
3. Place floor slabs and balcony;
4. Fix solid wall panels;
5. Fix glazed panels and fins;
6. Fix roof trusses and tension rods;
7. Place roof deck;
8. Finish roof deck.

Services

Connection to the underground drainage and mains water supply is by flexible hose. Heating is by heat exchanger fed from a district heating system distributed through the house by underfloor ducts (see Figure 2.2). Electrical supply is from sockets located at ceiling height, switched manually or by remote control from the central control unit.

The air-conditioning ducts are insulated and suspended from below the floor deck (Figure 2.6). A single rainwater outlet is carried through partition walls to drains below.

References

Anon., 'Dutch courage', *Architects' Journal* (building feature), 7 August 1985, pp. 30–34.

Berni, L. and Leroy, A., 'Holland: a constructive workshop', *Ottagono*, March 1987, pp. 20–33.

Buchanan, P., 'High-tech and high style', *Architectural Review*, January 1985, pp. 56–57.

Buchanan, P., 'Barely there – sculpture pavilion at Arnhem', *Architectural Review*, September 1987, pp. 81–84.

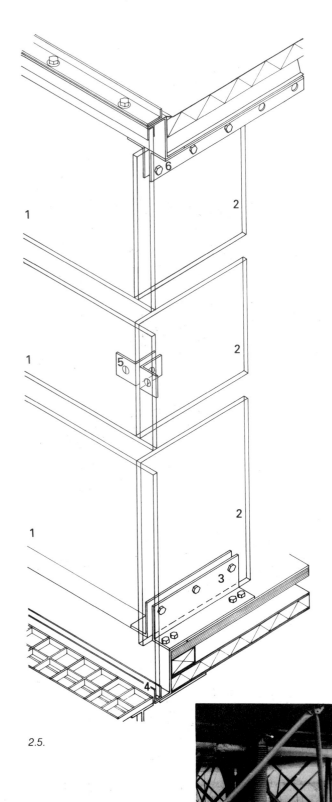

2.5.

2.6.

2.8.
Section through roof fixing. 1
0.75 mm thick corrugated metal
sheeting; 2 50 mm 'Styrofoam'
insulation board; 3 locating
washer fixed to steel decking with
self-tapping screws; 4 1 mm
EPDM membrane; 5 push-fit inner
sealing clip; 6 screw-down
sealing cap

2.9.
Method of fixing external panels.
1 Steel Z angle (25 × 50 ×
25 mm); 2 perimeter angle (50 ×
20 mm) bolted to Z angle; 3
sealant joint; 4 cover strip angle
(30 × 70 mm) riveted to panel; 5
40 mm polyurethane foam/
plywood composite panel; 6 30 ×
90 mm batten glued to panel; 7

panels fixed to Z angle with coach
screws; 8 EPDM membrane loose
laid on 50 mm extruded
polystyrene fixed to profiled steel
roof decking; 9 18 mm plywood
flooring screwed to 37 × 67 mm
timber battens bonded to upper
face of composite panels

2.10.
Sequence of assembly

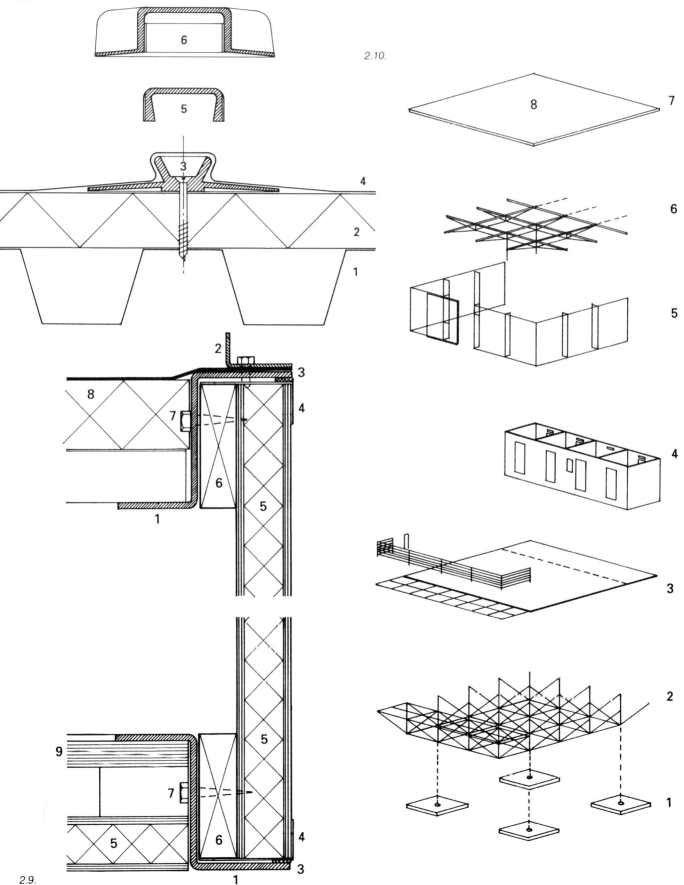

2.8.

2.9.

2.10.

The Burrell Gallery, Glasgow
Architects
Barry Gasson

General

The Burrell Gallery was built in 1983 as the winner of a competition to design a structure to house the Sir William Burrell Collection, which was bequeathed to the city of Glasgow in 1944 (Figure 3.2). This museum uses a wide variety of environmental control technology to enable it to protect its exhibits from pollution and damaging sunlight while at the same time being largely glazed to command views of the surrounding woodland, therefore placing the collection in the rural setting Burrell desired.

Traditionally built mainly in a variety of materials, the structure incorporates parts of the collection such as carved stone doors and windows into its own fabric, so that visitors walk through the doorways and experience them more fully and closely than they would had they been exhibited as objects simply to look at (Figure 3.1).

No overall grid governs the design: rather, each space is individually considered according to the particular exhibits' requirements. The spaces are then unified by the use of materials, which is a language of concrete columns, natural timber and stone and glass throughout. Gasson collaborated closely with James R. Briggs and Associates (environmental control system designers) from the start, to create a building specifically geared towards the ideal maintenance and display conditions its exhibits require.

3.1.

Structure

The architects have refined the structure to a point of simplicity, and the elegance of the junctions between its parts can only be admired. The tall 400 mm diameter concrete columns that still bear the two casting marks from the glassfibre moulds support a variety of laminated timber roof members manufactured by Kingston Craftsmen 1981 by means of bolted galvanized mild steel connector plates (Figure 3.3).

In the restaurant area and stained-glass gallery, 500 × 210 mm laminated timber perimeter beams are bolted to the columns using galvanized mild steel connector plates. These steel connections also support the rafters (105 × 333 mm) that are connected to vertical mullions of the same material and dimension by halving joints with glued and bolted timber connectors. The rafters are connected at their head to the perimeter beam by means of a galvanized mild steel T-shoe, bolted to the beam and rafter, and the mullion-to-floor junction is made by a flush-fitting mild steel shoe bolted to the concrete floor slab. The mullions and rafters are braced together by

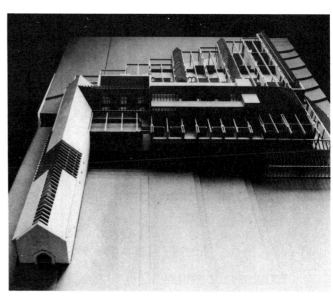

3.2.

3.1.
View along gallery to woods
beyond

3.2.
Model showing overall massing of
gallery

3.3.
Steel connector plates. 1 Primary
laminated timber beam (767 ×
210 mm) supported on steel plate
connector bolted to 400 mm
diameter concrete column; 2
laminated timber roof joists (267
× 105 mm); 3 motorized vertical
external aluminium roller blinds; 4
24 mm thick double glazing; 5
laminated timber perimeter beam
(500 × 210 mm); 6 laminated
timber rafter/mullion (333 ×
105 mm); 7 steel plate connector
bolted to beam and columns

3.4.
Horizontal glazing joint. (a)
Original design, (b) refined and
simplified joint

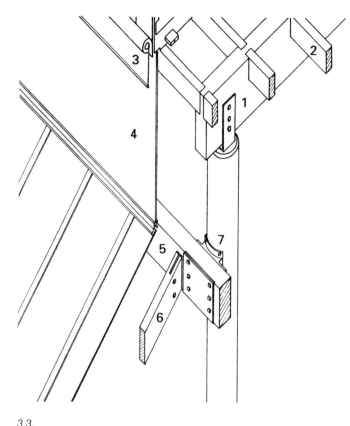

3.3.

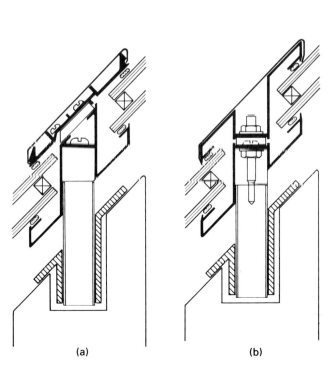

(a)   (b)

3.4.

means of mild steel tie bars.

An interesting feature of the glazing is the patent glazing bar detail to the angled restaurant wall. Gasson has refined the design so that one aluminium extrusion is used in the final design whereas initially two were required (Figure 3.4). It is this level of refinement that gives this building its great simplicity, as do the steel connector plates to the column heads which hold the laminated timber rafters away from the concrete columns.

Environmental control system

The Burrell Gallery employs a wide variety of environmental control devices. In order to control temperature and humidity, the building has been divided into 22 zones, each with its own air-handling plant. Each zone thus reacts independently to its location, environmental requirements according to function (restaurant, exhibition spaces, restorers' rooms, courtyard, etc.) and number of occupants. The system is designed to maintain 19°C ≮ 10°C with a relative humidity of 60% + 5% where there are exhibits, with slightly higher temperatures in 'people' spaces, such as the lecture theatre. Running costs are substantially reduced by limiting fresh air intake for the six air changes per hour required to 12–31 m^3 per second, with the double-glazing seals being very efficient and heat from lighting and other incidental heat sources also being recovered.

The Burrell Gallery has been described as a giant-sized showcase with a system of blinds acting as the cover-cloth. External blinds on the south-facing glazing are operated by a push button from inside the gallery when the lighting level exceeds the recommended maximum (Figure 3.5). The blinds (PVC-covered glass fibre) can shade both vertical and sloping glazed faces. The sloping face blinds are on extruded aluminium rollers on cast aluminium brackets fixed with stainless steel pins through glazing bars to the laminated timber rafters. The blind rail travels on pulleys along stainless steel cables, with the last blind, being motorized, controlling all the others. In the vertical glazing areas the extruded aluminium blind roller brackets are fixed back to the fascia by stainless steel pins. External awnings over office spaces provide a controllable shading device, while internal blinds on the east-facing glazing provide the necessary control there. Thus, because the museum has opened itself up to the environment it has to employ an array of protective devices to prevent the damaging effects of that environment.

11

3.5.
*External view of restaurant and
stained-glass gallery*

3.5.

Costs

In this type of building, services contribute a large amount towards the total costs. In this case over 42% of the total costs was for services, with ventilation accounting for 22.7%. The structure itself – including all partitions, doors and ironmongery as well as the frame and walls – accounted for 23.2%.

References

Anon., 'The Burrell Tour', *Architects' Journal*, 19 October 1983, pp. 65–70.

Anon., 'The Burrell Tour', *Architects' Journal*, 19 October 1983, pp. 81–85.

Brawne, M., 'The Burrell museum machine', *Architects' Journal*, 19 October 1983, pp. 86–93.

Bugg, V., 'The Burrell costs/credits', *Architects' Journal*, 19 October 1983, pp. 97–98.

Glancy, J., 'The Burrell – art and architecture', *Architectural Review*, February 1984, pp. 28–37.

Boyatt Wood Hostel for the Disabled
Architects
Hampshire County Council Architects' Department: (David White)

General

This hostel for physically disabled young people is situated in Selbourne Drive, Boyatt Wood, Eastleigh, in Hampshire. It was designed by David White of Hampshire County Council Architects' Department (County Architect: Colin Stansfield Smith) for Hampshire County Council Social Services Department, Raglan Housing Association. It provides six sheltered flats intended for permanent occupation and 24 bedsitting rooms grouped in fives and sixes around shared dining and sitting areas. Staff accommodation, a hairdressing service, bar, work-

The accommodation is housed in units of loadbearing brickwork construction with flat roofs providing sound and heat insulation. The 'umbrella' of PVC above it provides rain-shelter, but it is not sealed at the edges or gable ends; instead these remain open to guard against excessive heat gain within the building (Figure 4.5).

The flats/bedsitting units

These are constructed of a golden buff-coloured brick, which is also used (this time without mortar) to form the floor covering of the arcade. Doors from each unit relate

4.1. General view

ohop and recharge station for wheelchair batteries are all provided. This accommodation is arranged around a central 'street', and a lightweight profiled PVC roof on light steel frame spans the entire space (Figure 4.1), reaching out at the east and west sides of the small 'town' to provide sheltered gardens and carports. The complex deliberately attempts to avoid the institutionalized corridor, and instead provides a meandoring street, liberally planted, which runs from north to south with a central entrance from the west next to the communal 'forum', which forms a centrepiece in the arcade (Figures 4.2(a) and (b)). The trelliswork forming the walls and ceilings in this area is echoed in the furniture, designed by David Morriss and built by a local disabled persons' workshop (Figure 4.4).

into the central street arcade, with porches of the same brick jutting into the street Clerestories provide additional light into the living rooms of tho flats and bedsit groups.

The roof

The roofing material is carried on a frame of circular hollow section mild otool finished in a white paint. Five triangular cross-section lattice trusses run from north to south, supported at 6 m centres on the brick loadbearing walls of the accommodation below. The trusses are braced together in the line of the gable walls and also diagonally in the plane of the roof, with 48.3 × 4 mm c.h.s. Glazing purlins of the same section run in the line

4.2.
(a) Plan. 1 Main entrance; 2
vehicular entrance; 3 forum; 4
internal street; 5 sheltered flats; 6
bedsits with communal lounge; 7
car parking; 8 gardens. (b)
Section. 1 Gardens; 2 bedsit; 3
communal lounge; 4 internal
street; 5 sheltered flat; 6 car
parking

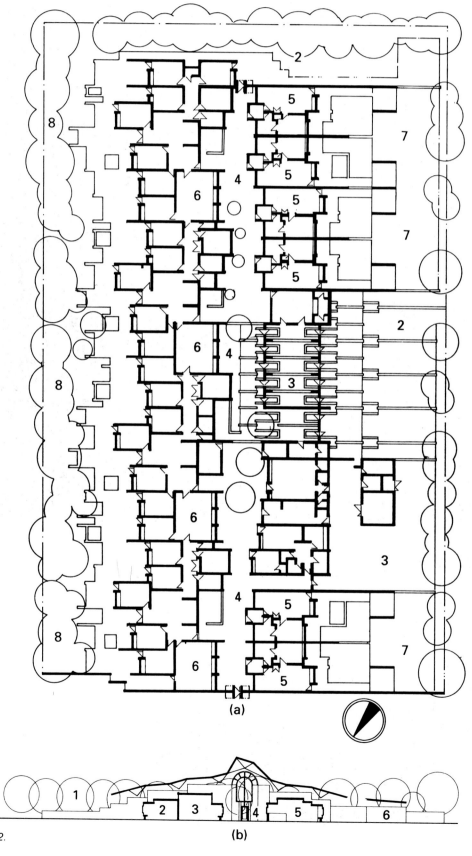

(a)

4.2.   (b)

4.4.
Trelliswork echoed in furniture design in communal 'forum'

4.5.
Internal street showing 'umbrella roof'

4.3.
Roof gutter and gargoyle discharging into pond. Note PVC skirt on underside of outer truss

4.3.

4.4.   4.5.

4.6.
Exploded view of roof arrangement. 1 PeVe Clair TKP 150/45 × 2.5 mm thick sheeting; 2 GRP flashing; 3 60 × 5 mm continuous mild steel flats; 4 roof trusses; 5 48.3 × 4 mm c.h.s. bracing members; 6 mild steel bracket; 7 concrete padstone; 8 glassfibre gutter unit with 'gargoyle'; 9 brickwork support wall

4.7.
Detail of roof fixing. 1 PeVe Clair TKP 150/45 × 2.5 mm thick sheeting; 2 GRP flashing; 3 Fakband V self-adhesive tape; 4 Sela 35 washer head drill screw (flashing and sheeting to have 15 mm diameter holes predrilled); 5 60 × 5 mm continuous mild steel flat; 6 65 mm long × 5 mm mild steel cleats at 600 mm centres; 7 5 mm thick gusset at 600 mm centres; 8 48.3 × 4 mm c.h.s.

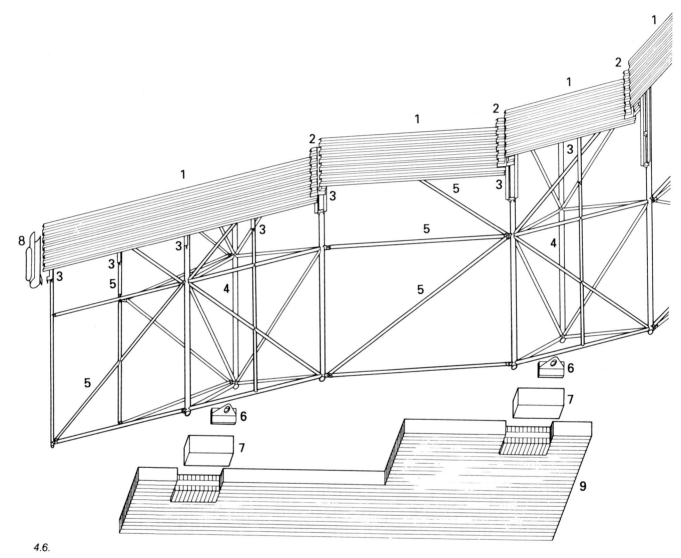

4.6.

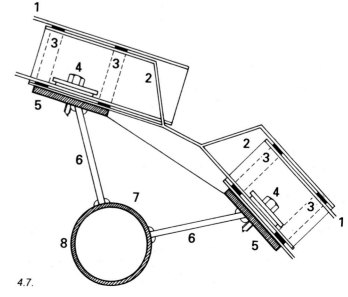

4.7.

of the trusses, the entire roof covering an area of 33.6 × 75.0 m (Figure 4.5). The roof finishes used are PeVe Clair clear (Isobelic) glazing (TKP 150/45 × 2.5 mm) and Plannja Profile Sheet roofing (45 × 0.55 mm) with PVF^2 finish. The sheet roofing is used over the flat-roof areas of the accommodation except where clerestory lighting is required.

The sheeting spans between trusses, and is supported on and connected to continuous 'flats' of mild steel (60 × 5 mm) welded to 5 mm cleats which are in turn welded to the top chord of the truss at 600 mm centres (Figure 4.6). The cleats are made rigid by means of 5 mm mild steel gussets welded between them at 600 mm centres.

A seal is made between two spans of roof finish by means of glass-reinforced polyester flashings, which are formed in the same profile as the sheeting. The flashing fits *below* the upper sheet and *above* the lower one, except at the apex of the central ridge, where it fits over both. Two strips of Fakband V tape (compressed size 10 × 3 mm) are used to seal each sheeting-to-flashing joint.

The PeVe Clair glazing and Plannja Profile sheet roofing are screwed to the mild steel support flats using Sela washer head drill screws (35 mm and 20 mm, respectively), allowing for expansion of 2.5 mm. The PeVe Clair glazing lengths have widths of 1200 mm, and the side laps are pop-riveted at 600 mm centres, also using a sealing strip. The Plannja sheet roofing has sealed rivets at 300 mm centres along the side laps. The GRP flashing is manufactured in widths corresponding with the PeVe Clair sheeting, plus 150 mm laps.

A PeVe Clair TKP 150/45 × 2.5 mm thick skirt is attached by means of flats (53 × 5 mm m.s.) welded to cleats (5 mm thick m.s. at 600 mm centres) to the underside of each of the two outermost trusses. These prevent rain from entering, but are not sealed and, together with the open-ended gables, allow air movement and are intended to reduce the possibility of heat gain under the 'umbrella'. A series of air vents are also provided in the roof plane above the uppermost truss (Figure 4.3).

Rainwater from the roof is collected in glassfibre gutter units, bolted to brackets welded at 1200 mm centres to the outer mild steel 'flats' which support the roof sheeting. Lengths of guttering are connected by means of a 50 mm spigot and socket joint, with seal-bolted connection. Instead of downpipes, the gutter is formed into 'gargoyles', each 600 mm wide, which discharge into ponds in the gardens below them.

References

Darley, G., 'Hampshire symbol', *Architectural Review*, **179**, No. 1072, June 1986, pp. 58–61.

Stansfield Smith, C., 'Public tribute', *Architects' Journal*, **183**, No. 5, 29 January 1986, pp. 20–23.

5.1.

Clarke Ascot House, Brisbane
Architect/owner
Chris Clarke

General

Built in 1985 on a steep hillside in the suburb of Ascot overlooking Brisbane, Australia, this unashamedly modern and finely detailed house is supported on a pristine white-painted r.h.s. steel frame sprung from just four foundation pads and is linked to a timber deck, surrounding a swimming pool, by two bridges (Figure 5.2). Owner/architect Chris Clarke designed the building with Mark Whitby (structural engineer) while nearing the end of a 15-year stay in England, having worked for John Winter for 10 years (he was involved in Winter's own Highgate House) and for Foster Associates, on the Hongkong and Shanghai Bank.

Clearly, Clarke has been influenced by Craig Elwood and Mies van der Rohe's ideas, and the house was conceived as a series of prefabricated elements which could be brought to site and bolted together as quickly as possible, thus eliminating the need for extensive work on a site virtually inaccessible to heavy machinery because of its slope (Figure 5.1). The low site costs offset the relatively high building costs, the result being an elegant re-interpretation of the local terrace lifestyle, suited to the subtropical climate, with house, terrace and pool interacting (Figure 5.3). Sliding glazed panels, aluminium louvres and strut-supported canopies finely

5.2.

control the environment, with water heated by a roof-mounted solar collector, but an air-conditioning unit is still required.

The Clarke house won an honourable mention in the 1986 Royal Australian Institute of Architects awards and represents a very high standard in component building design as an example to architects throughout the world.

5.3.

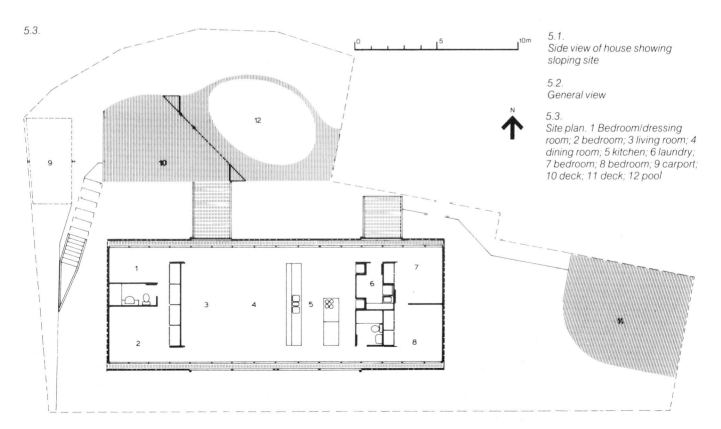

5.1.
Side view of house showing sloping site

5.2.
General view

5.3.
Site plan. 1 Bedroom/dressing room; 2 bedroom; 3 living room; 4 dining room; 5 kitchen; 6 laundry; 7 bedroom; 8 bedroom; 9 carport; 10 deck; 11 deck; 12 pool

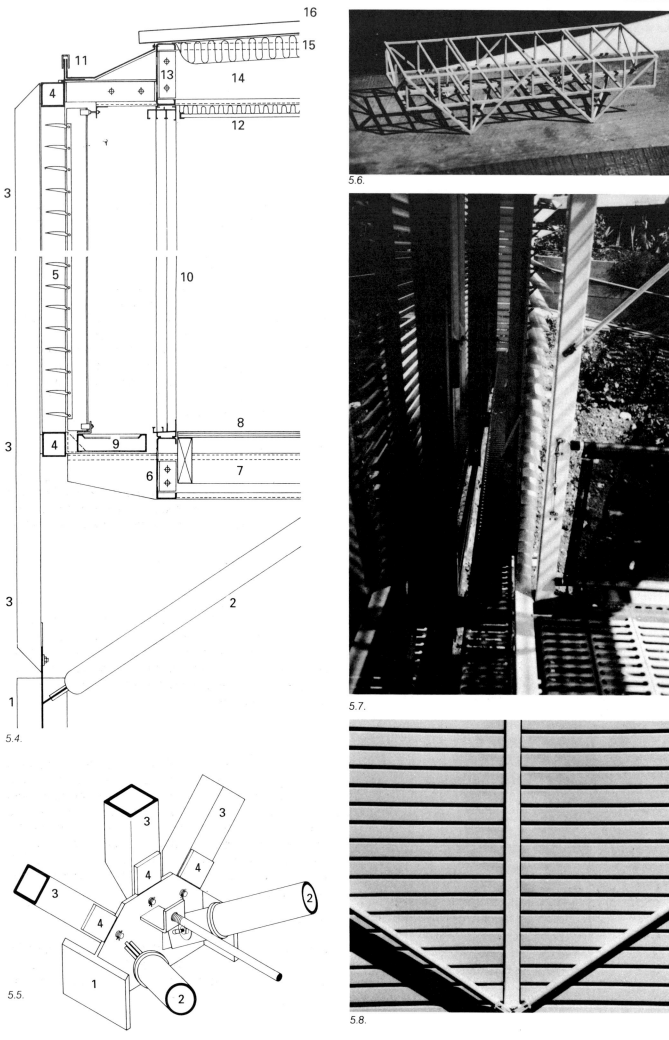

5.4.

5.5.

5.6.

5.7.

5.8.

5.4.
Construction details. 1 356 × 171 mm mild steel stanchion; 2 80 mm diameter mild steel c.h.s.; 3. 80 × 80 mm r.h.s.; 4 80 × 80 mm mild steel r.h.s. forming frame structure; 5 adjustable aluminium louvres; 6 perforated steel channel forms edge beam; 7 150 × 50 mm hardwood joists at 450 mm centres; 8 20 mm tongue and groove silver ash floorboards; 9 walkway formed from steel grating units; 10 sliding anodized aluminium patio doors; 11 gutter support formed by 76 × 76 × 5 mm mild steel angle with continuous fillet weld to steel frame; 12 perforated aluminium ceiling strips with 25 mm acoustic lining; 13 perforated steel channel forms fascia; 14 pressed steel roof beams; 15 75 mm foil-backed glassfibre insulation quilt; 16 roof formed from interlocking colour coated galvanized steel profiled roof decking fixed to 125 × 50 mm hardwood purlins

5.5.
Support bracket. 1 356 × 171 mm UB cut to provide support bracket; 2 80 mm diameter c.h.s.; 3 80 × 80 mm r.h.s.; 4 bearing plate welded to back of diagonal member

5.6.
Architect's own model shows clear structural intent

5.7.
Zone between louvres and glazing with standard floor grating as walkway

5.8.
End-wall cladding

Structure

The key to this building is the box structure on four triangulated legs, as shown on the architect's own model (Figure 5.6). The simple geometric relationship, with the legs springing from the top corners down to the foundation pads and back to the centre, where they meet, results in the elegant final structural solution. All the main framing is constructed in 80 × 80 mm r.h.s. mild steel. The raking struts are tubular (80 mm diameter) and the tertiary structure is made up from standard cold-rolled sections. Roof studs and floor joists are mainly formed of hardwood.

The complete structure is bolted to four concrete foundation pads (Figure 5.5), the extra height on the south side being made up by 356 × 171 mm mild steel I-beam stanchions.

In detail, the inherent jointing complications of the rolled steel sections was overcome by cutting the ends at 45 degrees, thus facilitating face fixing.

Sequence of assembly (Figure 5.4)

The simplicity of the design depended upon an accurate and predetermined sequence of assembly as follows:

1. Lay and level foundation pads.
2. Then prop four identical four-bay storey-height frames on the long north and south elevations.
3. Bolt each pair together, forming an eight-bay wall.
4. Insert two-bay east and west elevation wall frames.
5. Insert roof and floor structure, thus stabilizing the entire building.
6. Apply roof finish and gutter.
7. Insert timber floor joists and floor decking.
8. Fit louvred ceiling with acoustic pads.
9. Fit internal partitions.
10. Fix perimeter glazed sliding doors and walking grills.
11. Complete internal plasterwork of end walls and painting.

Cladding

The long walls are entirely glazed in fixed and sliding anodized aluminium patio doors which are set back by 300 mm from the structural frame. This also supports the aluminium louvres in front of the window with standard steel grating units, forming a walkway between them (Figure 5.7). Using the same standard grating units, Clarke created the main entrance bridge with canopy above, leading from the entrance deck on the north

(sunny) side to the main living area. This canopy, with its adjustable struts, can be lowered to secure the house in the event of severe hailstorms, prevalent in the area, like a medieval castle.

The end walls are formed using fixed profiled aluminium sections (a Luxalon type 84R, Figure 5.8) on stringer supports fixed to 6 mm Versilux insulation board on 64 × 34 mm Gyproc boxed steel studs with 12 mm plasterboard forming the internal linings.

The roof is covered by an interlocking Klip-Lok profiled steel deck supported on 125 × 50 mm purlins and cambered to purpose-made 300 mm wide pressed steel gutters on both the long elevations with 75 mm foil-backed insulation below.

Internal finishes

Internally, the suspended ceiling is formed using perforated Luxalon 84C with 25 mm acoustic pads. The floor finish is silver ash, gun nailed to the joists, and coated with an ultraviolet light-stabilized polyurethane clear finish.

Services

Hot water is supplied by a solar collector mounted on the roof comprising a 300-litre tank and two black nickel-coated collectors. Air conditioning has also been installed. All rain and waste water runs to a point in the centre of the house and drains to the ground via a purpose-designed hopper and pipes attached to either side of an electrical ladder rack.

Costs

The high building costs ($600 per square metre) were offset by the inexpensive site and the small amount of foundation work necessary. Also, the steel frame was less susceptible to fungal and ant attack than the local timber buildings and thus has a longer life expectancy Some similarities can be made between this building and the Yacht House by Richard Horden (Case Study 30), both architects perhaps influenced by their time at Foster Associates.

References

Brookes, A.J., 'A modern metal home', Roof Cladding and Insulation, July 1987, pp. 32–36.
Carolin, P., 'Brisbane bridge house', Architects' Journal, 6 August 1986, pp. 20–27.

Conservatory at Kew
Architects
Property Services Agency (Gordon Wilson)

General

Completed in 1986, this £4 million tropical conservatory was designed by the government's Property Services Agency for the Royal Botanic Gardens at Kew, south-west London (Figure 6.1). The design concept of a 'glazed hill' led to a stepped and staggered plan form, facing east–west, of five structural bays and clerestory-like gables glazed to let in a maximum amount of winter sunlight (Figures 6.2 and 6.3), covering $4490\,m^2$ (twice the area of the 1846 Palm House at Kew by Turner and Burton).

Portal-framed structure

The multi-span steel portal-framed structure is composed of a series of welded portal frames at 5.4 m centres. In some cases these frames span over five bays with props at each bay. Where the roof line changes, welded I-section mullions connect the top and bottom beams into the chords of a rectilinear lattice truss (Figure 6.4). The structure is braced against the wind by Vierendeel tubes (144 mm diameter) rigidly connected to the top flange of the I-beam forming the portal (Figure 6.5). In addition, these Vierendeel tubes also provide a secure anchorage for maintenance access. The roof pitch is 26.5 degrees, with the roof sloping down from the 11.4 m maximum ridge height to various ground levels externally.

6.1. General view

6.2.
Site plan. 1 Main gate; 2 Kew
Road entrance; 3 Princess of
Wales Conservatory; 4 Palm
House; 5 Temperate House

6.3.
Photograph of model showing
staggered plan form

6.4.
Lattice truss formed where roof
steps back

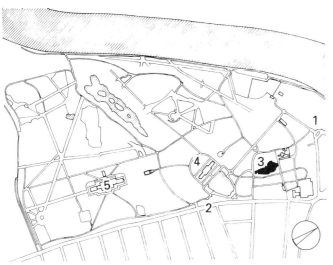

6.2.

6.3.

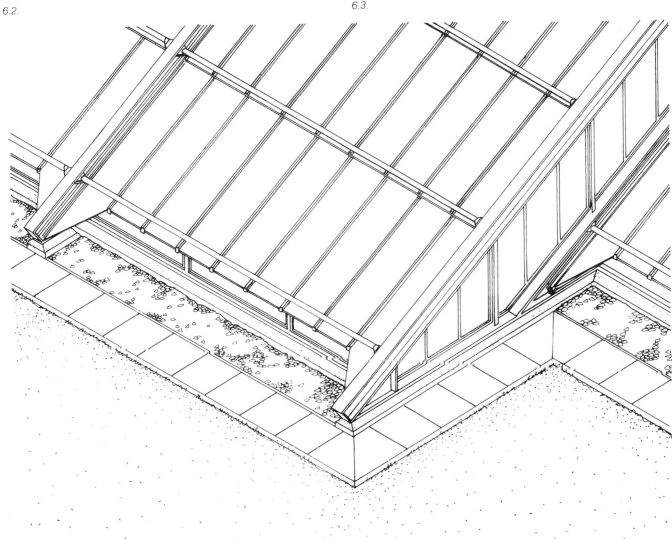

6.4.

Cribbs Causeway Warehouses, Bristol
Architect
Building Design Partnership
Project architect
Gennaro Picardi

General

This development was built in 1986 for the Prudential Assurance Company, adjacent to junction 17 of the M5, at Bristol, and designed by BDP. It consists of two blocks of retail warehousing space providing 7000 and 9000 m² apiece (Figure 7.1). Built as empty shells for unspecified occupants, each structural bay can become a separate unit of approximately 1500 m² with individual service connections (Figure 7.2).

Structure

Both buildings are based upon a 3 m grid in both plan and section. Building A has a free-span structure of 21 × 21 m, and Building B a clear span of 18 × 12 m. The buildings are divided into bays by the main structural framework:

Building A: six bays, 21 m apart;
Building B: four bays, 21 m apart.

A secondary arched beam spans across each bay at 6 m centres. These, in turn, support the roof sheeting rails (Figure 7.3).

The gable walling is supported by vertical cladding rails of gable posts at 3 m intervals, with cross-bracing (Figure 7.4). This very straightforward sequence of structural parts is a model to a student attempting to understand a hierarchy of beam sizes for a rectangular structural form.

Roofing

The roof shape takes the form of a shallow curve with a building height varying from 6 m at the gutter line to 8 m at the apex. The roof overhangs the front and rear elevations by 1 m, providing shading and weather protection (see Figures 7.2 and 7.4). Its construction is twin-skinned steel sheeting with site-assembled insulation (Figure 7.6). The roof profile used is the 'Architectural Profiles' (AP 22) for the external and internal metal roof sheets, separated and supported by zed spacer bars and the thermal break provided by a plastic spacer ferrule. Insulation is obtained by using 60 mm Rockwool insulation at 23 kg/m² density (to provide a U-value of 0.6 W/m²/°C) (Figure 7.5).

Wall sheeting

The wall-cladding construction on the side walls is similar to the roof specification with both internal and external sheeting using Architectural Profiles AP 22 profile. Sheeting is coated with PVF² Kynar 500, which consists of a primer coat, two coats of PVF² and a clear final coat with a total thickness of 50 microns. The colour is a special pale yellow. The profiled walls and roof were carried out by Hermcrest Southern Ltd, for Sir Robert McAlpine Ltd (main contractor).

Curtain walling on the end gables

There are two types of curtain walling on the building. Hermcrest provided the Slimwall system of curtain walling on the side walls. The gable facades are an interchangeable system of glazing and aluminium panels by Hans Schmidlin AG. These glazed panels are double-glazed in toughened glass, 6 mm thick anti-sun green externally and 6 mm clear float toughened internally to the bottom-glazed units. The remaining units, with a reduced requirement for impact resistance, have 6 mm clear float internally.

The pressed aluminium panels, downpipe and hoppers are coated in Colorsec powder coating, colour metallic silver to the external sheeting, off-white to the internal sheeting and bright yellow for the downpipes and hoppers.

As with all curtain wall systems, adjustment is required to allow for inaccuracy of the adjacent construction. In this case it is provided by the cast aluminium spacer bracket specially made by Schmidlin for this project. This translates the tolerances of the gable posts and allows alignment of the vertical sheeting rails (Figure 7.7).

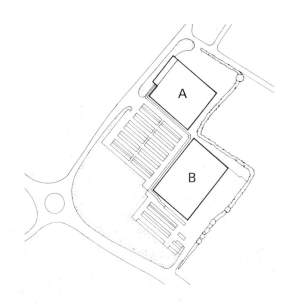

7.1.

7.1.
Site plan

7.2.
Rear elevation of bays

7.3.
Arched beams at 6 m centres with
sheeting rails

7.4.
Gable wall prior to cladding

7.2.

7.3.

7.4.

7.5.
Construction details

7.6.
View of roof at eaves shows twin skins of profiled steel sheeting with site-assembled insulation

7.7.
Foot of gable post with cast aluminium curtain walling support bracket and curtain walling mullion

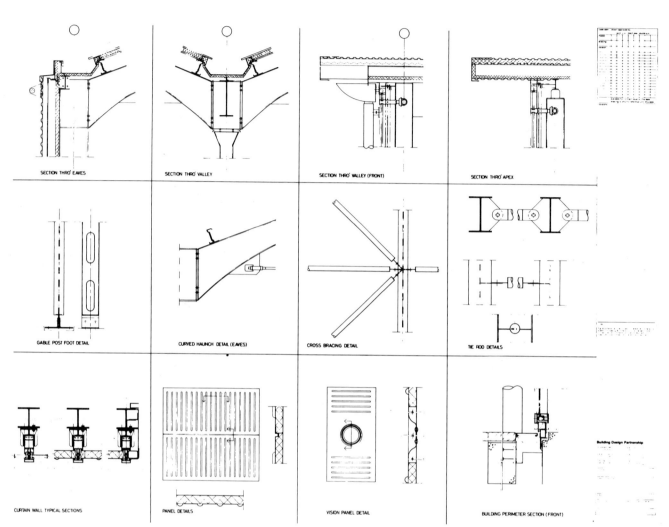

SECTION THRO' EAVES

SECTION THRO' VALLEY

SECTION THRO' VALLEY (FRONT)

SECTION THRO' APEX

GABLE POST FOOT DETAIL

CURVED HAUNCH DETAIL (EAVES)

CROSS BRACING DETAIL

TIE ROD DETAILS

CURTAIN WALL TYPICAL SECTIONS

PANEL DETAILS

VISION PANEL DETAIL

BUILDING PERIMETER SECTION (FRONT)

Building Design Partnership

7.5.

7.6.

7.7.

7.8.
Details of hopper head

7.9.
Covered walkway

7.10.
Escape door and ladder rail

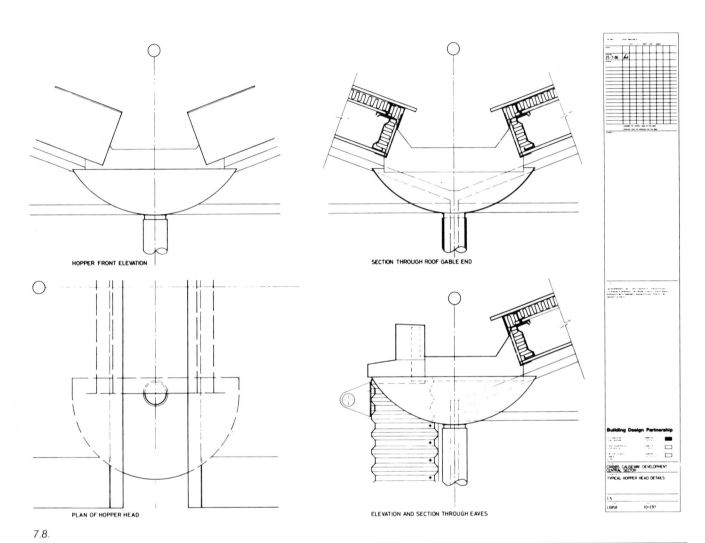

7.8.

HOPPER FRONT ELEVATION

SECTION THROUGH ROOF GABLE END

PLAN OF HOPPER HEAD

ELEVATION AND SECTION THROUGH EAVES

Building Design Partnership

CRIBBS CAUSEWAY DEVELOPMENT
CENTRAL SECTION

TYPICAL HOPPER HEAD DETAILS

1:5

L6858 (0-)97

7.9.

7.10.

Covered walkway

A continuous 3 m wide tubular steel covered walkway provides both a visual and physically protective link for customers to the front elevation of both retail warehousing blocks. The covering is formed by a green translucent polycarbonate dome with the detail of the column head with its four projecting flanges providing not only support to the beams but also a means of allowing tenant signage. It also allows further extension of lightweight structure to the walkway canopy (Figure 7.9).

Accessories

An interesting feature of this building is the careful choice of hopper fronts and gutters, as detailed by BDP (Figure 7.8). These add a refinement to the overall appearance. Similarly, fire doors have been carefully detailed to match the profile of the cladding. Also, ladder support rails have been provided in various positions in 75 mm diameter aluminium with plastic protection to allow roof access without damaging the edge guttering (Figure 7.8). The high quality of detailing for an industrial building of this type is illustrated by the concern for junction conditions between components and quality control over such items as thickness of sheeting carried out by the architect.

There are some interesting parallels that can be drawn between this approach to detailing and that by the Australian architect Glen Murcutt in his Kempsey Museum (Case Study 17).

References

Brookes, A.J. and Stacey, M., 'Fast facades', *Building Products*, December 1987, pp. 81–91.

Copeland, S., 'Development economics', *Architects' Journal*, 18 February 1987, pp. 61–66.

The Customs House, Hazeldonk
Architects
Benthem and Crouwel

General

This prototype for a number of customs houses is situated in Hazeldonk, near Breda in the south of Holland, close to the Belgian border, and was built in 1984 (Figure 8.1). It consists of a rectangular plan of raised offices below a space-frame roof with two storeys of smaller offices and ancillary rooms separated from the main space by a glazed corridor (Figure 8.2). The offices look out over a carpark which contains a further space-frame structure used for customs inspection of containers (Figure 8.3).

Structure

The space-frame structure (seven bays wide by 38 bays long, each bay 1800 mm) is held on two pairs of seven V-shaped legs at 10.8 m centres, thus forming a series of squares each seven bays × 1.8 m on their lower booms and eight bays × 1.8 m on their top ones. This could be seen to be an ideal arrangement for a space-frame construction of approximately 1.8 m in depth.

The connection between the space frames made by Octatube (Delft) uses an unusual method of bolting the flattened ends of the tubular steel chords onto a specially welded plate (Figure 8.4), thus avoiding the expensive node connection normally associated with space decks. (This system was used in Benthem and Crouwel's house in Almere: see Case Study 2.) The legs of the structure

8.1.

8.1.
General view

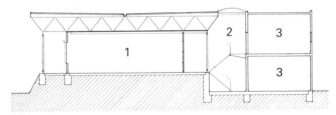

8.2.
8.2.
Section through Customs House.
1 Customs hall; 2 glazed corridor;
3 offices

8.3.
Inspection shelter with Customs
House in the background

8.3.

8.4.
Space-frame nodes and V-shaped support legs

8.5.
Welded steel base bracket

8.6.
Section through curtain walling

are bolted at their base to welded steel brackets bolted to the concrete block (Figure 8.5).

Cladding

The cladding to the main office areas is constructed using the Astrawall system and assembled by J. Hermans of Tienen. The overall assembly of 4 no. solid or glazed panels each 745 mm high is connected back to an aluminium carrier system with a box section approximately 120 mm and 50 mm (Figure 8.6). The two centre bands consist of double-glazed units, one of which is openable, and the top and bottom solid panels are made using a sandwich panel of 6 mm glass, 50 mm polyurethane and 1.5 mm aluminium inner skin (Figure 8.7). The corners of the curtain wall assembly are formed by a solid L-shaped panel mounted into the curtain wall section and painted black to match (Figure 8.8). Cill detail to the upstand concrete slab includes an aluminium strip fascia mounted into the carrier transom (Figure 8.9).

Roof

Strangely, the building has a double roof layer with the outer skin comprising a single-skin profiled steel roof deck and the inner one supported by purlins which are hung from the bottom booms of the space deck. These form the thermal and acoustic barrier as a continual box around the office areas. The edges of the roof deck support the curtain wall framing by means of a 120 × 80 × 10 mm roof-edge member (Figure 8.10).

The roof of the container shelter is a metal deck suspended from purlins fixed to the bottom booms, thus inverting the upper roof structure of the office block accommodation. The classic problem of roof drainage from an overhanging roof has been dealt with in this case by the somewhat uncomfortable detail using downpipes following the shape of the structural props. Large deflections can also be expected in a roof of this type.

Services

Services to the customs house are provided by ducts mounted within the depth of the space frame, between the two roofs. External blinds are mounted on the curtain walling assembly above the opening windows.

References

Berni, L. and Leroy, A., 'Holland: a constructive workshop', *Ottagono*, March 1987, pp. 20–33.

Buchannan, P., 'High tech and high style', *Architectural Review*, January 1985, pp. 56–59.

8.4.

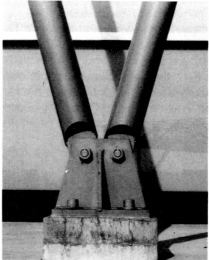

8.5.

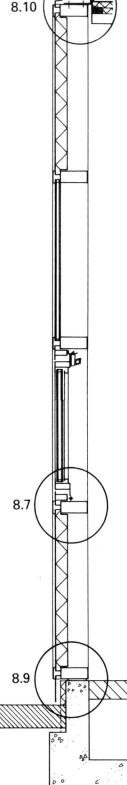

8.6.

8.7.
Section through cladding transom. 1 50 × 115 mm extruded aluminium transom section; 2 sandwich panel: 6 mm glass, 50 mm polyurethane insulation, 1.5 mm aluminium inner skin; 3 gasketed cover strip; 4 opening glazed panel

8.8.
Plan of corner detail. 1 50 × 115 mm extruded aluminium mullion sections; 2 L-shaped corner panel; 3 30 × 30 × 2 mm aluminium angle; 4 fixed glazed panel; 5 opening glazed panel; 6 gasketed cover strip

8.9.
Detail at base. 1 50 × 115 mm extruded aluminium transom; 2 5 mm thick aluminium strip; 3 35 mm thick 'foamglass' insulation; 4 sandwich panel: 6 mm glass, 50 mm polyurethane insulation, 1.5 mm aluminium inner skin; 5 gasketed cover strip; 6 concrete perimeter edge beam

8.10.
Detail at roof. 1 120 × 80 × 10 mm roof-edge member suspended off bottom of space frame; 2 50 × 115 mm extruded aluminium transom section bolted to roof-edge member; 3 gasketed cover strip; 4 aluminium coping; 5 profiled aluminium decking with 60 mm polyurethane insulation; 6 single-skin membrane roof covering

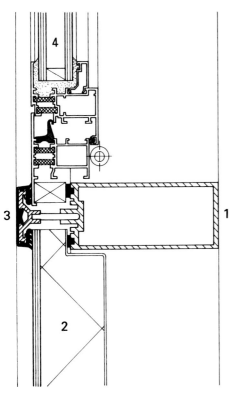

8.7.

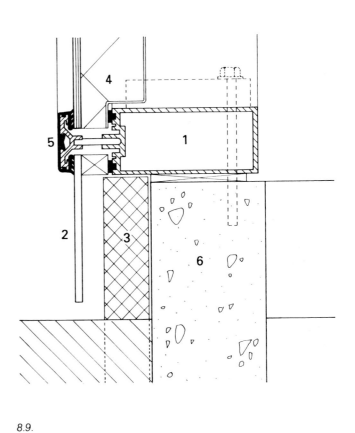

8.9.

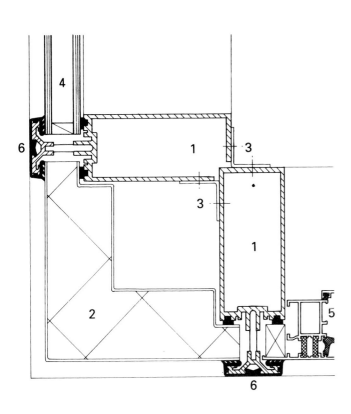

8.8.

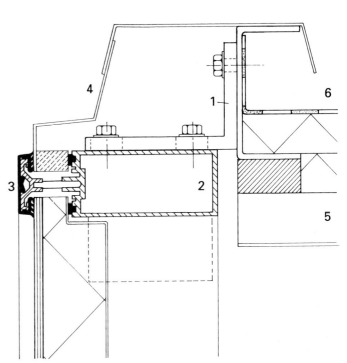

8.10.

9

Darling Harbour Exhibition Centre
Architects
Philip Cox and Partners

General

This building, with its tall-masted structure, is situated near the Chinese area of Sydney, Australia, and is part of the dockland redevelopment of Sydney's Darling Harbour. The site is bisected by a series of elevated motorways from which the roof of the building can be seen (Figure 9.1). This creates an unusual requirement for the building, whose construction can be observed from all levels. The plan shape is a series of five staggered bays following the line of the freeway overhead (Figure 9.4), each bay being independently structured by four supporting masts, forming the large exhibition centre with a height to the underside of the main beams of 13.5 m.

The project was a mangement contract by Leighton Contractors Pty Ltd, using architects Philip Cox and Partners and engineers Ove Arup and Partners.

Structure

A typical structural bay is shown in Figure 9.3, and consists of four masts, each being a group of four c.h.s. steel columns arranged in a square and bolted at their base to the concrete slab (Figure 9.5). From these masts four sets of triangular trusses spanning 15 m are supported by rods at their ends. These are pinned at their ends to allow movement using stainless steel pins (Figure 9.6).

From the ends of these trusses and from the masts span four main beams pinned at their centre, spanning a total of 92 m, with rods from the masts supporting these beams along their length (Figure 9.7) and with a triangular cross-section lattice outrigger 13.5 m long, also suspended at its ends by rods from the masts. The method of separating out these rod connections at the head of the mast to avoid complicated junctions is of interest (Figure 9.8), and this should be compared with Victoria Plaza (Case Study 31). The ends of the rods have cast fork connectors through which pass the steel pins into the welded plates on the beams and columns.

Comparison can also be made with Stansted Airport (see case Study 27). Both structures have four columns per mast which are bolted down to the concrete base. Stansted has 4 no. 457 mm c.h.s. at 3 m' centres supporting a structure which spans 36 m in both directions. Darling Harbour has 4 no. 406 mm c.h.s. at approximately 1 m centres supporting a structure which spans a total of 92 m in one direction and 26.3 m in the other, using cable supports. Between the main beams the roof beams spanning 26.3 m are curved to allow a roof slope. These then support curved purlins taking the

9.1.

9.2.

roof sheeting (Figure 9.2).

It is this hierarchy of structural members that should interest students of component assembly. However, it is likely that the weight of steel is more than normally expected for a structure of these spans. The result, with its white-painted steelwork against a bright blue Australian sky, is a very graceful and elegant design solution.

Cladding

Cladding panels consisting of 35 mm steel faced sandwich panels by H.H. Robertson, 900 mm in height, span onto vertical cladding rails bolted to a secondary frame (Figure 9.9) and are surrounded at their edges by glazed strips between the roof and at the main mast positions. These panels are finished with an embossed epoxy coating in two colours to produce a striped effect. The glazed strips between the panels are formed using conventional curtain wall framing fixed back onto the cladding supports (Figure 9.10). The composite panels

9.1.
View of roof from motorway

9.2.
Curved purlins

9.3.
General arrangement of one
structural bay

9.4.
Site plan. 1 Entrance; 2 foyer; 3
main halls; 4 loading bays

9.3.

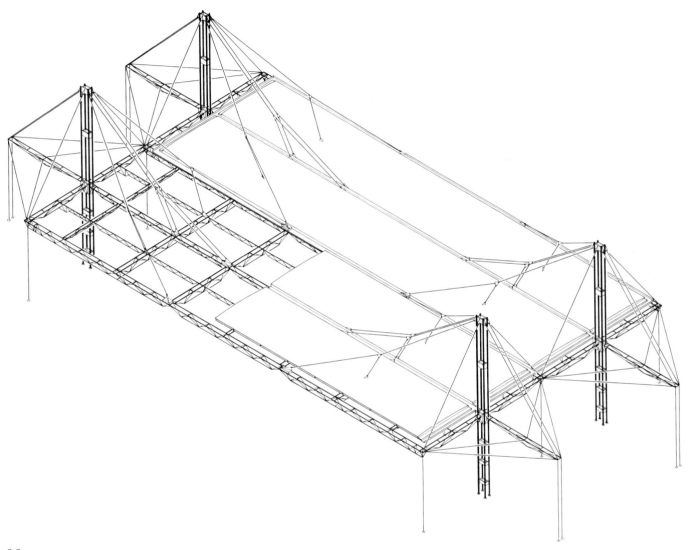

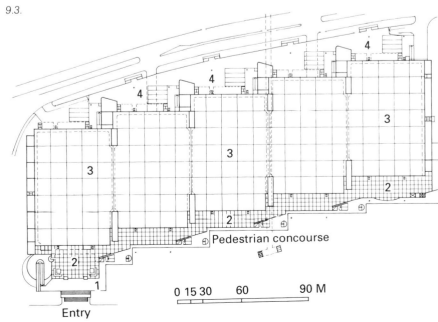

Pedestrian concourse

0 15 30   60   90 M

Entry

9.4.

9.10.
Curtain wall with glazed zone

9.11.
Cladding fixed back to blockwork

9.12.
Cladding cleats. (a) Factory welded. (b) Site welded

9.10.

9.11.

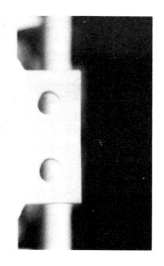

9.12a.

9.12b.

are also fixed back to solid walls in some positions, using aluminium cleats bolted through to a galvanized top-hat section, fixed to the blockwork (Figure 9.11). Corner panels are formed by cutting the back skin of the panel and re-sealing with a silicone joint.

An interesting site problem of fixing the cladding rails to their cleats resulted in these having to be re-welded and site drilled to take up deviations in alignment (Figure 9.12b). The problem of tolerances in component assembly cannot be overemphasized, and any means of taking up three-dimensional variations, particularly in the main structure, should be employed (i.e. using slotted connections). (See also Case Study 32 for curtain wall fixing to the Hongkong and Shanghai Bank.)

References

Ogg, A., *Architecture in Steel, the Australian Context*, RAIA, 1987, pp. 191–198.

Quarry, N., 'Darling development', *Architectural Review*, February 1987, pp. 70–73.

The Devonshire Building, Boston, Mass.
Architects
Steffian and Bradley Associates

General

Situated in Devonshire Street, Boston, Massachusetts, USA, near the Boston City Hall, this mixed-use high-rise structure was built in 1983 as a speculative development of offices, apartments and a top-floor health club with swimming pool and underground parking for 220 cars. This building represents a faction of current architectural design leaning towards sleek, smooth, flat facades using aluminium as a curtain wall skin in front of a more traditional construction to achieve the performance requirements for thermal, fire and acoustics (Figure 10.1). As such, although it cannot be considered particularly significant in the context of world architecture, it may be interesting for the student of construction to note the relatively low-cost nature of the curtain walling assembly now described.

Construction of external wall

The entire exterior surface of the building is clad with Fluoropolymer-coated aluminium Alucobond panels, consisting of two sheets of aluminium (Peralumen NS41) each 0.5 mm thick, bonded to a low-density polyethylene core. These panels, formed to shape, are combined with anodized aluminium windows (Figure 10.2).

Detail

At each of the 40 floor levels a 100 × 38 mm continuous steel channel section is fixed by adjustable brackets back to the floor slab. To this is mounted the extruded aluminium carrier system for the windows and Alucobond panels formed into a tray, which is also fixed into the same section. These aluminium panels are formed by cutting the inner skin of the Alucobond and the core and allowing the outer 25 mm of aluminium skin to bend inwards at a 90-degree angle. Extruded aluminium stiffeners running lengthwise were attached to the back of the panels using silicone cement. The stiffeners also support the panel by resting on adjustable clips fixed back to the continuous steel channel.

Opening and fixed double-glazed window sections are also attached to the carrier system and the whole assembly is face sealed using Silpruf sealant on a Denver foam backing strip (Figure 10.3). The visual expression of both the vertical and horizontal joints is then created using these 63 mm wide × 3 mm aluminium plates, face fixed through into the carrier system with a

10.1.

1.5 × 18 mm neoprene isolator cemented to the mullions and transoms to form a thermal break.

Clearly, the main problem with this kind of face-fixed plate is the butt-joint junction between the plates and the face-fix screws and washers (Figure 10.4). Accuracy in the cutting of the ends of the plates and the method of sealing between them would be extremely significant in a building where this detail could be immediately noticed at eye level. On a 40-storey building in a busy city street, such as the Devonshire Building, this may not be quite as significant. At the back of the assembly, metal stud and dry wall lining is used with insulation provided by fibreglass bats.

10.1.
General view down Devonshire Street

10.2.
Detail of opaque panel and opening double-glazed window. 1 125 × 75 mm steel angle anchored to concrete slab; 2 100 × 38 mm continuous steel channel; 3 extruded aluminium carrier system; 4 Alucobond tray; 5 aluminium stiffener; 6 adjustable clip; 7 opening

double-glazed unit; 8 Silpruf sealant with Denier backing foam; 9 63 × 3 mm aluminium cover plate fixed back with stainless steel screw on neoprene washer

10.3.
Single- and double-glazed windows. 1 Extruded aluminium carrier system; 2 fixed double-glazed panel; 3 fixed single-glazed panel; 4 63 × 3 mm aluminium cover plate fixed back with stainless steel screw on neoprene washer

10.4.
Isometric of cladding assembly. 1 Concrete floor slab; 2 125 × 75 mm steel angle; 3 100 × 38 mm continuous steel channel; 4 extruded aluminium carrier system; 5 Alucobond tray; 6 63 × 3 mm aluminium cover plate fixed back with stainless steel screw on neoprene washer; 7 double-glazed unit

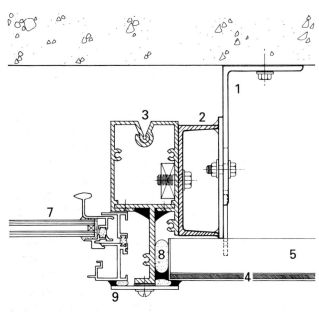

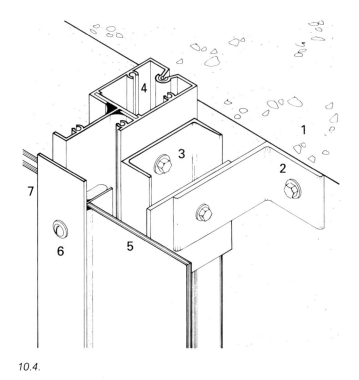

10.2.

10.4.

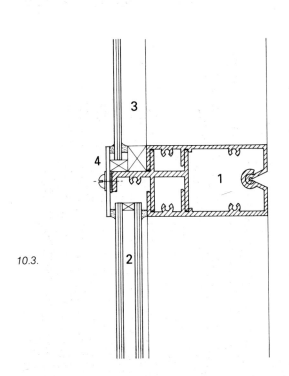

10.3.

1 Finsbury Avenue, London (Phase 1) Architects/Engineers/Quantity Surveyors Arup Associates

General

One Finsbury Avenue is part of a three-phase development built on land owned by British Rail (Figure 11.1). Greycoat Estates were the developers and Arup Associates the architects, engineers and quantity surveyors.

Arup Associates designed an eight-storey atrium building which, by stepping back from the elevation at the sixth floor, maintains the existing urban scale (Figure 11.2). The architects have created a series of planted balconies at the upper levels on all but the south facade. The design of the facades incorporates a system of sunscreens and maintenance walkways which also create a human scale (Figure 11.3). Balconies, sunshades, screens and planting add richness to the central atrium space which is enclosed by a glazed lantern (Figure 11.5).

This building, designed on a square grid, is beautifully detailed and represents a new approach in speculative office building, where the quality of the workplace is important as well as simple efficiently used space. Arup Associates have carefully detailed the interior to allow a great versatility in planning and subdivision. Ceiling tiles, light fittings and air inlets are all easily movable.

Structure

The developers' need for a rapid site erection, coupled with recent requirements for steel fireproofing, allowed spraying of fireproofing onto the steel as an alternative to complete encasement of steelwork in concrete. This led the architects to design a steel-framed structure with steel decking and concrete slab floors. The frame made up from a total of 1500 tons of steel, was in UB and UC sections, and in order to achieve maximum economy the design was based on a simple rectilinear form with repetitive elements and simple bolted connections. Horizontal stability is achieved by diagonally braced frames in the core area.

The floor slab is 130 mm deep overall, constructed on 1.1 mm profiled steel sheeting spanning 3 m and using a lightweight aggregate pumped concrete mix. The concrete slab then acts compositely with the profiled steel sheeting as well as the frame beams by steel shear studs welded to the beams through the profile sheets.

The frame and slabs took 13 weeks to erect on site. The entire process from start on-site to completion of the building took 21 months at a cost of £20 million. External columns at ground-floor level were encased in concrete

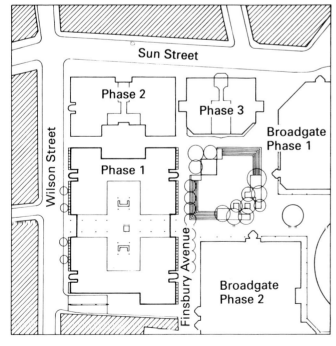

11.1.
Location plan

11.2.
East elevation showing stepped-back balconies on sixth floor, thus reducing the visual bulk of the building

11.1.

11.2.

11.3.
North–south section showing central atrium with floors stepping back

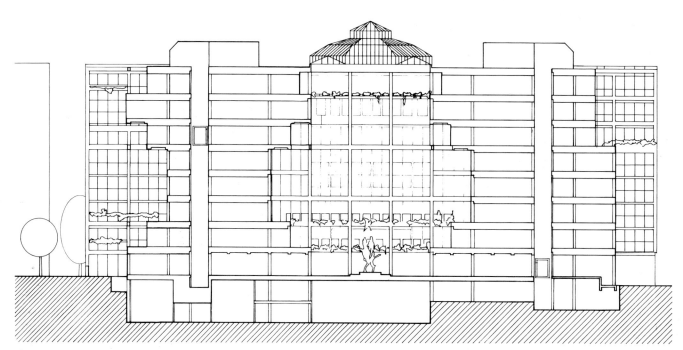

11.3.

and, wherever possible, this process was carried out at the fabrication works. Exposed columns within the building are faced in metal-faced fireboard for protection.

Cladding

The integrated curtain walling system by Joseph Gartner incorporates a patented system whereby hot water is circulated through the r.h.s. members forming the mullions and the transoms of the subframe to which the glazing carrier system is fixed. This provides the only heat source necessary in the building to counteract the main heat loss at the perimeter. The curtain walling is in bronze-anodized aluminium, with panels of the same material being used to clad the frame itself and the externally exposed stairwells. Bronze-coloured glass is used for the spandrel panels. At the ground floor, polished granite is used instead of the bronze-anodized aluminium as the cladding material, and the unpolished variety of the same stone is used as a paving material.

The external louvred sunscreens, which also act as maintenance walkways, are in bronze-anodized aluminium, with elegant edge beams and vertical supports in cruciform aluminium sections (Figure 11.4). Because of the uneven storey heights it has not been possible to maintain a square grid and thus the cross bracing is not lined through. The sunscreens provide shade on the east and west elevations, reducing the load on the air-conditioning system while providing visual interest to the street.

Details

Internally, the atrium opens out after first-storey height. All metalwork is aluminium finished in white synthapulvin, except for the grey-finished mullions and handrails, which employ the same aluminium extrusion as is used in the internal sunshade frames. The structural members of the octagonal glazed lantern also act as the glazing bars, rather than using separate systems. A swivelling gantry enables access to each surface to allow cleaning and maintenance. However, it is the layering and cruciform detail of the support to the external walkway which demonstrates the commitment by the design team to the use of modern materials to enhance the overall scale of the building.

As Peter Buchanan says: 'Arups have provided an object lesson for all architects. They prove that spec. offices can make a sensitive contribution to a civic environment, and that even a huge office building can have a richness and delicate scale suggestive of the human beings who work within – and who will no doubt be enjoying the building too.'

References

Anon., '1 Finsbury Avenue, London: Phase 1', *The Arup Journal*, pp. 2–7.

Buchanan, P., 'Urban Arups', *Architectural Review*, May 1985, pp. 21–30.

Davies, C., 'Craft or calculation', *Architectural Review*, May 1985, pp. 19–20.

11.4.

11.5.

11.6.
*Section through integrated
curtain walling/heating system*

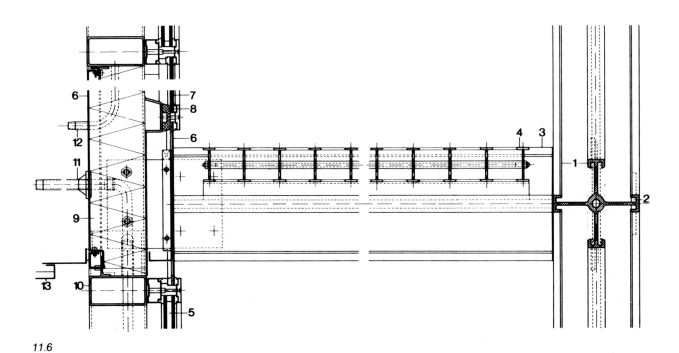

11.6

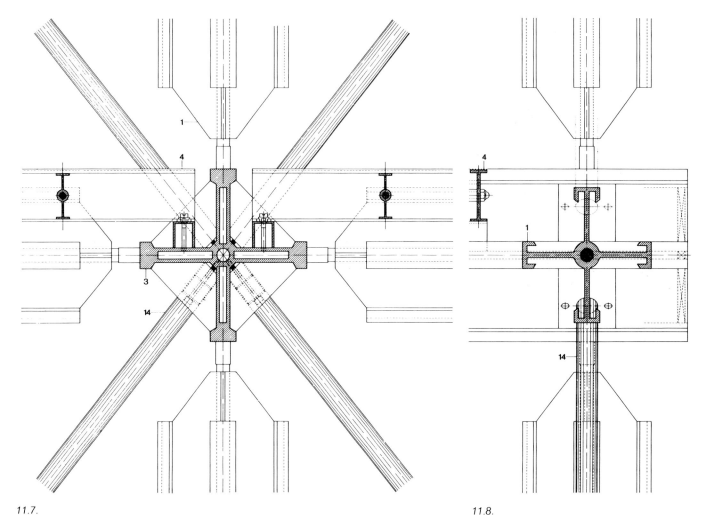

11.7.

11.8.

Details
1 Aluminium-shape 180/180 mm
2 Angle 50/50 mm
3 Aluminium-cantilever 230/230 mm
4 Aluminium-grill, sun-blinds
5 Double glazing

6 Aluminium-cladding 3 mm
7 Spandrel glazing
8 Gasket
9 Insulation
10 Steel section 120/60 mm, heated
11 Return pipe for heating

12 Supply pipe for heating
13 Suspended ceiling
14 Diagonal bracing,
    stainless pipe Ø 30/5 mm
15 Cantilever fixing
    steel plate 340/180/12 mm

12

IBM Travelling Technology Exhibition
Architect
Renzo Piano

12.1.

General

This unique demountable structure was used as a travelling exhibition for IBM during 1984/1985 with sites as varied as Madrid and Helsinki. Under the supervision of Chris Wilkinson Architects, the pavilion was assembled at the Natural History Museum in London and at York (Figure 12.1). Two pavilions were fabricated and erected by the Sicilian firm of Calabrese Engineering SpA, to the original design of Renzo Piano and developed with the assistance of Ove Arup and Partners. Twenty-three specially designed bright-yellow trucks were used to transport the exhibition.

Structure

The structure is composed of 34 three-pinned arches (Figure 12.3) to a radius of 5.3 m with a single timber chord at 5.9 m radius joining the tops of the polycarbonate pyramids forming the skin. Each half arch comprises six polycarbonate pyramids, with three pyramids moulded out of a single sheet. The key cross section (Figure 12.2) shows how the polycarbonate acts as diagonal struts joining the timber chord members made of laminated beech with cast aluminium connectors. For transport, each arch was separated into four major components:

1. Two outer-chord timber members;
2. Four inner-chord timber members;

3. Fourteen inner-chord cross members;
4. Four sets of three pyramids.

The 600 mm deep half arch was then assembled on site by fixing the outer timber chords to the two sets of polycarbonate pyramids using stainless steel washers glued to two faces of the apex of the pyramid (Figure 12.4) (Dini, p. 78, shows Renzo Piano's original method of connecting the polycarbonate to its supporting framework which was later developed for the IBM travelling exhibition.) Figure 12.5 shows the formed stainless steel plate (a Kinch plate, named after Robert Kinch, one of the engineers working at Ove Arup and Partners) bolted to these washers with a rubber block cast on a rod radiating from the plate. This rubber block has a push fit into the external aluminium nodes connecting the outer timber chords. The pyramids are connected to the inner timber by 200 mm long stainless steel rods (Figure 12.6). A stainless steel block with a rotating cross pin is glued to the polycarbonate and the rod is screwed into the cross pin (Figure 12.7). The other end of the rod has a rubber block cast on and pushed into the aluminium node of the inner timber chords. At the base of the assembly the inner chords are pinned to a stainless steel plate (Figure 12.8) bolted to the edge beam. An important feature of this construction is that these movable metal rods allow for the differential thermal movement between the polycarbonate and that of the wood and aluminium struts.

Thus the construction is significant both in the way it

46

12.1.
The IBM pavilion at York

12.2.
Cross section through pavilion

12.3.
Plan of pavilion

12.2.

overcomes the difference in thermal movement of the components used and the method of connecting the polycarbonate to the timber using the stainless steel connectors which made ease of assembly possible, even allowing for temperature and tolerance effects. Also of interest to the student of prefabrication is the elegant means of connecting the beechwood struts with the cast aluminium nodes (Figure 12.6), which shows how traditional craftsmanship of finger jointing can be translated into new material.

Polycarbonate panels

The polycarbonate pyramids were produced as a unit in sets of three, partly to ease transportation in relation to their length but also because 8.5 m was the maximum

length of sheet available for fabrication. These units were joined with an overlap detail at their horizontal joint. The vertical weather joint between the polycarbonate units was achieved by a thin transparent PVC strip fed down between the units which was disposable and replaced at each assembly (Figure 12.9). This system of pressed polycarbonate units forming the arc was originally developed by Renzo Piano as polyester frames at Genoa, Italy, in 1964/1965.

End wall panels

Perhaps the most disappointing feature of the pavilion was the solid timber-panelled end walls (a client requirement) (Figure 12.10) made visually lighter by the use of mirrors internally to carry through the effect of the structure.

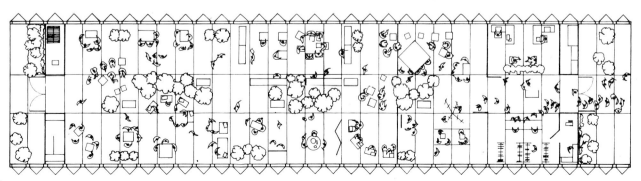

12.3.

12.4.
Exploded view of fixing at apex of pyramid. 1 Stainless steel (Kinch) plate; 2 stainless steel washers glued to each side of the polycarbonate pyramids; 3 stainless steel rod with rubber block cast on; 4 aluminium node finger jointed to outer beechwood chord

12.5.
Fixing at apex of polycarbonate pyramid

12.6.
Exploded view of fixing at base of pyramid. 1 Stainless steel block glued to polycarbonate pyramid; 2 freely rotating cross pin; 3 200 mm long rod fixed to the cross pin at one end, a rubber block cast on the other; 4 aluminium node finger jointed to inner beechwood chord. Note that node is pinned to base plate

12.7.
Rods connecting polycarbonate pyramid to inner timber chords. Note anti-condensation air nozzle on duct between chords

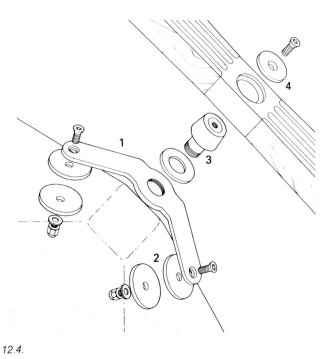

12.4.

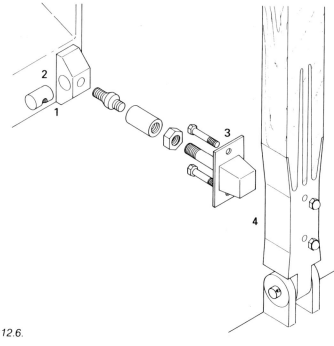

12.6.

12.5.

12.7.

12.8.
Pinned joint at base of arch

12.9.
Polycarbonate units with transparent PVC strip. Note fishtail air ducts

12.10.
Timber-panelled end walls. Note also at top of arch vein ducts branching off main spine duct

Services

All services were originally intended to fit within the floor space and exposed ducts were used to pass air between the services floor zone to the skin zone by means of 'fishtail' ducts (see Figure 12.9). It may be interesting to note the similarity of this method to that used by Richard Rogers at Lloyds of London, where a similar technique was used to pass the warm air through the glazed external walls.

In addition, condensation was controlled by passing small quantities of heated air onto the inner surfaces of the pyramids from aircraft-type nozzles from the 'vein' duct, which passes between the pairs of inner chords forming the arches from a central supply duct (see Figures 12.7 and 12.10).

Temperature control

The original concept of the transparent polycarbonate skin led to some problems from glare and heat build-up. To enable the internal temperature to be regulated, modifying devices comprising double-walled white insulated polycarbonate pyramids were fitted within the transparent pyramids. Additional thermal control and shading devices made from perforated aluminium panels were also used. A computer program had been developed to establish the thermal performance and to give the required heating and cooling capacities of the air-conditioning system.

References

Anon., Pavillon d'Exposition IBM, IBM Pavilion Pan 1984. *Architecture d'Aujourdhui*, 235, October 1984.

Dini, M., *Renzo Piano, Project and Buildings 1964–1983*, Architectural Press (now Butterworth Architecture), London, 1984, pp. 74–79. Describes early development of the 'electronic greenhouse' but the method of connecting the polycarbonate pyramids to the aluminium nodes was later superseded.

Hannay, P., 'Piano forte', *Architects' Journal*, 24 October 1984, pp. 24–27. Not a particularly useful technical reference but shows photographs of assembly of the pavilion at the Natural History Museum site in London.

Kinch, R. and Guthrie, A., 'The IBM travelling technology exhibition', *The Arup Journal*, **19**, No. 4, December 1984, pp. 2–6 (published by Ove Arup and Partners, London). By far the best source of information on the development of the structure and services, with clear photographs of the connection joint details and anti-condensation air nozzle.

12.8.

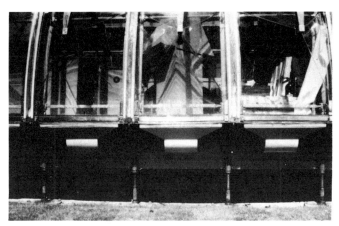

12.9.

12.10.

13

Johnson and Johnson World Headquarters, New Brunswick, New Jersey
Architects
I.M. Pei & Partners

General

This office complex, built in 1982 for Johnson and Johnson Inc., is situated within a 16-acre parkland setting, 501 George Street, adjacent to Rutgers University Campus in New Jersey, USA. The complex consists of a 16-storey tower linked to a series of connected four-storey blocks of offices. The tower, a modified square plan, and the serrated-shaped wing are clad in aluminium panels with continuous bands of clear glass (Figure 13.1). This early use of plate aluminium assembly is the main reason for its inclusion here.

The total floor area is 450 000 ft^2, of which approximately one third is contained within the tower and the rest in the serrated-shaped wing. Executive parking for 70 cars is located below the lawn fronting the tower, with space for a further 800 cars on the northern part of the site. The main contractors were John W. Ryan Company, NYC and the panel fabricators were Trio Industries. The total project value was $76 500 000.

13.2.

13.1.

13.1.
General view

13.2.
Aluminium panel fixed back to
concrete frame

13.3.
Sequence of assembly

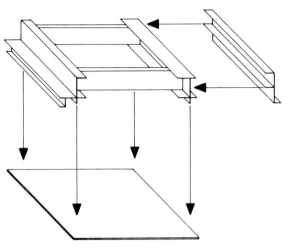

13.3 .1

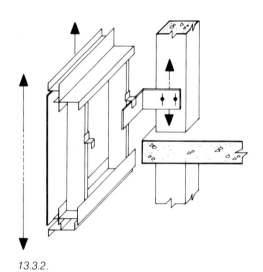

13.3.2.

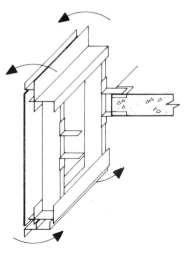

13.3.3.

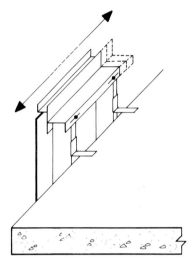

13.3.4

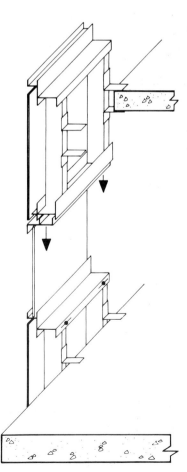

13.3.5.

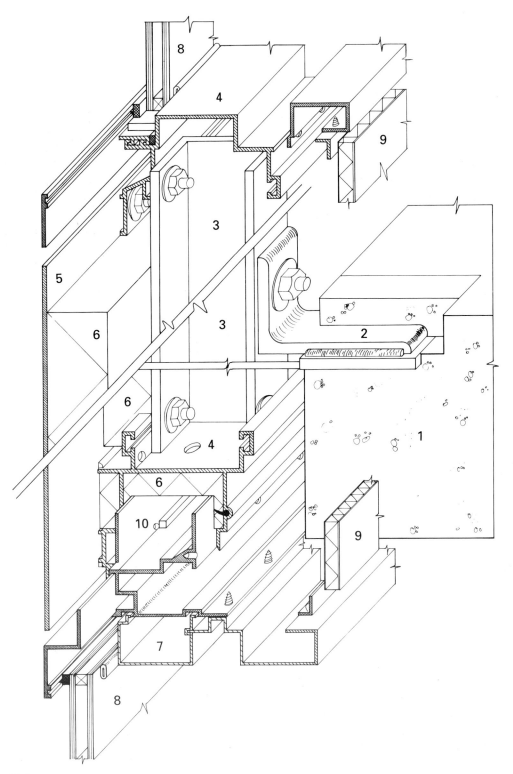

8

4

9

3

5

3

6

2

6

1

4

6

10

9

7

8

13.4.

13.4.
Sectional axonometric of fixing to slab. 1 Concrete floor slab; 2 steel angle site welded to steel inset cast into slab; 3 vertical member of panel frame; 4 horizontal member of panel frame; 5 4.5 mm thick aluminium sheet panel; 6 mineral wool insulation; 7 window head retainer; 8 double-glazed panel; 9 internal lining board; 10 weepholes

13.5.
Detail of horizontal joint. 1 4.5 mm thick aluminium sheet panel; 2 Silpruf seals; 3 weepholes and baffle in upstand gutter; 4 neoprene wipe seals; 5 back-up gutter section at top of panel; 6 9 mm diameter weeptube

13.6.
Aluminium top-hat section between aluminium sheets forming a false joint. 1 4.5 mm thick aluminium sheet panels; 2 Silpruf seals; 3 extruded aluminium top-hat section; 4 stiffener section

13.7.
Detail of glazed unit cill. 1 4.5 mm thick aluminium sheet panel; 2 double-glazed window unit; 3 Silpruf seal; 4 weepholes; 5 vertical member of panel frame; 6 internal lining

Cladding

Figure 13.2 shows the 4.5 mm sheet aluminium panel, colour off-white, mounted on an extruded aluminium framed fixed back by cleats to the concrete floor slab. The sequence of assembly (Figure 13.3) was as follows:

1. The panel sheet was bolted to the aluminium frame and a window head retainer was screwed to the bottom horizontal member for transportation.
2. A temporary bracket was fixed to the columns and the height of the window cill was corrected. Cleats were then bolted to the frame uprights in a corresponding position.
3. Alignment of the panel was then set and the cleats were welded to steel insets in the slab.
4. The panel was positioned horizontally by sliding the panel sheet and horizontal rails against the stationary verticals.
5. The window was positioned and the head restraint was released down onto it. Glazing strips and seals were then attached.

Mineral wool insulation was mounted *in-situ* within the panel frame and an internal lining board was fixed to the rear face (Figure 13.4).

The detail of the horizontal joint (Figure 13.5) shows the back-up drainage system using an upstand gutter with weepholes to discharge any water penetrating the neoprene seals at the base of the panel. An unusual feature of the design is a 3 mm thick gutter section at the top of the panel mounted between the vertical frame members, which also drains any water entering the panel past the Silpruf sealant down to the base of the panel via a 9 mm diameter weeptube. It was this obsession with self-draining systems which typifies the US aluminium curtain walling systems of the early 1980s, possibly because of the lack of confidence in long-term durability of the available sealants and gaskets.

Another interesting feature of the design is the false joints formed between the 5 ft high infill panel and the 2 ft 2½ in top infill panel making up the total height of panel assembly of 7 ft 4 in, including the joint. This was formed using an aluminium top hat bolted to the inner side of the aluminium outer sheet (Figure 13.6). This may have been used for aesthetic reasons, but it is more likely that 5 ft was the maximum width of plate aluminium available.

Windows

Double-glazed window units are mounted back into a similar aluminium framing member as the panels, which also includes weepholes below the glazing units (Figure 13.7).

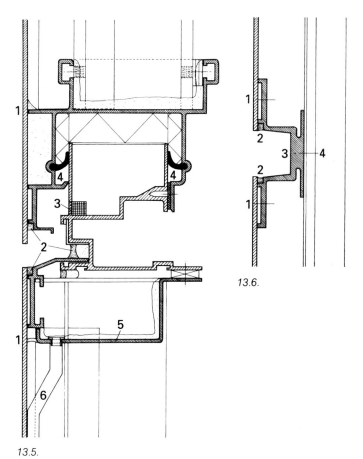

13.6.

13.5.

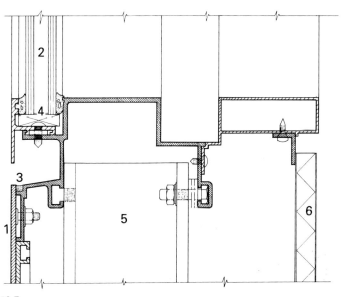

13.7.

14

Lloyds of London: Atrium
Architects
Richard Rogers Partnership

14.1.

14.1.
View of the Lloyds atrium from the south

14.2.
Detail of cast steel fixing bracket

14.3.
Atrium under construction

General

14.2.

As with the Hongkong and Shanghai Bank (Case Study 32), many articles have been written about the Lloyds Building and comparisons drawn between the two. The external cladding to the building has been described in Brookes, *Concepts of Cladding*, and this study is concerned only with the large atrium in the centre of the building with its prominent barrel-vault structure by Josef Gartner (Figure 14.1). Brief mention is also made of the staircase treads of the satellite service towers, which were formed by Nedal (Holland) and fixed by the Wessex Guild Ltd, this being one of the largest aluminium extrusions yet produced for the building industry.

Atrium structure

Although Lloyds was originally conceived of as a steel building, requirements for fireproofing eventually resulted in the use of a concrete frame. For the large glass enclosure of the full-height atrium, however, the fire-resistance requirements were less stringent and the preferred material could be used. Ove Arup and Partners were structural engineers for the primary and atrium structures. The main concrete columns, having performed their primary purpose of supporting the floors, extend up to the springing of the barrel vault to act as the main supports of the steel cage. The key component at this transition point from steel to concrete is a complex (two-limbed) cast steel bracket (Figure 14.2). These brackets thus form the bearing points for the steel structure, composed of a series of tubular lattices exposed on the outside of the building. The tubular arch lattices are supported on tubular steel triangular cross-section lattice beams which span between the concrete supports (Figure 14.3). Tubeworkers Ltd fabricated the atrium steelwork. The lattices use nodes of cast steel for bolting the steel members together, the cost of which was kept within reasonable limits by standardization of the members.

Cladding

The curtain walling is an aluminium-framed thermally broken carrier system fixed to the inner flanges of the

14.3.

tubular steel trusses (Figure 14.4). This supports the double glazing. A facility for a vertical cleaning track is also provided.

This is one of the few places in the building where a major component is not self-finished and maintenance-free. Elsewhere, stainless steel is used, but for the atrium it was decided to paint the structure, which is said to have a minimum life of 10 years before re-coating. A cleaning gantry is provided at the apex of the arch for external maintenance along which a crane runs. There is also an internal cleaning gantry at the springing of the arch.

One of the difficulties presented by the sequence of operations is that the large sheets of glass required for the curtain walling had to be fed between the exposed steelwork of the atrium and the concrete structure, and special tilting lifts were devised by Josef Gartner (Figure 14.6) to make this possible. Often the viability of a technical proposal is dependent on such ingenuity and experience of the fixing subcontractors, and architects would do well in understanding more of the means of assembly of components in building.

Services

A series of extract systems are used to draw up hot air from 'The Room', and the office above it, through the atrium by means of the chimney effect. These extract ducts are held by cantilevered steel supports connected to the triangular steel lattice edge beam and are expressed on the outside of the building.

Details

Although Lloyds is better known for the details of the external facade such as the 'fishtail' ducting (Figure 14.5)

55

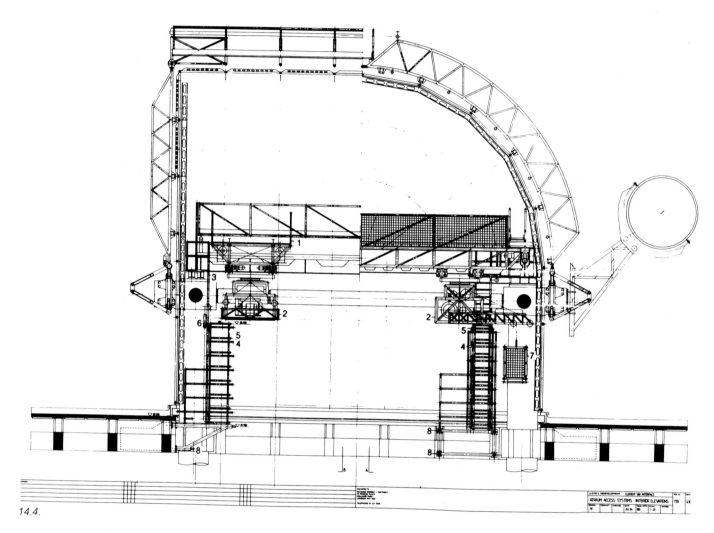

14.4.

or the fully assembled toilet modules by Jordans of Bristol, there are many less obvious examples of ingenuity in component detailing. One of these is the innovative use of large aluminium extrusions devised for the staircases of the satellite service towers. Rumour has it that Rogers, on visiting the Gartner works, saw the ends of a pile of square aluminium extrusions and suggested to job architects Frank Peacock and Amo Kalsi that these could be bolted together to form a system of aluminium staircase treads. On further investigation with one of the largest aluminium extruding companies in the world, Nedal (Utrecht), manufacturers of such products as yacht masts, flag poles and special extrusions for transport, it was found that the complete extrusion (requiring a die of approximately 500 mm diameter) could be made in one section (Figure 14.7). As a result, almost 2000 triangular profile treads, each the width of a staircase, were manufactured for this project and bolted to steel I-beams, which in turn were bolted to the *in-situ* concrete ramp which spans between floors (Figure 14.8).

14.5.

14.6.
Lifting equipment to offer double-glazed units up to frame

14.7.
Stair assembly

14.8.
Section through stair extrusion

14.6.a.

14.6.b.

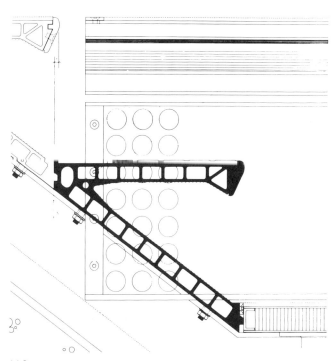

14.7.

Once assembled, rubber stair treads with aluminium nosings were clipped to the aluminium extrusions forming the treads. Although very ingenious and appearing to satisfy the philosphy of component assembly, one could envisage simpler and therefore less costly ways of forming such a staircase assembly, as it would appear that the bottom member of the extrusion in the plane of the pitoh of tho ctaircase is duplicating the purpose of the slab below.

References

Anon., 'Two engineered solutions', *Architects' Journal*, 22 October 1986, pp. 79–94.

Brookes, A.J., 'Lloyds redevelopment, London', in *Concepts in Cladding*, Construction Press, London, 1985, pp. 75–80.

Davies, C., 'Lloyds: putting it together', *Architectural Review*, 1986, pp. 69–80.

Murray, P., *Lloyds of London*, Edizioni Tecno, 1985.

Russel, F., *Richard Rogers, Architects*, Academy Editions, London, 1985, pp. 130–133.

14.8.

Locomotive Shed, Preston Dock
Architects
Brock Carmichael Associates

15.1.

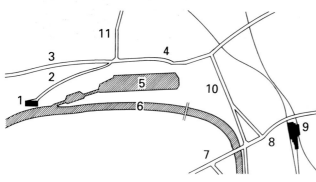

15.2.

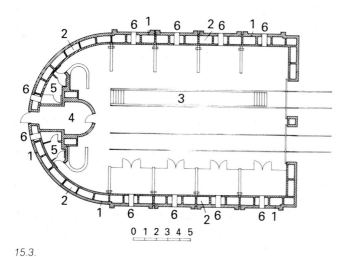

15.3.

General

Completed in 1986 for the Borough of Preston, in Lancashire, the new engine shed for the maintenance of the three locomotives that serve the Preston Dock was needed because extensive redevelopment of the Dock Estate for commercial and residential uses required the relocation of the dock railway (Figure 15.1). Located at the end of Chain Caul Road, Preston (Figure 15.2), the building provides both a landmark from the landscaped riverside walk and a visual end to the railway line. The architects decided to use traditional materials (bricks and slate) in a modern way to create a contemporary structure which, at the same time, would present an industrial image suitable for a railway building. It houses the locomotives with an inspection pit and lifting beam, toilet and shower facilities, mess room and supervisor's office (Figure 15.3).

Structure

The brick diaphragm walls with an external leaf of 215 mm and an internal one of 102.5 mm, separated by a 797 mm space, form a wall of 1115 mm total thickness (Figure 15.4). This supports a 675 mm deep precast concrete ringbeam on all walls. From this are sprung four 457×152 mm $\times$ 52 kg/m^3 universal beams with circular cutouts, supporting an arch-type structure made up from 219.1×10 mm c.h.s. with a 139.7×5 mm c.h.s. hoop above. Similarly, at the apse end, four $457 \times 152 \times$ 52 kg/m^3 UBs support the circular end of the arch structure above. The whole structure is braced around the perimeter by 114.3×3.6 mm c.h.s. cross bracings with additional ties in the four square roof bays and in one bay of the main structure (Figure 15.7).

The roof is supported by U-section purlins spanning between the main UBs which, in turn, support the timber rafters, battens and slate tiles above (Figure 15.5). The whole structure is supported by a 250 mm thick reinforced concrete raft with a 600 mm deep perimeter edge beam.

Glazed lantern

The glazed lantern consists of Haywood's Patent Glazing (System 4672) at 610 mm spacing with 6 mm Georgian wire polished glass. The patent glazing sections span between an anodized aluminium ridge piece propped from the top of the c.h.s. arches and an upstand r.h.s. clad with anodized aluminium profiled sheet cladding (Figure 15.6). A continuous cleaning rail runs externally around the lantern upstand. It is this sophistication of

15.1.
View of gable wall

15.2.
Site plan. 1 Locomotive shed; 2 Chain Caul Road; 3 Riversway; 4 Water Lane; 5 Albert Edward Dock; 6 River Ribble; 7 Liverpool Road; 8 Fishergate Hill; 9 Preston Railway Station; 10 Strand Road; 11 Pedder's Lane

15.3.
Plan. 1 Diaphragm wall; 2 precast concrete ring beam above; 3 inspection pit; 4 mess room; 5 toilets; 6 high-level vents

15.4.
Half section half elevation of locomotive shed. 1 Diaphragm wall construction, 215 mm thick outer leaf, 797 mm cavity, 102.5 mm thick inner leaf; 2 precast concrete ring beam 675 mm deep; 3 Universal Beams, 457 × 152 × 52 kg/m³ with circular cutouts; 4 steel arch formed from 219 × 10 mm c.h.s.; 5 high-level extract duct; 6 114.3 × 3.6 mm c.h.s. bracing; 7 lifting beam; 8 inspection pit; 9 circular louvred air vent

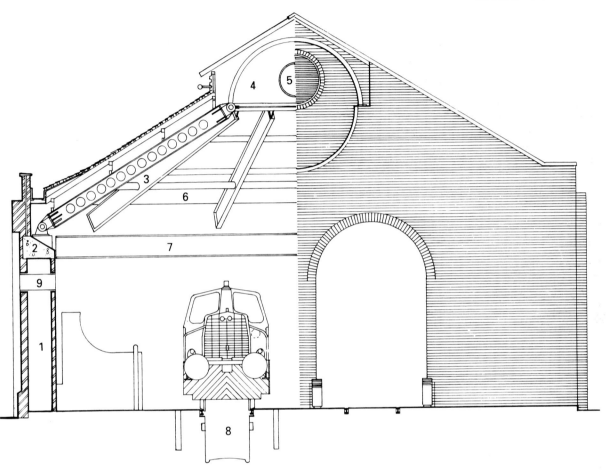

15.4.

Roof finish

The roof is composed of 457 × 254 mm Penrhyn Welsh slates on softwood battens, roofing felt, and 125 × 38 mm softwood rafters with 100 mm of mineral fibre insulation between. The rafters are firred at their ends to allow the rainwater to be discharged into a 400 × 400 mm pressed steel gutter supported by timber battens, which in turn restrain the parapet wall throughout its length at 1 m above its base (see Figure 15.5).

The brick walls

The exterior brickwork is mainly Blockley's Brindle Mix XVIII laid in Flemish bond. Nori Best Red Smooth facing bricks, manufactured by Accrington Brick and Tile Company Ltd and supplied as Procter and Lavender Red Smooths, are used for feature bands and arches. The interior is given a light, airy feel using Smooth Lumley Buffs (stretcher bond) with complementary detailing in Procter and Lavender Reds. Lumley Buffs are also used for the exterior plinth.

Other external features include four 215 mm deep arch details bonded to each side wall centred on bullseye ventilation openings (Figure 15.7). The front gable wall features two arched entrances and a central inverted arch at the apex of the gable: this required the use of permanent polystyrene foam formers above the ring beam. Twenty-five millimetre Jablite expanded polystyrene forms the wall insulation fixed to the inner leaf with cavity straps, the whole assembly being built from the inside outwards.

detailing which characterizes the construction of the building.

15.5.
Gutter detail. 1 Cavity parapet wall; 2 precast concrete ring beam; 3 diaphragm wall; 4 steel bracket bolted to ring beam; 5 Universal Beams, 457 × 152 × 52 kg/m³ with 244 mm diameter cutouts; 6 cross bracing; 7 steel channel purlins; 8 125 × 38 mm rafters firred at gutter ends; 9 100 mm mineral fibre insulation; 10 400 × 400 mm pressed steel gutter

15.6.
Lantern detail. 1 Haywood patent glazing; 2 aluminium ridge piece propped off c.h.s. arches; 3 high-level extract duct suspended off c.h.s. arches; 4 anodized aluminium profiled sheet cladding; 5 cleaning rail

15.7.
Site-progress photograph showing roof steelwork

15.8.
Model of locomotive shed

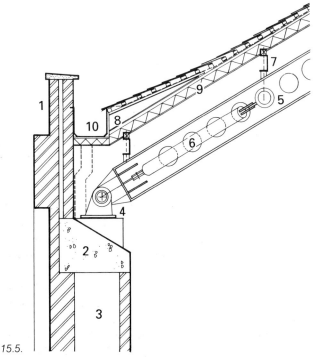

15.5.

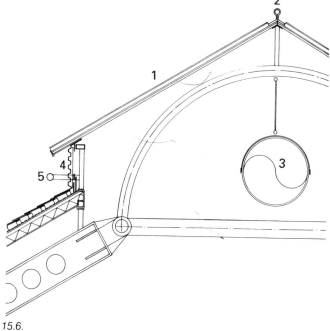

15.6.

Services

An ingenious system of exhaust and extraction is slung below the main roof structure. Designed by Rodney Environmental Consultants, the system is basically in three parts. First, a high-level general extract system is connected to a large circular louvre on the front facade. Second, a local high-pressure system is attached to the locomotive exhaust and ducted to circular louvres on the sides of the building. Two additional circular louvres with adjustable blades on the same elevation are used to equalize the pressure within the building. Finally, a gas-fired Reznov warm-air system is distributed by header ducts along each side of the building. Additional heating and low-pressure hot-water coils are provided in the maintenance pit and the small office and rest-room areas.

Lighting is sodium and electric services are also provided to a fixed beam to allow transverse lift of motors for inspection and maintenance.

References

Hetherinton, R. and Jamieson, B., 'The locomotive shed at Preston Dock', *BPA Engineers File*, Note No. 4, November 1986.

Marsh, P., 'Brick Development Association structural brickwork awards', *Building Design* (Bricks Supplement), 1986.

Ostler, T., 'Practice profile', *The Architect*, May 1987, pp. 47–50.

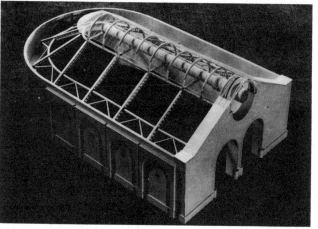

15.7.

15.8.

The Menil Museum, Houston, Texas
Architect
Renzo Piano

General

This museum was built to house the De Menil Collection of Modern and African Primitive Art in Montrose, Houston, Texas, USA (Figure 16.1). A close friend of the client, Pontus Hulten (Director of the Pompidou Centre's Art Museum), suggested Penzo Piano as the architect, and after a trip to Israel in late 1980 the idea for a museum where the use of controlled daylight to illuminate the display objects was first suggested. Although modified since the first proposals, the design concepts of Renzo Piano with Peter Rice and Tom Barker from Ove Arup and Partners were developed in association with Richard Fitzgerald Partners, Architects.

Occupying an entire city block (Figure 16.3), the museum with its module of 40 × 20 ft comprises a rectangle 402 × 142 ft with a maximum height of 45 ft. The visual theme of grey clapboard with white trim and black canvas awnings resulted from the client's requirements, but it is the platform roofs with their elegant leaf shapes that makes the Menil Museum more than just a simple box (Figure 16.2).

Roof baffles

Natural lighting without glare is achieved by Piano's ingenious roof formed from ferrocement leaves hanging from ductile iron trusses. The whole character of the building is determined by this elegant organic roof structure which has an uninterrupted span of 12 m (40 ft grid) across the bays (Figures 16.4 and 16.5). The ferrocement leaves were individually cast on a concrete formwork by Ferrocement Laminates Ltd of Leeds, specialists in concrete boat building. The underside of the leaf was hand finished while the top surface remained with its moulded form. The leaves were then bolted to a ductile iron (spheroid graphite) frames (Figure 16.6), which were made by North American Foundries Co., (and not Crown Foundry, as reported by Glancey). These frames were cast as individual triangular units which were bolted together and connected to the leaf to form 10 triangular truss bays spanning the complete 12 m. These frames were then fixed to trusses spanning across the 20 ft grid which also support the

16.1. General view

16.2.
Section through gallery

16.3.
Site plan. 1 Public entrance; 2
staff entrance; 3 temporary
exhibition gallery; 4 permanent
exhibition gallery; 5 conservation
laboratory; 6 staff lounge; 7
registration; 8 reception; 9 shop;
10 library; 11 orientation; 12 cafe;
13 administration

16.4.
Section across museum

16.5.
Internal view of gallery

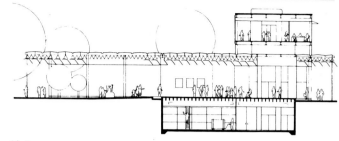

16.4.

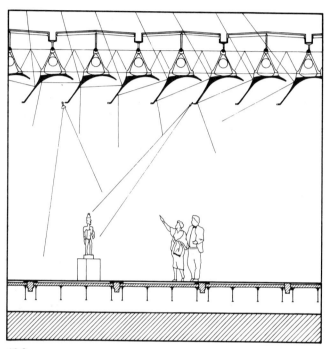

16.2.

16.5.

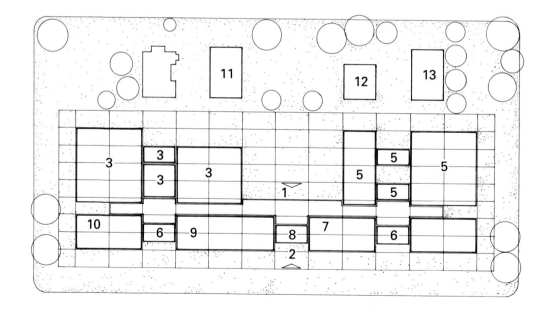
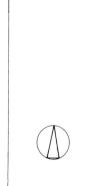

16.3.

glazed roof above. A common misunderstanding is that the ferrocement louvres are adjustable – this is not the case. They act simply as reflectors to diffuse the light and prevent direct sunlight entering the building. Their shape has been derived from the sunlight conditions in Houston.

The shape of the leaves evolved from months of study, involving specific properties of materials, structural behaviour and optimum lighting angles. According to *Progressive Architecture*, the initial concept was of leaves in the form of flattened quarter circles connected by a truss derived from the Arverdi tubular system. The final shapes were developed by computer-generated modelling and actual physical mockups (see *PA News Report*, September, 1982, p. 40). Dini's book on Renzo Piano's projects and buildings shows him in work sessions with Peter Rice and Tom Barker on his full-scale mockup of a typical exhibition room to study the true latitude of Houston, the results of research carried out previously on 1:10 scale models using theoretical mathematical analysis. It is this combination of design engineering and research that is so essential for the development of sophisticated component technology.

Piano has always been known for his interest in the craft of building related to the production of sophisticated components, and it is the choice of what are essentially traditional moulded materials (i.e. concrete and cast iron) which makes this assembly so interesting for students of the technology, and shows that architects need not be constantly looking for new materials (polycarbonates, etc.) but can use appropriate techniques to solve specific problems.

References

Anon., 'The responsive box', *Progressive Architecture*, May 1987, pp. 87–97.

Anon., 'Museo Menil, Houston', *Domus*, No. 34, August 1987, pp. 33–42.

Dini, M., *Renzo Piano, Projects and Buildings 1964–1983*, Architectural Press (now Butterworth Architecture), London, 1985, pp. 272–303.

Glancey, J., 'Piano pieces', *Architectural Review*, May 1985, pp. 59–63.

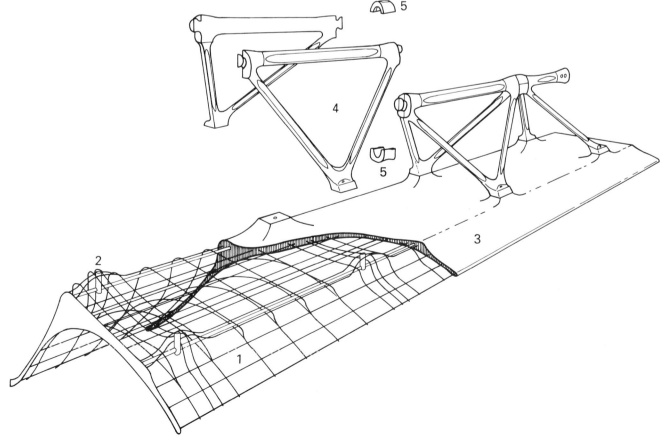

16.6.

Museum at Kempsey, New South Wales
Architect
Glenn Murcutt

General

Murcutt has been described by Alison Smithson as a 'timber and tin Miesian', and this building clearly displays his rational approach to building construction using low-cost materials such as corrugated steel roofing sheets to achieve an architectural simplicity. This building can be seen as a forerunner for his later work in Sydney (see *Architectural Review*, July 1987).

The museum at Kempsey, New South Wales, Australia, built in 1981, comprises three linked pavilions with vaulted roofs in corrugated steel (Figures 17.1 and 17.2). Light plays an important role in the design, with roof lights above the north pitch of the museum hall and in the smallest theatre pavilion (Figure 17.3). In order to control the internal temperature during the summer months, another characteristic of the design is the overlapping of the upper vault sheets. In addition, thin adjustable vents are provided along the tops of each wall, and two rows of rotary turbine vents either side of the central roof ridge exhaust stale air from the top of the building and form part of its character.

Structure

This is set out on a 4 m square grid (Figure 17.4), with tubular steel columns and bow-type trusses, whose bottom tension chords also support the centrally positioned fluorescent light fittings. The plate connector between the column and purlin has been deliberately enlarged to express its function. Below these purlins and spanning onto the loadbearing side walls a series of 100 × 38 mm pine rafters support the glazing where provided. Elsewhere, a secondary sheet of corrugated steel spans between purlin and wall.

Cladding

Roofs are a double skin of corrugated Lysaght 66 Zincalume, fixed with self-drilled screws and neoprene washers to mild steel Z-purlins at 900 mm centres (Figure 17.5). Insulation stops 50 mm clear at the purlins to allow air movement between the corrugations. The walls are 150 × 25 mm cedar panelling over 75 mm Insulwool, fixed back to the loadbearing brick walls. A glass block screen is positioned in front of the toilet block.

References

Bec, H., 'Detailing, national identity and a sense of place in Australian architecture', *UIA – International*

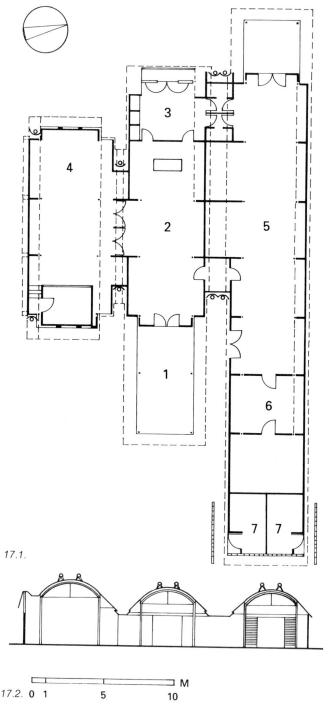

17.1.

17.2.

Architect, Edition 4, 1984, pp. 16–17.

Ogg, A., *Architecture in Steel – the Australian Context*, Royal Australian Institute of Architects, 1987.

Pegrum, R., *Details in Australian Architecture*, RAIA Education Division, 1984, pp. 16–17.

Spence, R., 'Museum boundaries', *Architectural Review*, February 1984, pp. 45–47.

17.1.
Plan. 1 Entry porch; 2 tourist information; 3 staff office; 4 theatre; 5 museum; 6 office and workshop; 7 public toilets

17.2.
Section

17.3.
Section through one pavilion. 1 Roof vents; 2 89 mm diameter c.h.s. curved to roof profile; 3 steel tie rod; 4 300 × 50 mm timber fascia beam; 5 brick wall; 6 mild steel Z purlins; 7 corrugated steel roofing with inner layer of corrugated ceiling lining; 8 600 mm wide steel through gutter

17.4.
Isometric of pavilion structure

17.5.
Detail of slat sunscreen. 1 75 × 3.2 mm aluminium louvres; 2 6 mm clear toughened glass; 3 aluminium glazing bars at 660 mm centres; 4 100 × 38 mm pine rafters under each glazing bar; 5 89 mm diameter c.h.s. lining; 6 150 mm mild steel Z-purlin; 7 insulation; 8 corrugated steel roof fixed with self-tapping screws

17.3.

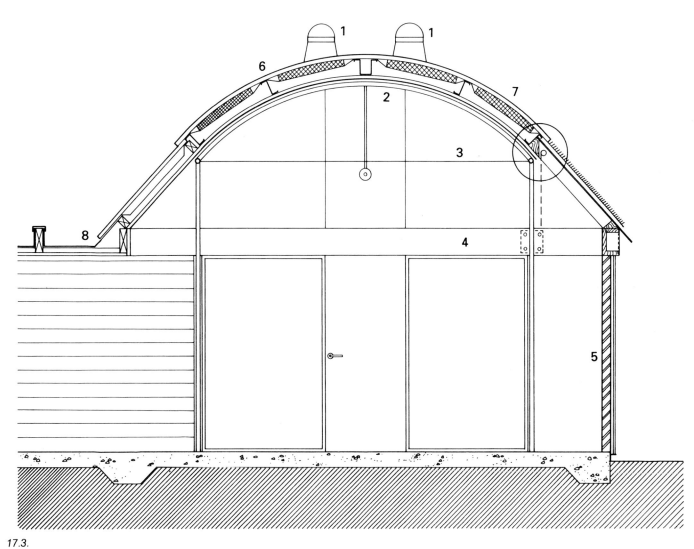

17.4.

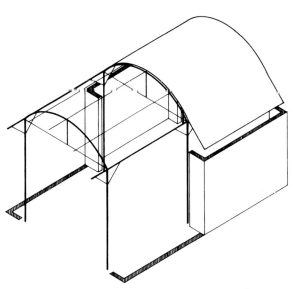

17.5.

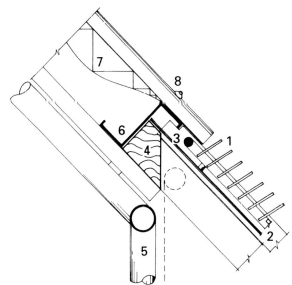

Oculenti Contact Lens Factory, Holland
Architect
Thijs Asselbergs

18.1.

General

Situated in north Hoofddorp near Amsterdam in Holland (Figure 18.1), this small factory by architect Thijs Asselbergs was completed in October 1985. It was built for a small manufacturer of contact lenses, and the square-plan building consists of office accommodation on the ground floor, comprising directors' offices, reception, general offices and central toilets, with a top-lit central staircase leading to the first-floor workshop areas, canteen and meeting room with stacked toilet unit.

The building has a modern image, complete with corner details obviously influenced by Mies van de Rohe's ITT building in Chicago (Figure 18.3). With a floor area contained within the square grid of ten bays each measuring 1.64 m, and an elevation of six bays each measuring 1.04 m all carefully designed around a grid, the building represents a clear demonstration of dimensional coordination (Figure 18.2).

Structure

The building appears to be supported by two box-like structures cantilevered from four masts, forming a square at the centre of the buildings. In reality, the ground floor comprises a precast concrete-framed structure (Figure 18.4) onto which the steel frame has been mounted. This probably has resulted from the building-

18.1.
General view

18.2.
Elevation, section and plan. 1.
Reception; 2 offices; 3 store
room; 4 staff entrance; 5 meter
cupboard; 6 toilets; 7 fitting room;
8 lens production; 9 meeting
room; 10 canteen; 11 services; 12
air lock

18.3.
Comparison of corner details. (a)
Asselbergs. (b) Mies van der
Rohe

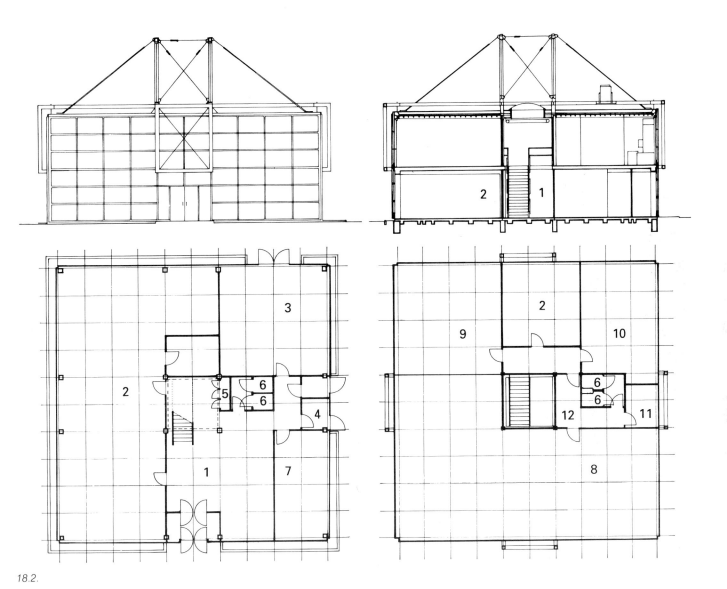

18.2.

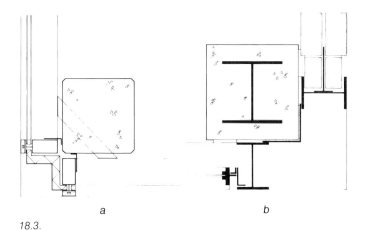

a   b

18.3.

control requirement allowing single-storey unprotected
steel frames (Figure 18.5).

The ground floor concrete ring beam supports a series
of precast concrete flooring units. The frame and the
first-floor slab are formed in reinforced concrete, with
four concrete columns set 3.28 m apart, defining the
central square of the building. These central columns
continue as steel r.h.s. section which are cross braced
together, and a frame consisting of four pairs of steel
H-beams, 210 mm square and 3.28 m apart, are welded
to them and have cantilevered supports from the floor
slab at the edge of the building. These vertical supporting frames are cross braced with steel cables (Figure
18.6).

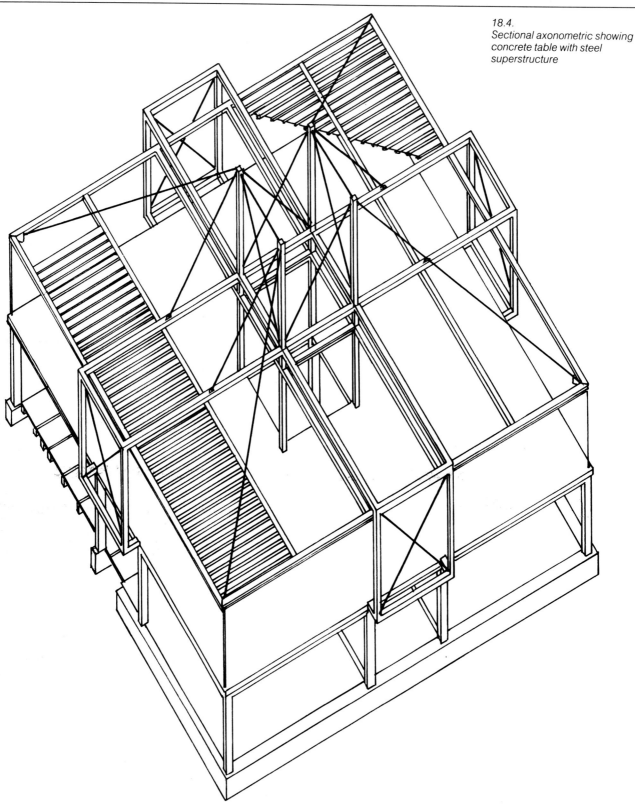

18.4.
Sectional axonometric showing
concrete table with steel
superstructure

18.4.

At the perimeter of the first floor there are no vertical columns, the roof edge beams being supported at their ends and one-third intervals by suspension cables, in the centre two points by the box frame and at their corners from the central masts. The corner junctions of the edge beams are also tied to the concrete slab below. It was necessary to prop these edge beams during construction prior to installation of the tension links.

Cladding

The cladding consists on both ground and first floors of a simple curtain walling section fixed at the head and base to the supporting structure. The black-finished aluminium

18.5.
The building under construction

18.6.
*Section through the building. 1
Concrete foundations; 2 concrete
table; 3 steel members supported
off concrete base*

18.7.
*Eaves detail. 1 Steel
superstructure; 2 adjustable steel
hanger; 3 roof membrane; 4
concrete roof tile propped on
rubber pads to allow drainage of
rainwater; 5 22 mm thick plywood;
6 perimeter steel channel; 7 steel
beam; 8 profiled steel sheeting; 9
min. 70 mm insulation laid to falls*

cover strips support sandwich panels of two skins of 3 mm aluminium and 35 mm of sheet polyurethane. Double-glazed window sections also clip into the same aluminium framework (Figures 18.2 and 18.7). One of the classic difficulties of passing the framework through external cladding is the joint around the projecting frame. This has been resolved using a plate fitting around the curtain walling assembly (Figure 18.9).

Roofing

Profiled steel roof decking spans 3.28 m in one direction onto steel purlins suspended from the frame above. In the central bays the suspension system was not required, as the purlins could span onto the central columns. Above the roof decking is 70 mm of insulation, with a continuous PVC finish. The roof drainage occurs at the centre of the building adjacent to the central rooflight and the drainage pipes are exposed below the ceiling at this point (Figures 18.8 and 18.10).

Internal detailing

It is satisfying to see the component nature of this building as expressed on the facade carried through into the internal linings and fittings. Many of the American examples elsewhere in this book, while expressing a modular aluminium skin on the outside, use conventional materials on the inside, and even Richard Horden, in his Yacht House (see Case Study 30), was required to provide plasterboard linings. In this case, however, Asselbergs has designed his building to express the nature of the construction, such as the soffits of the galvanized metal ceiling and the curtain wall framing. Designers seeking to create a similar constructional purity should ensure that these hard finishes and expressed services are to the client's satisfaction.

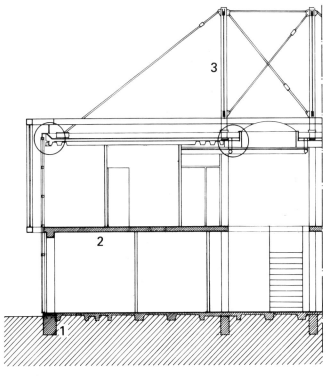

18.6.

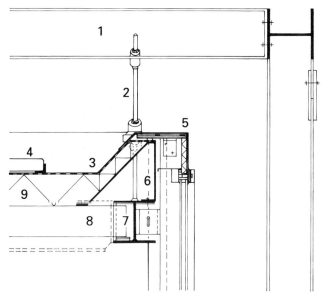

18.7.

18.5.

18.8.
Roof detail at skylight. 1 Steel
superstructure; 2 roof membrane;
3 insulation laid to falls; 4 profiled
steel sheeting; 5 insulated
drainpipe in steel casing; 6
perimeter drainpipe running
around skylight (see Figure
18.10); 7 metal capping; 8 2 m
square clear acrylic double-skin
skylight

18.9.
Steel frame projecting through
cladding

18.10.
View of stairwell showing
exposed drainpipes

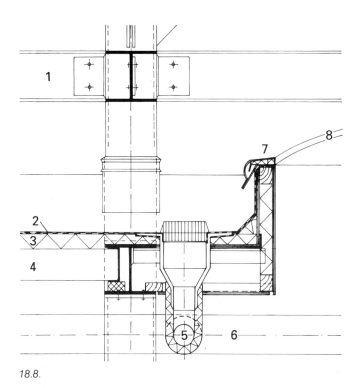

18.8.

18.10

References

Anon., 'Flexibiliteit leidt tot opmerkelijk bedrijfsgebouw',
  Bouwwereld, 13 December 1985, pp. 20–23.
Asselbergs, T., 'Bedrijfgebouw voor Oculenti',
  Architectuur + Bouwen, December 1985, pp. 17–20.
Van Heuvel, W., 'Een fragiele witte doos in Hoofddorp',
  Architetur Bouwen, December 1985, p. 21.

18.9

Operations Center for Philip Morris (USA)
Architects
Davis Brody & Associates

General

Located in Walmsley Boulevard, Richmond, Virginia, USA (Figures 19.1 and 19.2), this complex was designed for the makers of Marlboro cigarettes and comprises three linked pavilions clad with anodized aluminium panels and horizontal bands of glazing. A three-storey top-lit circulation route runs centrally through the administrative and research/engineering pavilions, and this is linked to the pilot plant building by a covered walkway which is finished in bright red. This colour is also used in the gateways which signal the entrances to the building.

The plan is arranged in 10 m bays around the circulation spine, offices enclosed in glass screens being located adjacent to the passage, allowing the open-plan areas to be situated next to the window walls. Semi-cylindrical stair wells, tubular balcony rails at upper levels and a careful use of colour create a pleasant enclosed street which unifies the diverse activities within the building.

One could compare the skin of this building with those of the Devonshire Building, Boston (Case Study 10) and the New Jersey Justice Complex (Case Study 23), all of which use aluminium panels. In this case, however, the architects have gone further in designing a coordinated facade system which incorporates its own environmental control mechanisms.

Cladding

The cladding (Figure 19.3), supplied and fixed by Zimmcor, Quebec, is mainly clear anodized 3 mm aluminium sheet, approximately 2 × 1 m, fixed to extruded

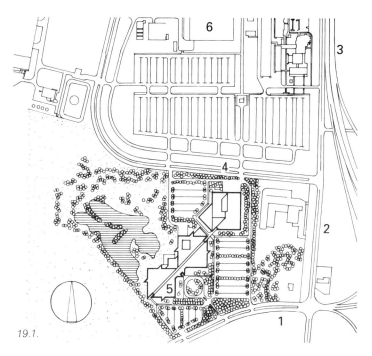

19.1.

aluminium mullions and transoms which are in turn fitted back to the main structure by angled cleats. The main spandrel panels consist of 3 mm plate aluminium mounted on an extruded aluminium frame with 75 mm fibreglass insulation and vapour barrier. These panels project approximately 170 mm from the front of the glazing with curved panels at the cills and parapet, which are finished in white fluorocarbon. The purpose of

19.1.
Site plan. 1 Walmsley Boulevard; 2 Commerce Road; 3 Interstate 95; 4 Bells Road; 5 Operations Centre; 6 cigarette factory

9.2. Entrance elevation

19.2.

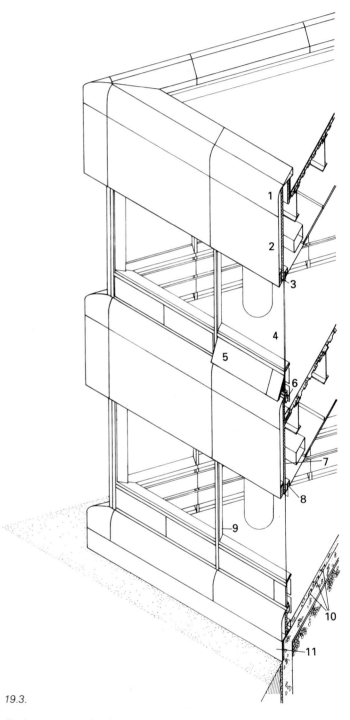

19.3.
Sectional axonometric through cladding. 1 White Kynar-painted aluminium trim; 2 clear anodized aluminium panel; 3 exterior aluminium venetian blind; 4 clear insulating glass; 5 operable vent; 6 fin-tube radiator; 7 insulation; 8 recessed motorized shades; 9 aluminium mullions; 10 power and telephone underfloor ducts; 11 natural cleft slate base

this additional space was originally to contain the outside sunshades which were later superseded by internal blinds. This modulation of the facade has some implication on the fixing screws to the joint cappings (see later).

In the same line as the windows, openable ventilation panels, also in aluminium, serve as a means of natural ventilation in the event of a breakdown of the mechanical air-circulation system (Figures 19.4 and 19.5). These panels are fabricated using two skins of 3 mm aluminium sheet with an aluminium frame and 50 mm of fibreglass insulation, top hinged to an extruded aluminium framing system mounted within the curtain walling assembly with a fixed aluminium mesh flyscreen behind.

The windows, 2 × 1.76 m double-glazed insulated units, are fitted within the curtain walling section in a way similar to the panels, using a pressure plate screwed to the mullions and transoms with an extruded aluminium snap-on cap (Figure 19.6). Face fixing of these pressure plates through the 12.5 mm slot between the projecting panels must have given some headaches to the fixing contractor (Figure 19.7).

The base of the building is faced with a small horizontal band of natural cleft slate edging to the concrete slab, allowing natural vegetation to be laid immediately adjacent to the facade.

The choice of white trim and dark anodized aluminium panels, while serving to emphasize the edges of the building, has two practical aspects. First, the curved corner pieces can be formed and post-coated in fluorocarbon and, second, any difference of colour matching, which is so difficult with anodized aluminium, is less obvious because of the bands of white.

Services

For energy conservation, the building was designed with exterior venetian blinds (also used in the Burrell Collection Building, Case Study 3). Supply problems delayed this installation and instead computer-controlled translucent fibreglass shades were installed behind the glass. The shades are automatically adjusted every 20 minutes for sun angle and desired sun penetration and heat gains. Heating is by perimeter fin tube and air-conditioning ducts are concealed above a suspended ceiling. The openable panels below the windows allow manual control in the event of a system failure.

In the skylight zones, air is moved by fans. Power and telephones are distributed in an underfloor duct system, with flat cables under the office carpets.

19.3.

References

Anon., 'Efficiency enriched and enlivened', *Architectural Record*, March 1983.

Anon., 'The staff gets the windows at Philip Morris', *Corporate Design*, November/December 1983.

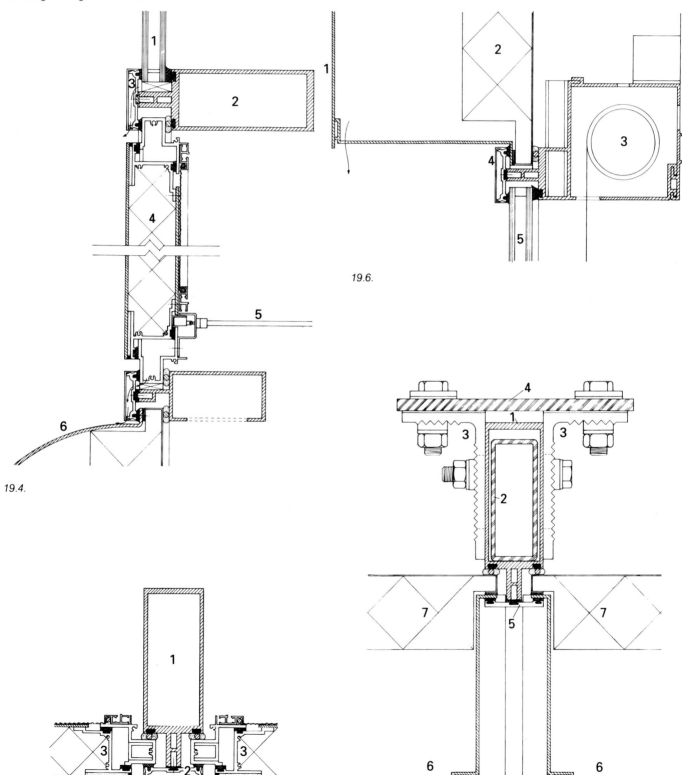

19.4.
Detail of window cill and operable ventilation panel. 1 25 mm double-glazed unit; 2 185 × 65 mm extruded aluminium transom; 3 extruded aluminium snap-on cap and pressure plate, with weepholes; 4 ventilator panel consists of 3 mm aluminium sheet, 50 mm rigid fibreglass insulation, 3 mm aluminium sheet and framed flyscreen behind; 5 underscreen operator; 6 curved aluminium spandrel panel with 75 mm rigid fibreglass insulation

19.5.
Plan of joint between ventilator panels. 1 185 × 65 mm extruded aluminium mullion; 2 extruded aluminium snap-on cap and pressure plate; 3 ventilator panel consists of 3 mm aluminium sheet, 50 mm rigid fibreglass insulation, 3 mm aluminium sheet and framed flyscreen

19.6.
Detail of window head. 1 3 mm aluminium sheet spandrel panel; 2 75 mm rigid fibreglass insulation; 3 motorized shade blinds; 4 extruded aluminium snap-on cap and pressure plate; 5 25 mm double-glazed unit

19.7.
Detail of vertical joint between spandrel panels. 1 185 × 65 mm extruded aluminium mullion; 2 continuous 125 × 50 mm steel r.h.s.; 3 150 mm aluminium anchor angle cleats; 4 structural steel frame; 5 extruded aluminium snap-on cap and pressure plate; 6 3 mm aluminium outer sheet of spandrel panels; 7 75 mm rigid fibreglass insulation

19.6.

19.4.

19.5.

19.7.

Parc de la Villette, Paris
Architects
Adrien Fainsilber and Rice, Francis and Ritchie

General

Completed in 1986, Adrien Fainsilber's conversion of the vast 270 × 100 × 45 m high abattoir into probably the largest scientific museum is, in many ways, a daring project. Four times the volume of the Beaubourg, the building rises from a sunken lake with three glazed bays projecting out over the surface of the water. Appropriately for a science museum, the stainless steel and glass structures are a showpiece of technology that tackle the problem of curtain walling with a radically different solution. Impressed by the quality of the glazed wall at Foster Associates' Willis Faber and Dumas offices, Fainsilber then worked in conjunction with Rice, Francis and Ritchie to make the structure of the glazed bays as light and transparent as possible (Figure 20.1). The whole assembly, including the stainless steel structure, was erected by CFEM.

Structure

Each of the three glazed bays on the south elevation is 32.4 m high by 32.4 m wide by 8.1 m deep. The 8.1 m square module forms the organizing principle for the primary structure, which is made up of stainless steel circular hollow sections. The main structure is braced along its top and sides by means of diagonal cross bracing in the plane of the structure. However, the main elevation is braced to the side elevations by a system of stainless steel compression struts and tension rods that act in a horizontal plane to counteract the wind forces (Figures 20.1 and 20.3).

Suspended glazing

In a conventional cladding system the cladding panels are supported off a secondary structure which, in turn, is fixed back to the primary one. At Parc de la Villette the secondary support system has been dispensed with: the glass is fixed directly to the primary structure and is provided with its own independent and much finer system of wind bracing (Figures 20.3(b) and 20.4). The structural glazing bay is an 8.1 × 8.1 m module subdivided into sixteen 2.025 × 2.025 m glass sheets (Figure 20.4). Each vertical row of four glass sheets is top hung and the load is taken on a central spring fixed to the top sheet. Every corner of the glass sheet is joined to the adjacent sheet by means of a moulded steel fixing with socket joints to allow movement in any direction. These fixings are restrained by the secondary wind bracing, devoted purely to the glazing. The glass sheets butt one another and the weathertight seal is provided by an *in-situ* applied clear silicone sealant.

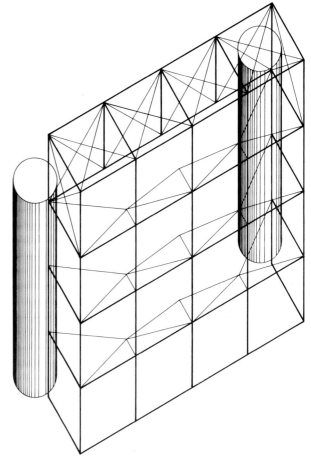

20.1.

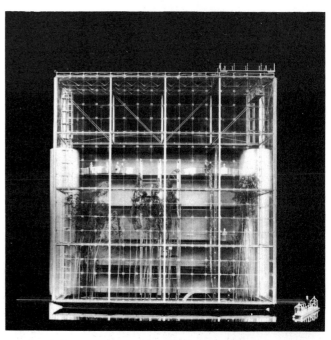

20.2.

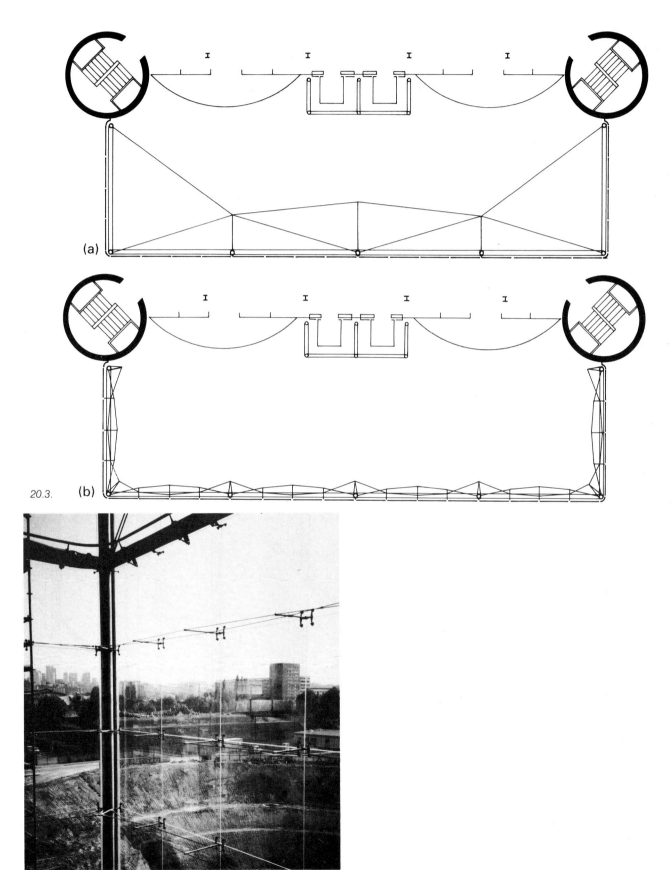

20.1.
Diagram of structural frame

20.2.
Model of glazed bay

20.3.
Structural hierarchy (see also Figure 20.4). (a) Tension rods and compression struts bracing the primary structure. (b) Tension rods and compression struts providing wind bracing to glass sheets.

20.4.
View looking out through glass bay

(a)

20.3.　(b)

20.4.

20.5.
Glazing fixing arrangement,
Renault Parts Distribution Centre,
Swindon

20.6.
Glazing fixing arrangement, Lime
Street Station, Liverpool

The flexible form of structure makes use of the little-appreciated property of toughened glass, which can tolerate a large amount of warping. This property, coupled with the idea of making the wind bracing out of cables which had the advantage of being elements of pure tension, were flexible and very fine, all combined to achieve the transparency that was desired.

The system should be compared with that used by Foster Associates at the Renault Centre (see Brookes, *Cladding of Buildings*, Case Study 21), where 1800 ×

4000 mm glazing was restrained using spider connections back to 114 × 68 mm horizontal framing at 810 mm vertical centres. In this case the pick-up points on the glass were then in 1800 × 1330 mm bays (Figure 20.5). At Lime Street Station, Liverpool, a similar principle was used, mounting 1950 × 1050 mm glazing, in this case back onto vertical supports 205 × 135 mm at 1960 mm centres (Figure 20.6), i.e. fixing pick-up points in bays approximately 1900 × 1000 mm. At Parc de la Villette these pick-up points are approximately in bays 2 × 2 m

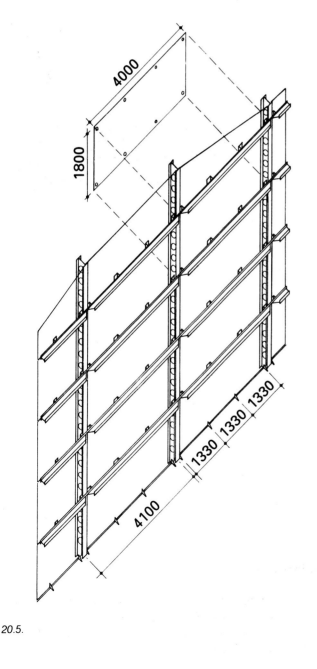

20.5.

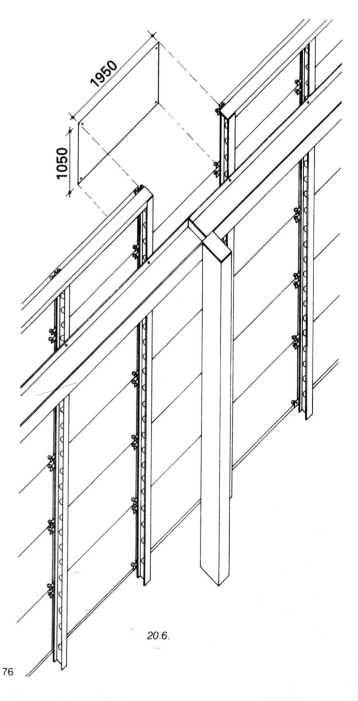

20.6.

20.7.
Glazing fixing arrangement, Parc
de la Villette, Paris

20.8.
Exploded isometric of swivel
fixing

(Figure 20.7). This demonstrates the gradual development of the technology, from the plate fixings as used at Willis Faber and Dumas to the drilled glass at Renault and Lime Street Station, with conventional fixing rails, to Parc de la Villette, with its tensioned fixing rails and a larger area of glass per fixing point and three-dimensional adjustment device.

Hanging four sheets of glass in this way induces stresses around the milled hole in the glass, of the order of fifteen times those in a single glass sheet. The innovative design introduces a system of swivels within the fixing that isolates the stresses and avoids any torsional stress, so that all the vertical forces are kept within the plane of the glass and horizontal forces can be taken out by the bracing (Figure 20.8).

Tests carried out on an 8.1 × 8.1 m sample proved the principle of the system, which literally breathed and flexed under positive and negative pressures producing deflections of up to 60 mm.

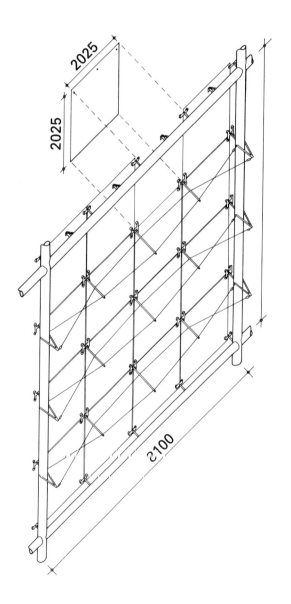

20.7.

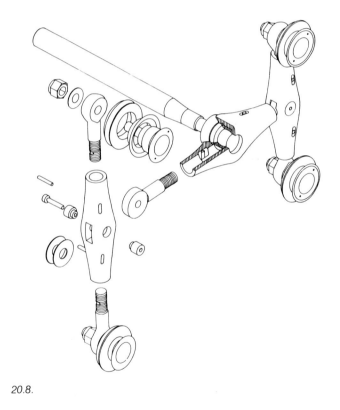

20.8.

References

Anon., 'Martin Francis – le discours de la méthode', *Architecture Ajourd'hui*, April 1986.

Ellis, C., 'Tomorrow's World', *Architects' Journal*, 30 April 1986, pp. 28–37.

Parsons House, London
Architect
Peter Bell and Partners

General

The Hall Place Estate, off Edgeware Road in Maida Vale, London W2, was completed in 1970 for Westminster City Council, and like so many high-rise, high-density schemes of this time, has proved an inadequate solution to poor housing conditions, mainly due to the poor quality of the infill panels, of cavity brickwork, and the cold bridge formed by the exposed *in-situ* concrete floor slabs (Figure 21.1).

The external fabric

The untreated softwood window frames had rotted to the point of failure by 1983, and the exposed concrete was spoiling around the reinforcement (Figure 21.2). Badly fitting draughty windows and inadequate insulation added to the problem. There was also a complete lack of any form of insulation. Peter Bell and Partners were asked to investigate repair work, but in their report of April 1983 suggested overcladding as an alternative. They proposed that, for an amount similar to that needed for the repairs, they could overclad the defective building in a rainscreen of aluminium-ribbed panels with insulation behind the new windows, which could be placed before the old ones were removed, thus minimizing disruption to the tenants (Figure 21.3).

For the final built scheme, completed in 1986, the architects consulted three cladding firms, and Hans Schmidlin (UK) Ltd was appointed cladding subcontractor, with Michael Barclay Partnership acting as structural engineers.

Structure

In overcladding, a series of support rails were first fixed to the existing structure with adjustable brackets. Because the brick infill panels were considered unstable, these rails had to be fixed between each floor slab, which required a fairly deep section. The architects decided to expose these cladding rails, and to use them as guides for maintenance cradle wheels (Figures 21.4 – 21.6).

The rails are made of extruded aluminium, 200 mm deep and 5.2 m long, with circular section outer flanges and channel section inner ones. The perforated webs reduce weight and aid air flow around the structure. Cutting the holes in the webs would, however, have increased their manufacturing costs, and it is doubtful whether this would in reality have offset the savings in main structure costs because of the reduced weight. The rails are fixed back to the concrete floor slab at each

21.1.

21.2.

storey by a pair of aluminium brackets, and vertical joints are formed by a spigot at the top of each tube which fits into the socket of the tube above. The aluminium used in the cladding structure is polyester powder coated with Colorsec (Figure 21.7).

Cladding

Cladding panels are hooked onto stainless steel support rods which span the U-section of the inner flange and they can be removed and replaced individually (Figure 21.8). The panels are also powder coated, 2 mm thick pressed (deep-drawn) aluminium with stiffened ends, profiled with a horizontal rib which is closed at the edge. Various sizes of panel were used, with widths of 480, 960 and 1440 mm. The edges are stiffened by folding back the sides of the panels, which are then perforated to form the hooks which clip to the support rods. The top and bottom panel edges overlap to prevent rain entering, but all-round ventilation is made possible by the fixing method.

21.1.
Parsons House before
overcladding

21.3.
Parsons House after
overcladding

21.4.
Cladding rails fixed to existing
fabric with adjustable brackets

21.2.
Deteriorated building fabric

21.5.
Insulation quilt fixed back to brick
walls

21.6.
Cladding panels hooked onto
rails

21.3.

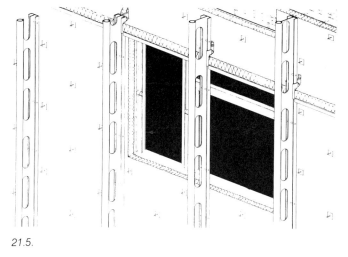

21.5.

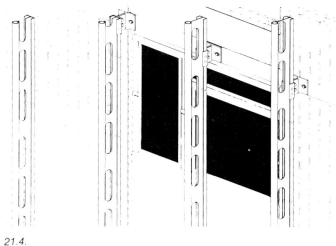

21.4.

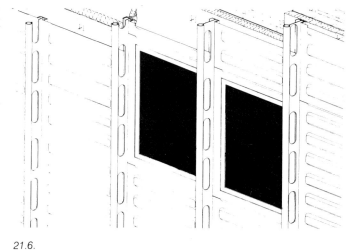

21.6.

The architects chose to use tilt-and-turn windows in aluminium sections, sealed back to the existing building with a waterproof skirt hidden by an internal timber lining.

The old walls are covered in an 80 mm thick blanket of mineral wool, fixed over the window infill panels with self-adhesive patent fasteners to prevent the need for drilling and fixing. This insulation covered all the cold bridge areas, isolating them from the outside.

The rails, panels and windows together form a rainscreen, which does not try to keep rain out altogether. Instead, any moisture trapped between the existing structure and new screen (both rain and condensation) drains down the ventilated gap at the back and exits through the open joints at the base of each panel. The mineral wool insulation is vapour permeable, but is not affected by water – it is also non-combustible. Note also the inclusion of cavity fire stops.

Under the terms of guarantee from the powder-coating manufacturers it is normal to require regular cleaning of the panel surface. Cleaning and maintenance have been made easier by the provision of a permanent 'runway' for the maintenance cradle, raised on davits circling the entire building. The cladding rails act as vertical wheel guides.

The ground floor and first floor up to cill level has been tiled, with the new face finishing 280 mm forward of the existing structure (thus further forward than the overcladding). This allows the water behind the panels to drain out at their base into a concealed gulley. The cavity conceals the insulation, which is continued to ground level. The new tiles blend into the surrounding groundcover, and are hoped to be vandalproof.

Comment

The Parsons House scheme is seen as a superior example of overcladding, which is a rapidly expanding construction method. The cost in 1986 of the overcladding system – about £220 per square metre – is seen by

21.7.
Close-up of adjustable bracket and cladding panel support rod

21.8.
Detail of cladding rail and double glazing. 1 Cladding rail with cladding panel support rod; 2 panel edge; 3 tilt-and-turn double-glazed window

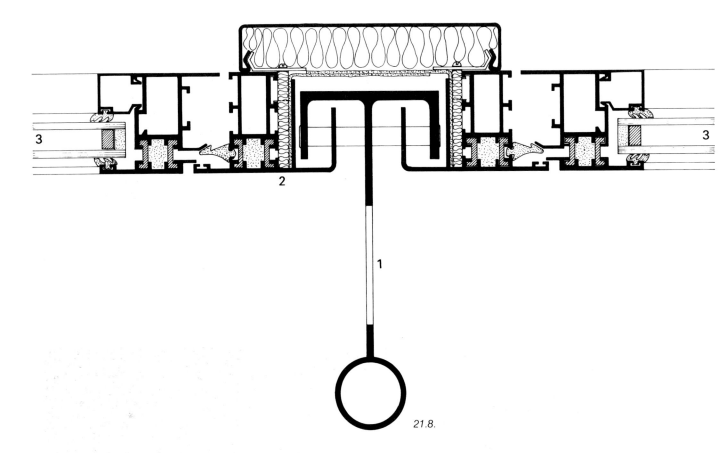

21.8.

21.7.

Roger Bloomfield of Bickerdike Allen Partners (building-failure experts and consultants to the architects) to be a long-term investment and therefore worthwhile. The cladding and windows should not require repainting for 40 years and the fuel bill has been reduced by 20%, as predicted. However, the panels and windows may require regular cleaning, and a stock of panels will have to be stored for potential future use since they are not standard designs.

References

Anon., 'A new suit of shining armour for decaying high-rise flats', *Aluminium Applications*, Summer 1986, p. 7.

Davies, C., 'High coverage', *Building* Supplement, 7 March 1986, pp. 8–11.

Harrison, H.W. *et al.*, *Overcladding – external walls of large panel system dwellings*, (BRE report) Case Study No. 1, pp., 52–53.

Pawley, M., 'New coat for a long life', *Guardian*.

Peter Bell and Partners, *Parsons House Overcladding*, Report to Westminster City Council (Client), November 1983.

Patscenter, Princeton, New Jersey
Architects
Richard Rogers Partnership

General

Patscenter is a new research facility for P.A. Technology, designed by Richard Rogers Partnership in Princeton, New Jersey, USA. It offers a high level of freedom of circulation, staff contact and maximum flexibility in the arrangement of offices, laboratories and services and the provision of a wide structural grid of totally free space. The client wished the building to have a strong visual presence that would emphasize P.A. Technology's innovative technical purpose. The architects responded by producing an expressive structure that is the antithesis of its neighbours in the think-belt around Princeton. The shock tactics of turning 'bland-box' inside-out are given maximum effect. By exposing the architectural images of science and technology the building provides an environment that seduces and stimulates a response (Figure 22.1).

Structure

The basic building concept is a central spine 9 m wide (Figure 22.2). The lower zone forms an enclosed glazed arcade providing main circulation, and above, slung on suspended frames, are the services plant. On either side of this spine two large single-storey enclosures, each 72 m long by 22.5 m wide, provide research space. To achieve the required flexibility these research areas are organized on a 9 × 4.5 m planning grid and are column free. All vertical structure within the building envelope is placed in the central spine (Figure 22.3). The large single-storey building with its general roof level only 4.5 m above ground level is enlivened by the deliberately dramatic steelwork frame with integral services (Figure 22.4).

The main structure, which is repeated at 9 m intervals, consists of a 7.5 m wide rectangular portal which acts as

22.1. General view

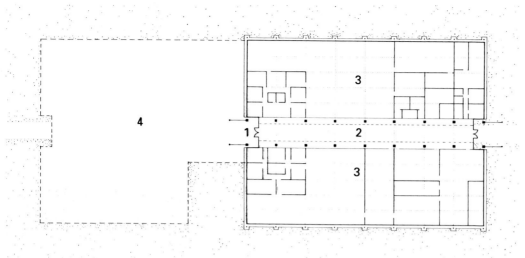

22.2.
Plan. 1 Entrance; 2 administrative spine; 3 research laboratories; 4 Phase 2 extension

22.3.
Isometric and section. 1 Administrative spine; 2 research laboratories; 3 bipod masts; 4 services platform

22.2.

22.3.

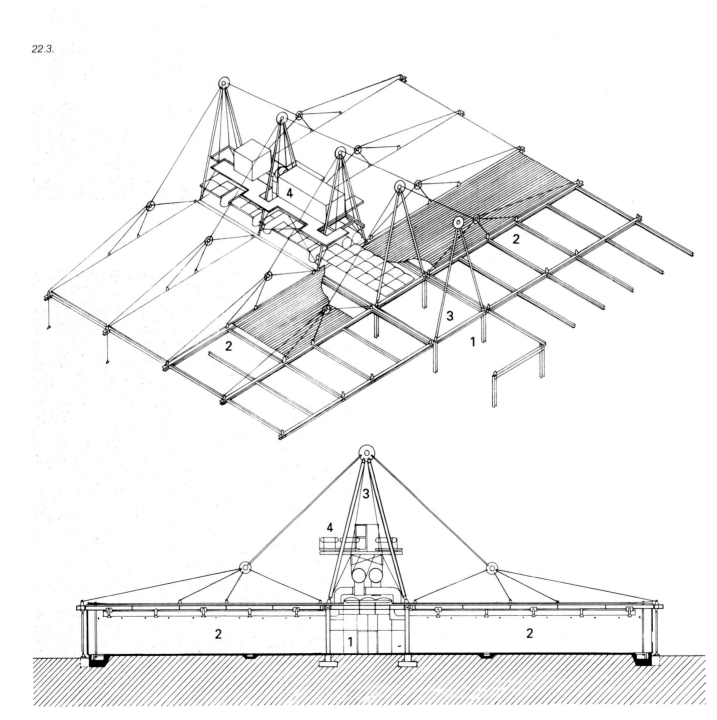

a base for the impressive 15 m high bipod mast. Inclined members are attached to the top of the mast to provide mid-span support for the main roof beam of the single-storey structure. The final form of the suspension system resulted after a long process of development and analysis. One problem in tension structure design is the effect of wind uplift: a perimeter column tie is needed to resist this. At his earlier building for Inmos in Cardiff, UK (see Brookes, *Cladding of Buildings*), Rogers used a V-shaped truss spanning from the central spine to the edge of the building. At Patscenter, although the span is much smaller, the truss is still required but it is less emphatically stated. When there is no uplift loading the two centre members supporting the roof structure are required to act as compression struts: consequently they are slender tubes. The two outer members act in tension and are rods. The structure is designed by Ove Arup and Partners.

One of the ways that the architects and engineers have managed to achieve a classic simplicity is the lack of diagonal bracing at high level between masts. Longitudinal stability is provided indirectly by making use of the suspended services platforms and their support hangers. As a result, the masts thrust upwards apparently independently, emphasizing the bay-by-bay flexibility of the building (Figure 22.5). Out-of-plane loadings on the masts and suspension systems are transmitted down to the main roof level, via the structural chassis of the services platform, then to ground level through the central portals and diagonal bracing at the ends of the building. Thus the building services help to justify the structure and vice versa. The overall weight of structural steelwork equates to 45 kg/m^2.

Cladding

Richard Rogers Partnership were keen to incorporate a large proportion of glazing into the wall cladding and yet conform to the insulation criteria set by the American codes. A successful compromise was achieved by the use of Kalwall translucent cladding. This system uses a sandwich made up of two light-transmitting fibreglass sheets bonded in an interlocking aluminium grid frame. To increase the thermal insulation of the panel gap between the two leaves, this was filled with translucent fibreglass inserts, their density selected to achieve the required insulation and light transmission. The overall panel thickness is 70 mm. The panels were prefabricated in 1.5 m wide and full storey-height frames to be erected on site.

The wall cladding provides a 20% clear glazing area, the remaining 80% Kalwall and a 17% light-transmission value and a 1.3 W/m^2°C U-value. The overall effect is

22.4.

22.5.

22.6.
Side view at night

22.6.

pleasing and similar to that of a translucent Japanese screen. (See the night-time view in Figure 22.5.)

Services

The planning concept of a central spine is ideal for the distribution of primary services and enables all the plant to be located centrally (Figure 22.6). Mechanical and electrical plant are in fact located at ground-floor level adjacent to the spine with air-handling and condenser plant on the suspended services platforms. The larger primary air ducts are external to the building envelope while smaller electrical and piped services are at high level within the spine. Secondary distribution runs laterally into the research enclosures.

Comment

This building is a pronounced refinement of its precursor for Inmos in Cardiff: solid-looking rectangular towers have been replaced by dynamic A-frames and complex joints have developed into simple geometrical 'washers'. The structure has achieved the inevitable simplicity that is the symbol of great architecture. A long, hard look at the structural principles and the solutions proposed is amply rewarded.

References

Gardner, I., 'Patscenter', *Arup Journal*, **21**, No. 2, Summer 1986, pp. 8–16.

Russell, F., *Richard Rogers and Architects*, Architectural Monographs, Academy Editions, London, 1985, pp. 44–45.

Sorkin, M., 'Another low-tech spectacular', *Architectural Review*, No. 1063, September 1985, pp. 38–43.

The Richard J. Hughes Justice Complex, Trenton, New Jersey
Architects
Grad/Hillier

General

This very large complex of law courts and tax offices for the State of New Jersey, USA, was completed in January 1982 at a total cost of $93.4 million. For such a project, two large architectural practices, the Grad Partnership of Newark and the Hillier Group at Princeton, worked together as the Grad/Hillier joint venture (Figure 23.1).

Built on an unusual chevron-shaped site, the overall design of the complex consists of an L-shaped office building with eight floors of accommodation and a ninth floor for mechanical services. The two equal wings of the L embrace the separate six-storey cube-shaped building containing meeting rooms, etc., which is suspended over a three-storey open-space mezzanine. The two parts of the building are separated by an atrium which begins at street level and rises the full nine floors of the building. Each of the cube's four floors are connected with the office accommodation by a series of bridges spanning the atrium space (two floors are two storeys high), which has structural silicone glazing with glass supporting fins.

Structure

The structural engineer was Daniel Sturn of Di Stasio and Van Buren. The most interesting aspect of the structure is the method of supporting the cube by four 7 m cylindrical columns 25 m centres apart, the load being carried on four trussed columns of structural steel within the

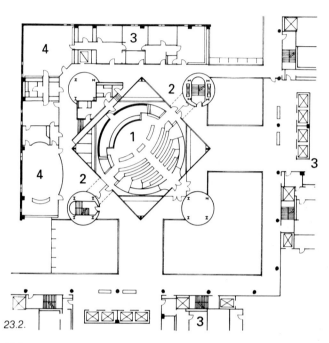

23.2.

23.2.
Plan of the central suspended cube housing the court rooms. 1 Court room; 2 lobby; 3 offices; 4 conference

23.1. General view

23.3.
Structural skeleton with columns,
trusses and cube clad

23.4.
Structural skeleton with external
cladding and atrium

23.5.
Exploded structural skeleton
showing suspended cube
housing the court rooms

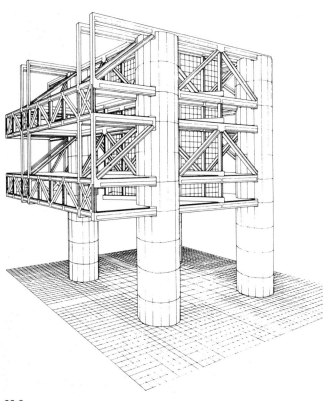

23.3.

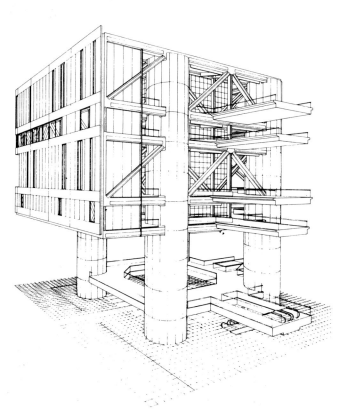

23.4.

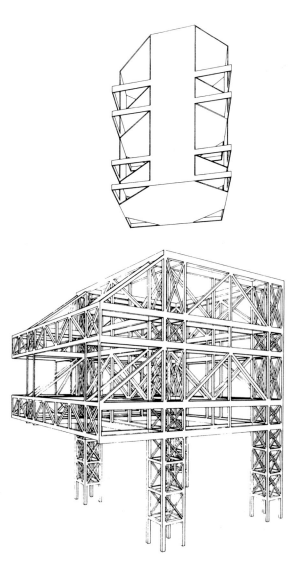

23.5.

23.6.
Internal view of atrium

23.7.
Detail of window cill. 1 25 mm thick double-glazing; 2 vinyl thermal break; 3 hinged door for natural ventilation with inset screen; 4 site-applied sealant with backing rope; 5 4.5 mm thick aluminium plate with factory welded Z-cleat; 6 75 mm thick insulation; 7 gypsum board lining

cylinders. It is interesting to note the change of direction of these supporting I-section stanchions (Figure 23.2).

Four two-storey trusses intersect the columns at the second and fourth court building levels. These support two single-storey trusses at the exterior of the first court level and two on the third (see Figures 23.3–23.5). The main trusses have been exposed as a feature of the building, allowing people to walk through them (Figure 23.6). These approximately 9 m high trusses were sprayed to achieve a three-hour fire rating and then covered with aluminium. To some extent, this principle of fire rating can be compared with the Hongkong and Shanghai Bank by Foster Associates (Case Study 32).

Such large and complex trusses would require substantial welding, and to keep site welding to a minimum these were fabricated off-site, disassembled, transported and then reassembled on-site with bolted connections. The surrounding office buildings consists of a conventional structure with bays of 10 × 10 m.

Cladding

The exterior skin of anodized aluminium panels with horizontal bands of grey reflective insulating glass fabricated and assembled by Flour City Architectural Metals at a cost of $8 million represents a high standard of panel-to-panel curtain walling assembly mounted between the columns set back behind the facade and restrained at intervals by the floor slab. The 1.5 × 10 m panels consist of 4.5 mm aluminium plate on an extruded aluminium framework with 75 mm of USG Thermafiber insulation and an inner lining of gypsum board. The total panel thickness is 160 mm. It is interesting to note the method of fixing the framing to the plate aluminium outer panel, using a welded Z-cleat clipped into the extrusion with a space to allow thermal movement and a silicone joint factory applied between the two parts of the assembly. Thus the panel arrives on-site with the frame attached to it. A further weather seal is applied at the cill condition on-site (Figure 23.7).

Aluminium-framed double-glazed windows with solar reflective glass fit within the assembly with a total frame width of 160 mm (Figure 23.8). Continuous ventilation slots occur below the windows with a hinged cill-type section to allow natural ventilation. Also note the aluminium mesh insect screen mounted above the slots.

Another interesting feature of the assembly is the window-washing equipment, track mounted within the jambs of both the windows and panels, allowing access for cleaning gantries for both windows and anodized aluminium panels (Figure 23.9).

23.6.

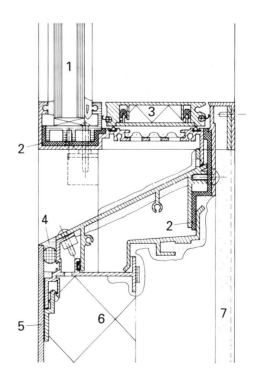

23.7.

23.8.
Window head detail. 1 25 mm thick double-glazing; 2 continuous polystyrene foam insulation; 3 hex head screws sealed at works; 4 4.5 mm aluminium plate with factory welded Z cleat; 5 75 mm thick insulation; 6 gypsum board lining

23.9.
Window jamb detail. 1 Track for window-washing equipment; 2 continuous vinyl foam self-adhesive tape; 3 thermal break; 4 25 mm thick double-glazing

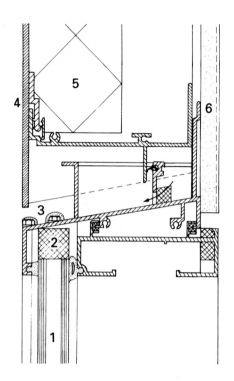

23.8.

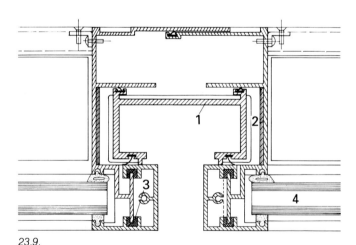

23.9.

Finishes

Generally, the aluminium is anodized and protected with one spray coat of Dupont 1234 clear laquer. This type of plate panel with welded stiffeners is difficult to manufacture, and it was the architect's requirement that these should be free of any bow or oil-canning, and that the stiffening rails should not 'read through' when installed in the building. The thickness of the plate (4.5 mm instead of the more usual 3 mm) would help in achieving the architect's specification for a maximum bow of 3 mm in 1 m. All columns are sheathed in the same aluminium that is used on the exterior and interior facades.

Mock-ups

With asemblies of this type it is necessary to provide a full-size mock-up complete with panels, openable vents, framing members, corner returns, window-cleaning guide tracks, spliced joints, sealants, glass and fixings, all with their correct finishes for the architect's approval. In this case there was an additional requirement for air- and water-penetration tests to be carried out by Construction Research Laboratory, Miami, Florida. Later modifications of the interlocking aluminium sections, designed to facilitate installation, resulted in the subsequent problems of air and water penetration in the completed building.

Costs

Costs of the structure represented approximately 20% of building costs, and mechanical services were of the same order. External walls were almost 9% of total costs with a similar allowance for the interior construction.

Services

In the interests of energy conservation, 172 solar collectors are located at 40-degree angles on the south side of the roof to heat domestic hot water. In addition to the top-floor mechanical services the building appears to depend upon the adjacent boiler plant in the nearby State Building as a source of heating and air conditioning.

References

Thomas, R., 'Unique design simplifies new justice complex', *Building Design and Construction*, June 1983.

Sainsbury's Supermarket at Canterbury
Architects
Ahrends Burton & Koralek

General

ABK won the 1982 limited-entry competition to design a new supermarket for Sainsbury's at Canterbury in Kent (Figure 24.1), which was completed in 1984. The brief reminded the competitors of the historic nature of the site, which was within sight of the medieval cathedral, and asked them to respect the local vernacular materials. It is perhaps surprising, then, that this masted and suspension cable structure of unashamedly modern design and materials should have won. In their entry, ABK claim that the masts echo the towers of the distant cathedral: they do in that they give vertical emphasis to an otherwise horizontal building, but the reader may feel that they have rather more nautical than ecclesiastical references.

The supermarket is on a difficult site on the Kingsmead Road and Northgate junction in Canterbury, with the River Stour bordering the western edge (Figure 24.2). The carpark is at the rear of the building, but because the road frontages are not owned by Sainsbury's and are to be built on, the main elevations of the building face the carpark.

The three functions of unloading, storage/preparation and sales are each housed in a separate structure of different length linked by service areas. Around these are grouped various offices, meeting rooms, etc., with the customer entrance located to the west of the sales area. Thus the building is composed of three blocks of masted structure linked by cross bracings over the 3 m service zone.

Structure

As the model shows, the roof structure of the largest of the blocks is composed of nine bays of paired 406 mm diameter c.h.s. mild steel columns supporting the mild steel main beams (356 × 368 mm × 153 kg/m I-sections) spanning 36 m. In the other two blocks, these main beams span 24 m. In all cases the beams are picked up by the suspension cables from the masts at 12 m intervals. The size of these paired mild steel rods is 60 mm diameter, and they connect to the beams via a 60 mm thick mild steel connector plate welded to the roof beams (Figure 24.3). Apparently there is no thermal break between the plate and the main beam.

Spanning 7.2 m between the main structural beams are mild steel purlins (203 × 133 mm × 25 kg/m) which

24.1. Model of competition design

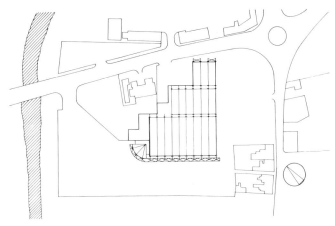

24.2. Site plan

support the lightweight roof composed of 70 mm profiled steel deck, supporting a vapour barrier, 40 mm insulation and 13 mm fibreboard covered with three layers of felt and chippings.

The reader should note the mild steel castings welded to the 60 mm diameter tie rods, and compare these with those used at the Victoria Plaza (Case Study 31) and by Richard Rogers in the Fleetguard Factory in France to observe the development of this type of construction. The method of connecting these plates to the beam connector plate using a stainless steel pin should also be noted (Figure 24.3). A low-viscosity silicone seal is placed between the plates and the cast ends of the rods.

The very lightweight roof deck would be prone to uplift

24.3.
Vertical section and elevation of connector plate. 1 60 mm thick connector plate welded to roof beam; 2 mild steel spade casting welded to 60 mm diameter tie rods; 3 60 mm diameter stainless steel pins with stainless steel pin cap; 4 low-viscosity silicone seal; 5 8 mm thick mild steel plate; 6 roof composition: three layers of felt and chippings, 13 mm fibreboard, 40 mm insulation,

vapour barrier, 70 mm metal deck; 7 50 × 50 mm angle bolted to beam; 8 356 × 368 × 153 kg/m mild steel universal beam; 9 203 × 133 × 25 kg/m mild steel purlin

24.4.
Canopy suspended from outriggers

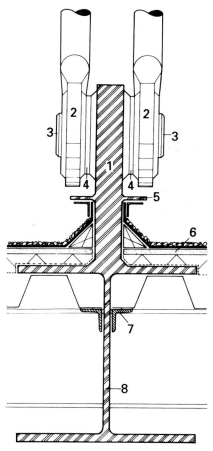

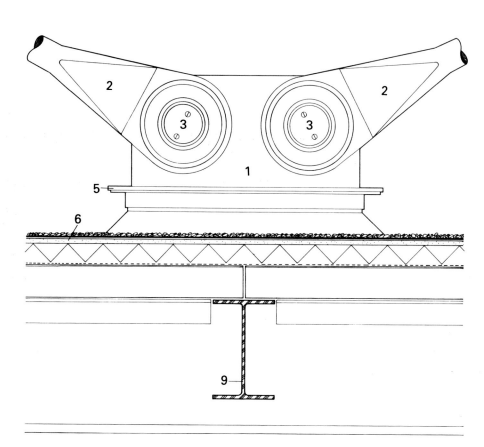

24.3.

24.4.

under certain wind conditions, but in this case the weight of steel supporting it is large enough to act as an anchor, thus eliminating the need for ties to keep the roof down. In addition, the main masts, with their projecting outriggers forming the compression member, support a fabric-covered ladder-type frame forming a covered canopy along the carpark elevation (Figure 24.4). These also link to a fan-shaped canopy with a fabric structure, suspended from its own mast arrangement.

Structural engineers for the competition scheme were Anthony Hunt Associates. However, the executive engineers were Ernest Green and Partners.

Cladding

Cladding to the sales floor block which faces the carpark is composed of 6 mm thick glazed panels and aluminium composite panels fixed to extruded aluminium curtain walling by Essex Aluminium. The interesting feature of this assembly is the cranked mullion spanning between

24.5.
*Section through eaves detail. 1
168 mm c.h.s. mild steel
outrigger; 2 plated steel
connector between paired masts;
3 roof composition: three layers of
felt and chippings, 13 mm
fibreboard, 40 mm insulation,
vapour barrier, 70 mm metal
deck; 4 aluminium–polythylene–
aluminium composite panel; 5
75 mm thick rigid insulation
bonded to panel; 6 insulated
panel; 7 extruded aluminium
cladding mullion*

24.6.
*Section through roof and internal
partition. 1 112 × 356 × 25 kg/m
mild steel universal beam; 2
50 mm thick mineral wool quilt
with wire mesh reinforcement and
aluminium interlayer; 3 190 mm
blockwork wall; 4 50 mm thick
mild steel connector plate; 5 mild
steel turnbuckle; 6 stainless steel
collar over torched-on roof finish;
7 paired 406 mm c.h.s.*

24.7.
*Section through base of external
cladding. 1 Paired 60 mm
diameter tie rod; 2 precast paving
slab; 3 6 mm toughened glass
panel; 4 extruded aluminium
frame with pressure plate; 5
paired 244.5 mm c.h.s.; 6
extruded aluminium cladding
mullion; 7 stainless steel
protection rails; 8 stainless steel
angle; 9 30 mm thick terazzo tiles;
10 friction piles; 11 reinforced
concrete perimeter beam*

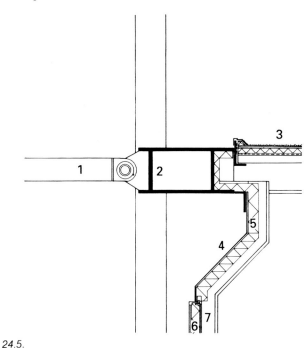

24.5.

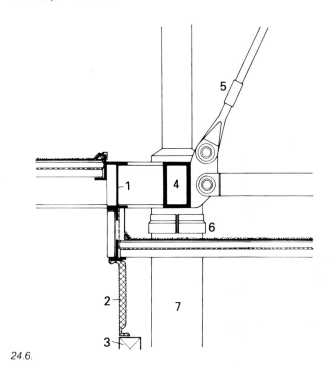

24.6.

the floor edge beam and the steel edge beam to the roof,
into which are fitted cranked aluminium panels forming
the recess at the head of the assembly (Figure 24.5). This
recess is continued on all the blocks, but in these areas
the walls have glazed 'Spectraglaze' concrete blocks.
The purpose of the recess is partly to emphasize the roof
plane and to act as a slip joint to take up the differential
tolerances between the roof structure and external walls,
which is always a problem with suspension structure of
this type (Figure 24.6, 24.7). At the Renault Centre by
Foster Associates a similar problem was solved using a
neoprene skirt.

References

Anon., 'Canterbury choice', *Architects' Journal*, 13 Octo-
ber 1982, pp. 44–46.
Outram, J., 'Supermarket forces', *Architectural Review*,
May 1983, p. 70.
Winter, J., 'Mast appeal', *Architects' Journal*, 5 Decem-
ber 1984, pp. 41–47.

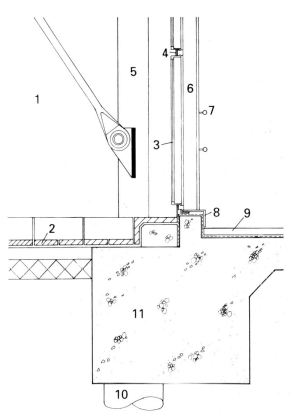

24.7.

Schlumberger Cambridge Research Centre
Architects
Michael Hopkins and Partners

General

Built in 1985 for research into rigs for oil exploration (which explains its section), the building is situated on the Madingley Road near junction 13 of the M11 west of Cambridge. With its cable structure, the project, designed by Michael Hopkins, Anthony Hunt Associates and Arup Lightweight Structures Division, represents the first large-scale example of the use of Teflon-coated glassfibre membrane in the UK (Figure 25.1). The shape of the building is determined by its use as an oil-drilling test station (Figure 25.2) and to ensure maximum contact between scientists of different departments.

The plan, composed of three central bays each 24 × 18 m, is defined on the east and west sides by five bays of office units with inset entrances dividing them (Figure 25.3). The building takes advantage of the contours of the site so that the test station and service yard on the north side are 2.5 m below the level of the offices and main entrance. To the south of the test station a large winter garden contains a restaurant and library to provide a stimulating environment for informal meetings.

Office bays

Each wing of offices consists of five Miesian-inspired modules, based on Hopkins' own design for the Patera system (see Brookes, *Concepts in Cladding*, p. 90) divided by inset entrances. Each of the five modules is made up of five bays, with external Pratt roof trusses spanning 13.2 m from which the roof is hung, pinned to hollow section steel columns at 3.6 m centres, forming a hybrid portal frame (Figure 25.4). The method of waterproofing the structure as it punctures the roof covering is attained using a split collar slipped over the hangers during the erection of the frame and welded together and sealed around the hanger after the roof member has been laid (Figure 25.6).

The front facades of the offices are composed of double-glazed and laminated 3 m high aluminium sliding glazed units (Figure 25.5) with polyester powder-coated frames. Imported from West Germany, new extrusions

25.1.

25.1.
General view from south-west

25.2.
East–west section. 1 Drilling test station; 2 offices; 3 services undercroft

25.3.
Plan. 1 Main entrance; 2 reception; 3 winter garden; 4 drilling test station; 5 offices/ laboratories

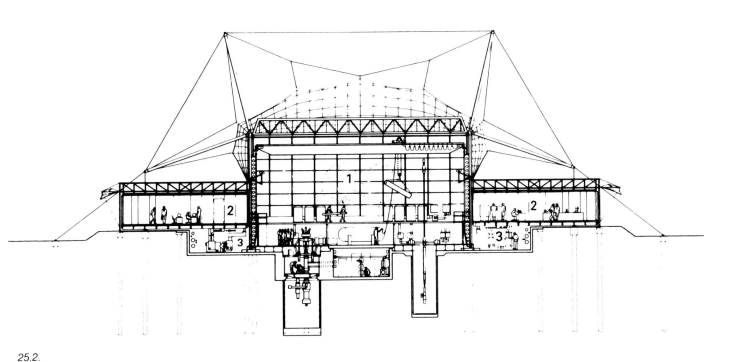

25.2.

were required to carry the weight of the glass. The ends of the long modules are clad with Plannja insulated profiled steel panels. Cold-rolled purlins 114 mm deep at 1.2 m centres support the 25 mm galvanized steel diaphragm roof, with a single-layer polymeric roof membrane laid to fall, with flashings and upstand (Figure 25.7).

The floor is galvanized steel decking, with 60 mm 'Styrofoam' insulation sandwiched between two layers of chipboard supported by 254 mm deep secondary beams at 1.2 m centres, on 406 mm deep rolled-section I-beams on the primary grid (Figure 25.8). Apart from the foundation slab, the entire system is dry assembly using prefabricated components. Lightweight demountable partitions by Classtech Ltd separate the office units. The internal glass walls are made of 21 mm thick laminated glass, acoustically sealed to protect office/laboratory accommodation from test-rig noise.

Structure

The roof membrane is attached to cables supported by an external steel framework based on a series of tubular lattice towers (2.4 m wide and 19.2 m apart) linked by prismatic beams (1.5 m deep spanning 24 m) with raking aerial booms connected by tension rods (Figure 25.9). The four-pinned portal formed by the main girder and beams is braced by triangular lattices positioned between the office units and braced in the other direction by ties between all main frames.

Throughout the courtyard structure, tie members have been used consisting of solid rods with threaded couplers and turnbuckles to allow adjustment of the ties. This number of threaded connections within a member must lead to a reduced factor of safety when compared with a more conventional welded solution. Due to this factor, and the critical nature of the tie elements, all ties which could cause collapse in the event of a failure have been duplicated and designed so that any one tie could support the working load of the building. The most detrimental effect of a tie failing would therefore be an increase in frame movements. Piled foundations of 450 mm diameter transmit high loads from eight double masts.

Membrane

Manufactured by the West German firm Stromeyer-

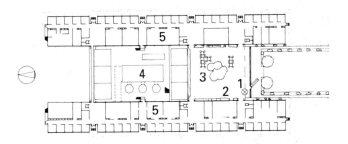

25.3

25.4.
Structural frame of offices. 1 Pratt truss: top boom 114.3 mm × 5 mm c.h.s., bottom boom 76.1 mm × 4 mm c.h.s.; 2 139.7 × 8 mm c.h.s. columns; 3 406 × 178 × 74 kg/m UB primary beam; 4 254 × 146 × 31 kg/m UB perimeter beam; 5 double glazing, 24 mm thickness overall, 6 mm toughened clear glass; 6 21 mm laminated clear glass; 7

services undercroft; 8 polyester powder-coated extruded aluminium louvres; 9 horizontal truss to brace main structural frame

25.5.
Glazed elevation to offices

25.6.
Detail of polymeric skirt flashing at joint between hangar and roof decking. 1 Bottom boom of truss; 2 hangar; 3 polymeric skirt flashing with stainless steel pipe clip (flashing bonded to polymeric roof membrane); 4 polystyrene insulation preformed to falls; 5 25 mm profiled steel decking; 6 galvanized 114 × 73 mm cold-formed steel purlins

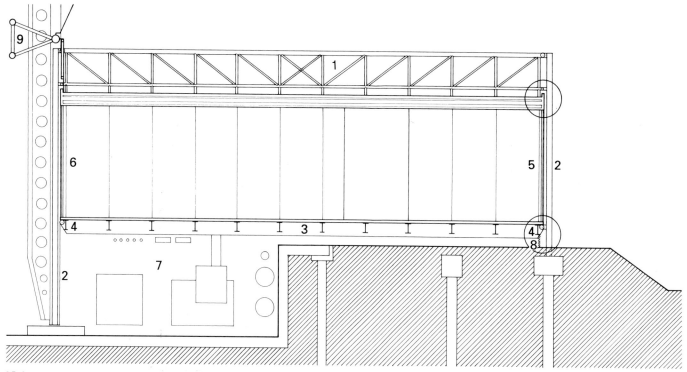

25.4.

25.5.

Ingenieurbau GmbH, the translucent Teflon-coated glassfibre membrane allows light into the testing areas. Because Teflon is an inert plastic, highly resistant to chemical attack and unaffected by ultraviolet light, it was claimed to offer a service life of more than 20 years with no discoloration with age (AJ, 24 October 1984, p. 4). The fabric is woven like cloth and the Teflon PTFE coating is applied by means of a dipping/sintering process.

A limitation in the width of the manufactured cloth has led to the membrane being constructed from a number of flat strips, the seams of which are lapped and heat welded in the factory. The edge of the fabric is then wrapped over a 20 mm galvanized steel strand cable (for a fuller description of this process see AJ, 24 October

25.7.
Office roof parapet detail. 1 Steel column 139.7 × 8 mm c.h.s.; 2 bottom boom of truss 114.3 × 5 mm c.h.s.; 3 preformed polymeric flashing fixed by steel clips; 4 single-layer 1 mm polymeric roof membrane over polystyrene insulation preformed to falls on 25 mm profiled steel decking; 5 extruded aluminium fascia panel; 6 galvanized steel 114 × 75 mm cold-formed purlin; 7 mineral fibre insulation 100 mm

thick suspended from decking; 8 continuous 100 × 75 mm steel glazing fixing angle attached to purlin hangar; 9 aluminium glazing frame; 10 24 mm thick overall double-glazing units; 11 perforated steel acoustic ceiling tiles

25.8.
Office floor/edge beam detail. 1 Aluminium glazing frame; 2 carpet on 22 mm T & G chipboard on 60 mm expanded polystyrene on chipboard; 3 perimeter fan-assisted convectors; 4 profiled galvanized steel decking; 5 edge beam 254 × 146 × 31 kg/m UB; 6 polyester powder-coated aluminium louvres; 7 galvanized steel primary beam 406 × 178 × 74 kg/m; 8 concrete blinding and kerb

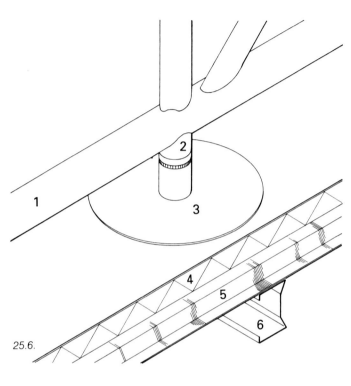

25.6.

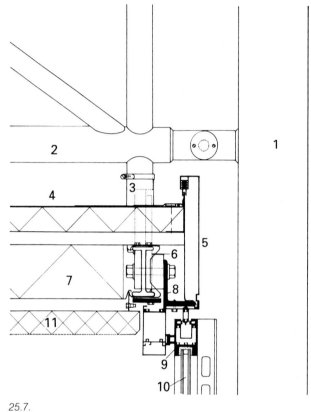

25.7.

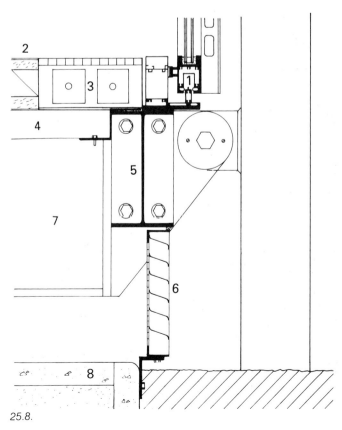

1984, p. 54). The completed membrane is then transported to the site and clamped to the main structural cables, which evenly distribute the tension on the fabric when tightened.

The membrane's resistance to snow and wind loading and its double curvature were modelled on a computer by Arup Lightweight Structures Division. To fine tune the membrane once erected, its superstructure of masts, rods and cables incorporates adjustable pinned joints which also rotate according to changing live loads.

Services

The services for both laboratory/office units and the test-rig zone run below the floor level in undercrofts with

25.8.

95

25.9.

access for maintenance. Heating is provided by a gas-fired boiler and a central chiller is located in the services compound. Offices are heated by fan-assisted perimeter convectors. The laboratories are air conditioned in the summer: extract grills are located in the floor and fumes are extracted and ducted to flue towers. The test-rig zone is partially heated. Electrical supply and data telecom cables run underfloor, rising to distribution points in the floor or office furniture. Cold water from the storage tank and hot water from the gas boiler are distributed via underfloor suspended piping: drainage is also suspended underfloor.

The tests rigs are isolated on resilient bearings to stop vibration transmission. Office/laboratory units are acoustically insulated with 21 mm laminated glazed wall and acoustic metal ceiling tiles.

Costs

Previously published articles indicate a cost of approximately £4 million, which suggests a building cost related to 5650 m² of offices and laboratories of approximately £675 per square metre after making allowance for external works. Of this figure, the work below the lowest floor finish accounts for nearly 20% of the building costs and the main frame, comprising eight double-masted tubular towers and the steel portal frames of the office blocks, 13%. The fabric roof and associated cables accounts for nearly 7%. Service costs are modest for a building of this type, mainly due to inexpensive heating and ventilation systems.

References

Architecture Aujourd'hui, No. 3237, February 1985, pp. LIX–LX,11–58 (English Summary pp. LII–LIV).

Architecture Movement Continuité, No. 9, October 1985, pp. 4–45. 'British Arch'.

A & U, No. 9 (192), September 1986, pp. 13–22.

Baumeister, **83**, No. 11, November 1986, pp. 34–39.

Croak, S., 'A Cambridge test: Hopkins for Schlumberger', *Architects' Journal*, **182**, No. 38, 18 September 1985, pp. 43–59.

Deutsche Bauzeitung, **120**, No. 2, February 1986, pp. 24–29.

Dietsch, D.K., 'Ties that bind', *Arch. Record*, **174**, No. 4, April 1986, pp. 136–147.

Hannay, P., 'A glimpse of tomorrow', *Architects' Journal*, **181**, No. 20, 15 May 1985, pp. 28–31.

Haward, B., 'Hopkins at Cambridge', *Architects' Journal*, **179**, No. 5, 1 February 1984, pp. 40–47.

Herzberg, H., 'High flyer', *Architects' Journal*, **180**, No. 43, 24 October 1984, pp. 43–63.

'Anthony Hunt: an architecturally minded builder', *Techniques & Arch.*, No. 356, October/November 1986, pp. 128–138.

Tubular Structures, No. 38, August 1985, pp. 16–17.

Sorting Office, Hemel Hempstead
Architects
Aldington, Craig & Collinge

General

Built in 1985 and situated on the St Albans Road/Park Lane junction in Hemel Hempstead (Figure 26.1), this sorting office was designed for the Eastern Postal Region by Aldington, Craig & Collinge and was required to house new sorting machines which were too large for the Post Office's existing buildings. The brief called for a general warehouse/industrial building with a 6 m minimum eaves height and no internal columns, with a high-level loading area on one side that would be marketable should the Post Office move out. The design takes advantage of the natural slope of the site to create a ground-floor public entrance below the sorting office on the south-west corner, which is linked to the administrative building by workshop areas. Although both main buildings are constructed using a light steel frame with a profiled steel composite cladding panel system on both walls and roof, it is the form of the sorting-office building which creates the most visual interest (Figure 26.2).

Structure

The structure of the sorting office consists of a series of 12 triangular cross-section lattice trusses made of tubular steel by Tubeworkers Ltd, spanning 28 m with a 12 m cantilever and overall depth of tubular truss of 1.5 m (Figure 26.3). Although at first sight these trusses and their steel cladding appear to wrap completely round the building on both sides, in reality they are propped on one side to allow a cantilevered overhang to the loading

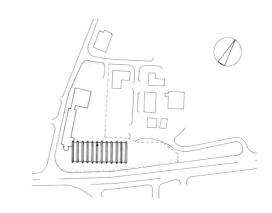

26.1. Site plan

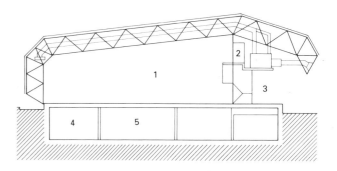

26.3.
Section through sorting office. 1
Sorting office; 2 watching gallery;

3 loading bay; 4 kitchen; 5
lounge/dining

26.2. General view from the south

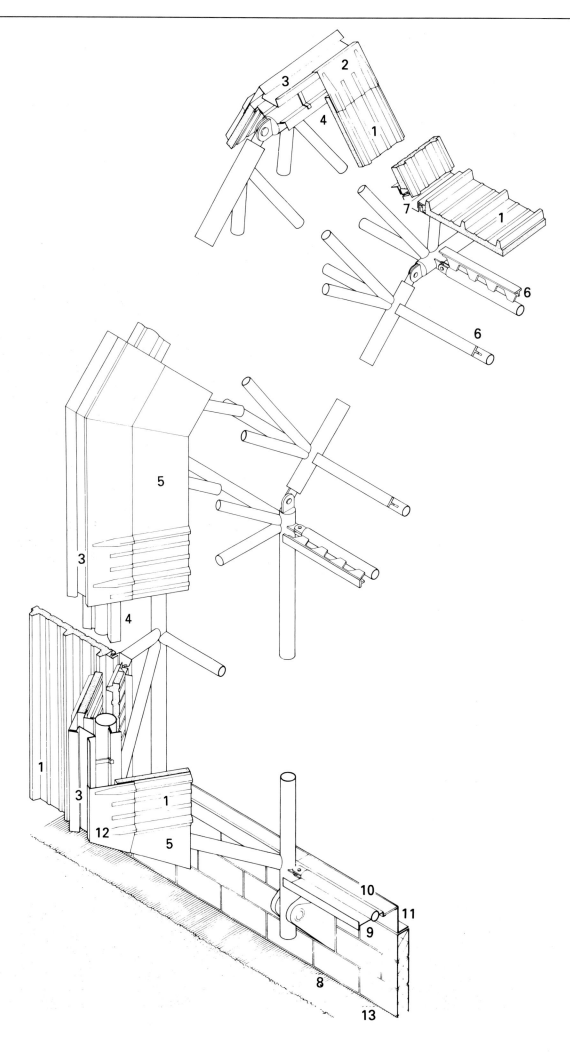

26.4.
Axonometric cutaway section through lattice truss and cladding. 1 Profiled Ondatherm panels; 2 standard pressed steel closer piece; 3 standard pressed steel gutter section supported on galvanized steel brackets; 4 steel fixing angles welded to c.h.s. at external apex of truss; 5 special insulated pressings used where cladding changes direction; 6 composite castellated purlin; 7 purpose-made extruded EPDM

gutter supported on 40 × 40 mm steel angles; 8 steel casting bolted to slab; 9 composite purlin; 10 rough-cast wired glass 6 mm thick; 11 200 × 100 mm steel angle kerbs bolted to blockwork; 12 special pressed steel closer piece; 13 fairface blockwork

26.5.
Profile of Ondatherm 101 composite panel

26.6.
·Detail of Don Reynolds glazing mullion. 1 Extruded aluminium mullion; 2 press-fit gaskets; 3 glazing

areas. Trusses are stabilized horizontally by half-castellated I-beams welded to c.h.s. forming the purlins which are fixed to the lower chords of the truss (Figure 26.4). In addition, the paired vertical propping columns are also cross braced in their top section.

The method of fixing the base of the truss to the concrete below used a special iron casting cast by Exeter Casting Ltd and a stainless steel connector bolted to the concrete slab. The lightness of the structure is cleverly emphasized by an infill of rough-cast wired glass (6 mm thick) sitting on steel angles and silicone glazed.

The cladding

Both roofs and walls are clad with Ondatherm profiled double-skin steel composite panels (Figure 26.5) supplied by Azimex and fixed by Harold Shaw Contracts. In this case, the panels have a 50 mm polyurethane insulation core and have a smooth white Plastisol finish to the steel. They span between the purlins on the flat planes and on the projecting plane span in the opposite

direction between the chords of the trusses using steel fixing angles and flats, welded to the outer chord of the truss.

Where the panels change direction, pressed closer pieces are used to close off the section. These (or flashings) also occur at the projecting ends of the sheets. The architects, faced with the use of these standard elements, have cleverly used ridge and valley gutters to also allow each side of the truss to be expressed externally as separate planes and to permit changes of direction to occur in the flat parts of the sheet. It is this detail that makes this building so interesting for a student of cladding, in that such an elegant solution has been reached using standard parts. However, details of this type are susceptible to potential rain penetration unless the tolerances of assembly and the inherent movement/shrinkage of the EPDM gasket can be controlled.

The ridge gutter (coated steel pressing) is supported on galvanized steel brackets and the valley gutters are specially formed in extruded EPDM with moulded corners tucked into the metal pressings forming the ends of the Ondatherm panels. The EPDM gutter was made up and welded together in the factory, brought to site and fitted as one continuous run.

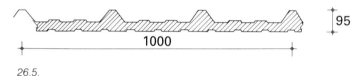

95
1000

26.5.

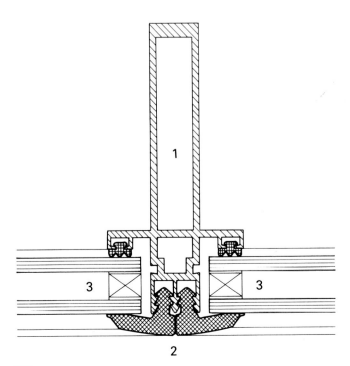

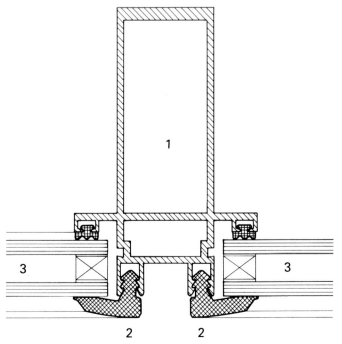

26.6.

26.7.

All roof rainwater is brought to ground level and collected in a continuous grill-covered ground gutter. In time there is some danger of the white cladding becoming streaked by the dirt in the rainwater, and it will probably need constant cleaning to maintain a pristine look.

Glazing

The west wall of the sorting office is clad in Don Reynolds double-glazed curtain walling composed of a polyester powder-coated extruded aluminium carrier system. This uses a split-section extrusion with a silicone glazing gasket (Figure 26.6).

Because of the height of the assembly (above 6 m), each of the curtain wall mullions is braced at its upper end by a triangulated c.h.s. frame descending diagonally from the outermost chord of the truss above, thus reducing the span of the transoms. The glazing supports are tied together at their base by stainless steel tie rods (Figure 26.7). Glazing is 24 mm double-glazed units formed in low E-glass inner leaf with tinted solar control glass outer leaf.

Services

The large plant required for heating the volume of air needed is situated outside, above the ancillary spaces and protected from the weather by the overhanging roof at the loading bays from which the ducts feed through the triangulated trusses. This allows easy access for maintenance without disrupting the sorting office, and is an excellent example of the integration between services and structure.

Costs

The building cost was £2.5 million, which, based on a total floor area, gives a cost per square metre of £424. Of this, the structural frame cost was £52 per square metre, the composite cladding forming the skin of the sorting office, inclusive of the gutter detail, cost £80 per square metre, while in the administration building the simpler roofscape cost £54 per square metre. The double-glazed aluminium curtain wall was approximately £200 per square metre. Thus the structural elements and shell of the building account for almost 50% of the building cost. However, the service elements are relatively inexpensive, being approximately 20% of the total cost, which compares well with other buildings of the same type.

Reference

Winter, J., 'Modern post architecture', *Architects' Journal*, 14 May 1986, pp. 37–58.

Stansted Airport Terminal Building, Essex
Architects
Foster Associates

General

The design of the Stansted Airport terminal building has tried to rediscover the simplicity and clarity of use characterized by the general aviation terminals of the earliest flying era. All public facilities are provided on a single concourse floor with arrivals and departures facilities planned side by side. With all baggage-handling systems, engineering plant, servicing and storage confined to an undercroft level below, the design is able to give a compact and flexible building which reduces walking distances for passengers and enables them to move through the building on essentially linear routes (Figure 27.1).

Another important aspect which has influenced the design is its context. For planning reasons, it was considered important that the building should not appear intrusive in the generally rural landscape of the locality. To this end, the undercroft has been partially excavated into the side of an existing rise in the ground, thereby establishing the concourse as an extension of ground level (Figure 27.2). The supports for the roof rise to 12 m at eaves level above the concourse, a height consistent with existing mature trees in the surrounding landscape (Figure 27.3).

The form and external appearance of the terminal are designed to have an assertive and low profile, but at the same time to manifest a strong and recognizable presence. The two main elevations are fully glazed. External structural elements support 18 m deep canopies, which provide sun shading and eliminate strong reflections in the glass walls, making them transparent rather than reflective. The two side elevations are constructed from translucent white glass and pale silver-grey aluminium panels for the undercroft, with a low horizontal band of transparent glazing separating the two at concourse level (Figure 27.4).

To allow the airport a high degree of flexibility for future alterations and modifications, a 36 m structural bay has been generated. All distribution equipment for heating, ventilation, air conditioning and lighting serving the concourse is contained within the clusters of steel columns on this grid (Figure 27.5). A secondary 1.2 m planning grid supports free-standing enclosures for shops, kitchens, lavatories, etc., and these can be easily dismantled (Figure 27.6). These enclosures are 3.5 m

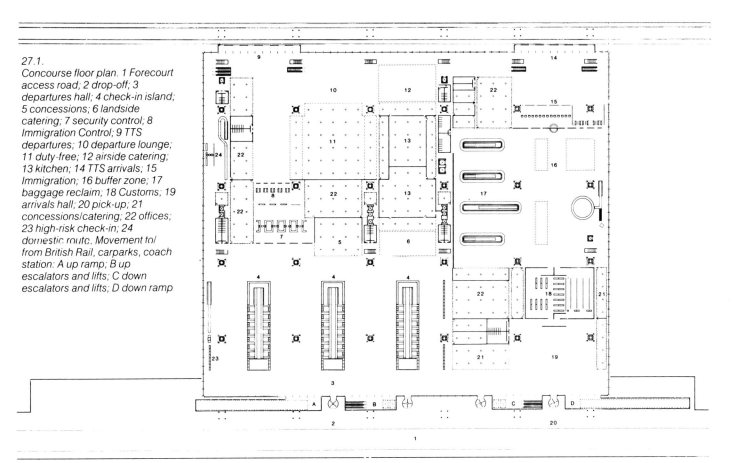

27.1.
Concourse floor plan. 1 Forecourt access road; 2 drop-off; 3 departures hall; 4 check-in island; 5 concessions; 6 landside catering; 7 security control; 8 Immigration Control; 9 TTS departures; 10 departure lounge; 11 duty-free; 12 airside catering; 13 kitchen; 14 TTS arrivals; 15 Immigration; 16 buffer zone; 17 baggage reclaim; 18 Customs; 19 arrivals hall; 20 pick-up; 21 concessions/catering; 22 offices; 23 high-risk check-in; 24 domestic route. Movement to/ from British Rail, carparks, coach station: A up ramp; B up escalators and lifts; C down escalators and lifts; D down ramp

27.2.
*Diagrammatic north–south
section through terminal*

27.3.
*Photomontage of terminal set in
landscape*

27.4.
*Corner view of model showing
rapid transit system*

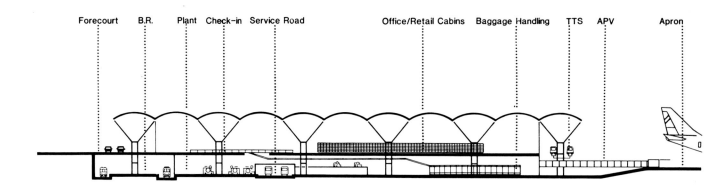

Forecourt B.R. Plant Check–in Service Road Office/Retail Cabins Baggage Handling TTS APV Apron

27.2.

high and are serviced by independent environmental engineering systems located in the undercroft.

Structure

The steel roof consists of 121 low-rise tubular section lattice shells, supported by 36 pre-stressed 'trees'. These trees are 21 m tall and are spaced at 36 m centres. The 'trunks' of the trees consist of a cluster of four vertical 457 mm diameter tubes. These are joined by 355 mm diameter horizontal tubes forming a three-dimensional Vierendeel structure cantilevered off of concrete foundation pads. At the 13 m level (4 m above concourse level) the vertical members reduce in size and are articulated diagonally outwards from pinned connection points. These elements now form the 'branches' of the trees, whose tips are at the corner of an 18 m square. The upside-down truncated pyramid shape thus formed is cross braced internally by a three-dimensional arrangement of four 163 m diameter tubes and pairs of 40 mm diameter high-strength pre-stressing rods. During construction this bracing is jacked taut by a force of about 70 tonnes. It is this pre-stressing which allows all the structural elements to be reduced to minimal sectional sizes.

Although these elements are principally fabricated, all primary node assembly components take the form of high-strength steel castings ranging in size from 25 to over 500 kg. In particular, this method of production has enabled the realization of the complex conical branch tapered sections. All castings have been designed to meet North sea oil-rig material performance standards and have been mechanically tested at the National Engineering laboratories in Scotland (Figure 27.7).

In fabrication, two types of welding process have been employed: first, submerged-arc automatic welding for all large-section tubular butt welds; and second, manually injected gas welding for small-section tubes and attachments. The selection and application of weld types have

been carefully considered in accordance with overall structural hierarchy and fabrication requirements.

The configuration of trees and shells has the advantage that, while the passenger concourse is interrupted by structure only every 36 m, the roof panels themselves have to span only 18 m (Figure 27.8). Both dimensional systems respond respectively to the integrated requirements of planning at floor level and of lighting and

27.3.

27.4.

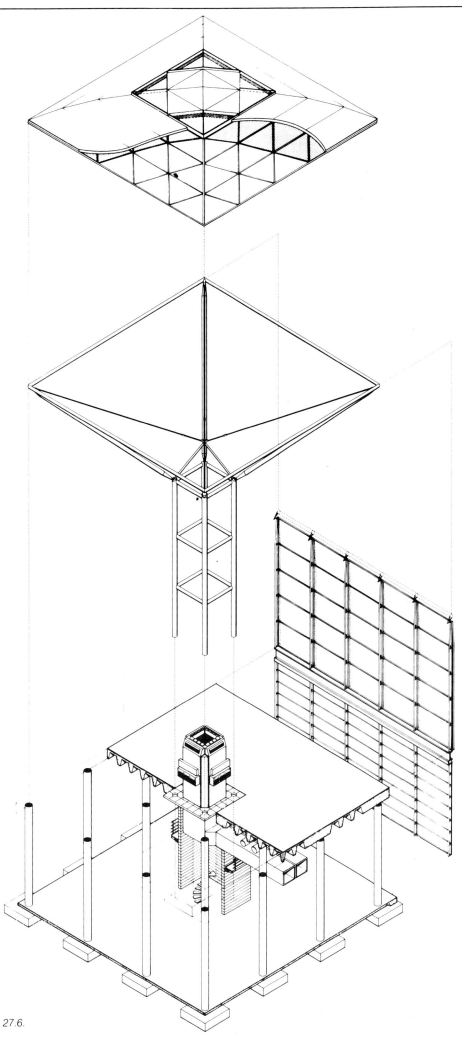

27.6.
Exploded isometric of cabin
structure and services

27.6.

27.5.
Exploded isometric of structural
tree and services

27.5.

acoustical behaviour at ceiling level. Additionally, the 2.5 m high lattice shells have been sized for constructability, since each is assembled fully on the ground, including profiled aluminium decking, and lifted directly onto the top of each tree and sets of interconnecting gridline beams by a large crawler crane (Figure 27.9). Similarly, the Vierendeel trunk structures are also fabricated entirely off-site and lifted into position as complete elements. Overall, the structural steelwork has been designed to minimize the amount of on-site assembly.

Another particularly unique feature of the structure is that, over its entire 198 × 198 m plan area, it possesses no expansion joints. Some slight rotational bending movement around gridline beam splice locations is allowed for, and this lets the structure react to wind and live loading without distortion. The gridline beam connection to the top of tubular steel wall cladding mullions allows for dynamic and thermal differential movement to occur. The decision to avoid expansion joints in the steelwork meant that they could also be avoided in the roof plane, thereby greatly simplifying the details.

Finally, the entire structure will be painted in a specially developed Isocyanate modified urethane acrylic decorative system, which allows for particularly fine colour

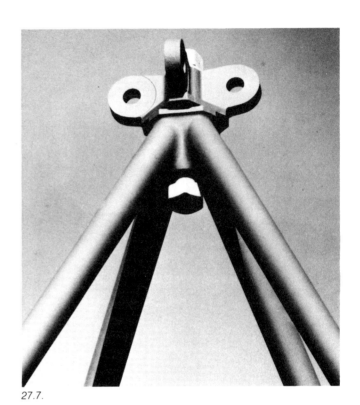

27.7.

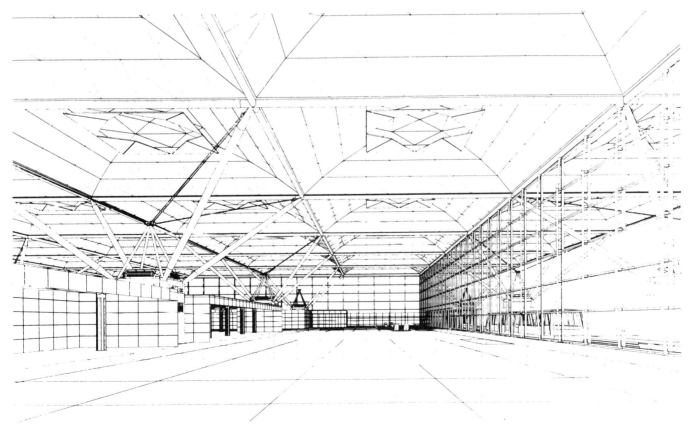

27.8.

27.9.

balancing with the indirect artificial lighting system and also exhibits significantly improved resistance to chemical and solar attack.

The total weight of steel in the structure is about 2800 tonnes and 4 hectares of profiled aluminium decking, also within the steelwork contract, are being used. Welded to the steelwork are about 110 000 cleats, lugs and brackets for the later attachment of cladding and high-level services. The steelwork contract was executed by Tubeworkers Limited of Claverdon in Warwickshire. Fabrication commenced in late summer 1986 and erection started on-site in spring 1987.

References

Davey, P., 'Stansted Structure', *Architectural Review*, No. 1072, June 1986.

Papadakis, A.C., 'Foster Associates, London Stansted Airport Terminal, *Architectural Design*, No. 56, May 1986.

Vitta, M., 'Steel trees in nature', *L'Arca*, June 1986.

Waters, B., 'Screws, nuts and teapot castings', *Building*, 11 September 1987.

Swindon Leisure Centre
Architects
Borough of Thamesdown Architects' Department
Borough Architect K.P. Sherry

General

This leisure complex, comprising sporting and social facilities together with bars and cafés, is situated in the development area to the west of Swindon, very near Norman Foster's Renault Centre, both of which use masted structures (Figure 28.2). Built in 1984, the complex has an ice rink, a 25 m swimming pool, a sports hall, squash courts, a health suite, arts and drama studios, snooker rooms, a youth club, a library and administration. A central mall connecting a café/restaurant, bar and information centre is located in the heart of the scheme to provide access to all these functions. The initial concept was based on a major roof structure embracing all the accommodation. Most of the building is at ground and first-floor levels with a small second-floor area. The site slopes north to south by just under a storey height, which allows the entrance from the buses to be at first-floor level.

The building was constructed in a remarkably short time between June 1983 and April 1985, using a prefabricated structure specially designed by structural engineers Anthony Hunt Associates.

Structure

The structure consists of a primary two-way lattice of 2.5 m deep girders at 14.4 m centres spanning from columns 93.6 m apart. The centre of the structure is formed by a $9\,m^2$ tower which also accommodates most of the air-handling plant (Figure 28.1). From these masts and those at the perimeter tension cables are used to assist the span of the lattice. These are restrained over the tops of the perimeter columns via outriggers to the base of the assembly (Figure 28.2). A series of smaller girders within this grid support the profiled steel sheeting forming the roof deck. The roof perimeter is formed by a triangulated lattice girder giving edge stiffness which is expressed as a cornice to the building.

28.2. Side view showing masted structure

Sequence of erection

The sequence of erection began from the central tower and progressed with each quarter of the roof completed in an anti-clockwise direction. (Was this because the crane driver was left-handed?) Stainless steel pins were used to connect the roof structure and nodes of the tension cables and the whole system was designed to maximize the number of repetitive elements to facilitate fabrication. An internal steel frame provides support for the precast concrete upper floors, and is fireclad where necessary and structurally independent of the main roof.

Cladding

This steel frame is also used to support the external cladding of profiled coated steel sheet and glazing. The cladding used is Glammett steel-faced foam-cored composite panels finished in silver PVF^2 and fixed by Metecno Contracts UK Ltd. Internal walls are generally fairfaced blockwork to supportspaces and public areas.

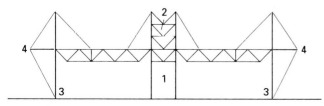

28.1.
Structural diagram. 1 Central tower; 2 services platform; 3 perimeter masts; 4 outrigger

28.3.

Services

The building is mechanically ventilated with air conditioning limited to the sports areas. Heat for the whole building is generated from the rink refrigeration plant, backed up by gas-fired boilers. Electrical services incorporate a BMS system for computer control and logging of all plant, and this level of sophistication is reflected in other systems of fire detection, security, public address and lighting.

Costs and comments

With a roofed area of 8760 m² and an internal floor area (including the two-storey block) of 12 500 m², the building cost of £9 million represents £720 per square metre,

which, for a building of this type, is a reasonably low-cost budget. Considerable innovation in the design and the attention to the form of the structural components and their expression make this building worth further study. For instance, the design of the canopies over the main entrances in simple frame and profiled cladding construction fit easily within the general sense of the building construction.

References

Anthony Hunt Associates, *Selected projects 1965–1985*, edited by Stratton and Reekie, produced in association with Book Production Consultants.

Ostler, T., 'The Swindon effect', *Building Design*, 17 October 1986, pp. 30–31.

The Trading Building, Haarlem
Architects
Cepezed

General

On an industrial estate near Haarlem, in Holland, this low-cost industrial unit with its highly visible mast structure is included here for its ingenious but simple use of components and the relationship between structure and cladding. It was built in 1985 by the architects Cepezed (Jan Pesman and Michel Cohen), and illus-

29.2.

29.3.

... the relating account approach is architects, Architectural use. These n about the which was ding, Haarit, therefore, h there may he simplicity y should be

rise 17 sets 30 m wide les, cantile-

29.1.
Section

29.2.
Boom pinned to 100 mm c.h.s.

29.3.
100 mm c.h.s. pinned to concrete slab

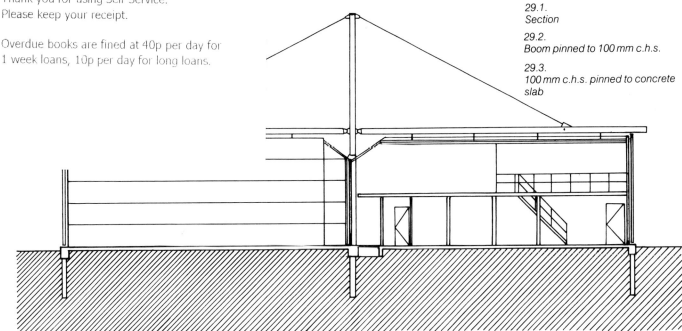

29.1.

29.4.
Side elevation showing 15 m long panels

29.5.
Detail at window jamb. 1 Sandwich panel; 2 50 × 30 × 3 mm pressed steel cleat; 3 70 × 260 × 2.7 mm multibeam; 4 50 × 50 × 3 mm r.h.s.; 5 site-applied insulation; 6 30 × 116 × 3 mm aluminium channel; 7 top-hat section; 8 T-shaped adaptor; 9 skylight glazing system; 10 100 mm perimeter c.h.s.

29.6.
Detail at door jamb. 1 Sandwich panel; 2 50 × 30 × 3 mm pressed steel cleat; 3 70 × 260 × 2.7 mm multibeam; 4 door jamb fixed to multibeam; 5 top-hat section; 6 30 × 116 × 3 mm aluminium channel; 7 50 × 50 × 3 mm r.h.s.; 8 100 mm perimeter c.h.s.

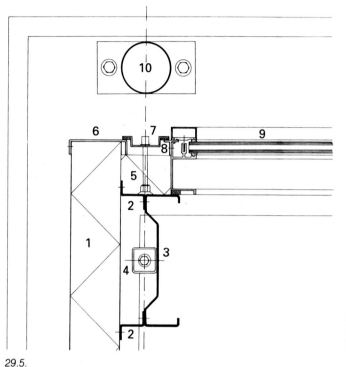

29.5.

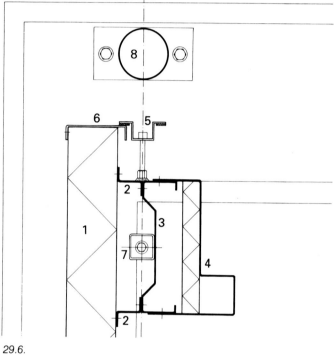

29.6.

vered booms each spanning 15 m. These booms (355 mm diameter c.h.s.) are tied at their ends to the ground slab by 100 mm diameter c.h.s. pinned at their bases (see Figures 29.2 and 29.3). Cross bracing is provided within each bay of the masts and outriggers are included at the ends.

Cladding

The cladding is composed of a 100 mm sandwich panel of two skins of 0.6 mm steel laminated to a polystyrene insulation, and the 15 m side panels are unusually long

(Figure 29.4) with interim supports at 5 m centres. The panel skins have been roll formed from 1200 mm wide coil resulting in panels 1155 mm wide. The panels are supported by vertical multi-beams, which are in turn fixed at their head to 100 × 100 mm r.h.s. suspended from the structural booms.

The panels are fixed to the structure by means of pressed steel cleats and the doors and windows are directly attached to the vertical multi-beam (Figures 29.5 and 29.6). The 102 mm vertical joints between the panels and windows consist of site-applied insulation and a top-hat section, painted to match the panels, which is screwed back into a nut welded to the multi-beam. The accuracy in placing these multi-beams is therefore very critical.

An interesting feature of this jointing assembly is the T-shaped adaptor to the windows to form a back plate against which the top-hat cover piece can be sealed. Similarly, the ends of the panels are capped in a aluminium U-section which is oversized on one side to allow a bearing plate for the top-hat cover piece. The same section with the outer flange bent by 45 degrees is used as a capping to the eaves detail (Figure 29.7).

Horizontal joints between the panel are tongue and groove joints formed in the polystyrene insulation, with a face-sealed silicone joint. At the base of the panel (Figure 29.8) an Omega 25 × 25 mm profile allows a similar upstand detail, also acting as a location slot.

29.4.

29.7.
Eaves detail. 1 Sandwich panel; 2 30 × 116 × 3 mm aluminium channel; 3 hanger; 4 100 × 100 × 4 mm r.h.s.; 5 106 mm deep profile roof deck; 6 355 mm diameter c.h.s. boom

29.8.
Detail at base of cladding. 1 Sandwich panel; 2 25 × 25 mm 'Omega' profile channel; 3 concrete slab

29.9.
Detail at skylight. 1 100 × 100 × 4 mm r.h.s.; 2 106 mm deep profile roof deck; 3 pressed metal edging; 4 'Skylight' glazing system

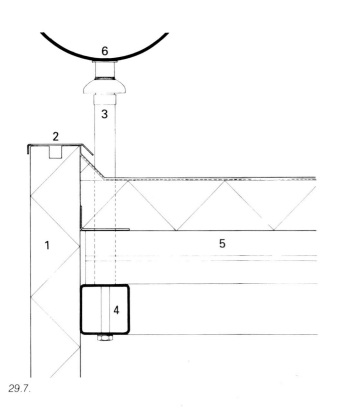

29.7.

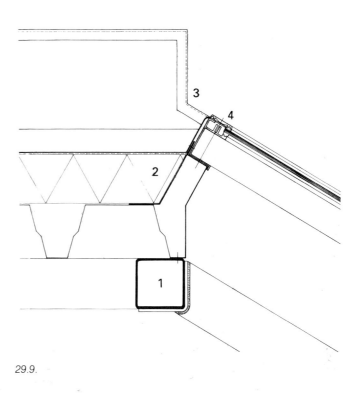

29.9.

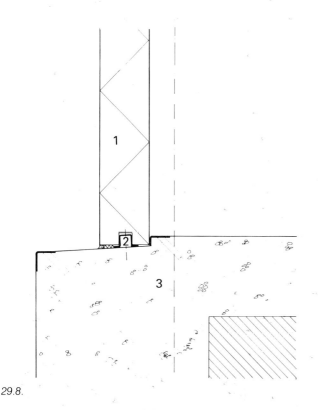

29.8.

Roofing

The 106 mm deep profile roof deck is supported by 100 × 100 × 4 mm r.h.s. suspended from the main boom. This kind of penetration of the roof by the supporting framework can be difficult to waterproof (see Figure 29.7). (See, for example, case studies of the Patera System and IBM Sports Pavillion in Brookes, *Concepts in Cladding*.)

The metal decking is sealed to provide a vapour barrier, with 100 mm polystyrene insulation and PVC roof covering above. In the centre of the building a continuous skylight-glazing system is provided. The detail of the junction between the glazing and the underside of the roof deck using a metal flashing is shown in Figure 29.9.

References

Berni, L. and Leyroy, A., 'Holland: a constructive workshop', *Ottagono*, No. 84, p. 23.

Mass, T., 'High-tech: het controleerbare beelt', *Architectur – Bouwen*, February 1987, pp. 23–26.

Van Douwen, A.A., 'Bedrijfsgebouewen in Nederland', Staaldocumentatie No. 1, *Bijlage Gebouwen met staal*, No. 81, June 1987.

30

'Yacht House' System, Woodgreen
Architect
Richard Horden Associates

General

Considering Richard Horden's previous experience with Foster Associates on the Sainsbury Centre and his enthusiasm for small boats, it is perhaps not altogether surprising that he should have been involved in the design of the 'Yacht House' modular frame building system in conjunction with Proctor Masts (manufacturers), Anthony Hunt (engineer) and the Scott Sutherland School of Architecture (development). As a prototype for a range of designs using the same structural system, Horden built a house at Woodgreen, in the New Forest, Hampshire, for his sister. Using entirely self-build parts (apart from the ground slab and drainage systems), the house was finally completed in 1985 at a price of around £300 per square metre, although Horden claimed a saving of £30 000 overall using self-build construction methods.

The house plan consists of a rectangle, four bays ×

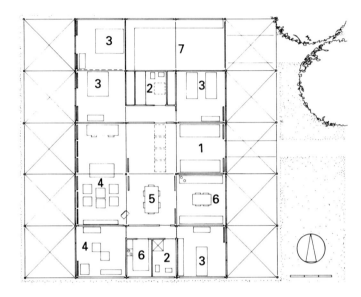

30.1.

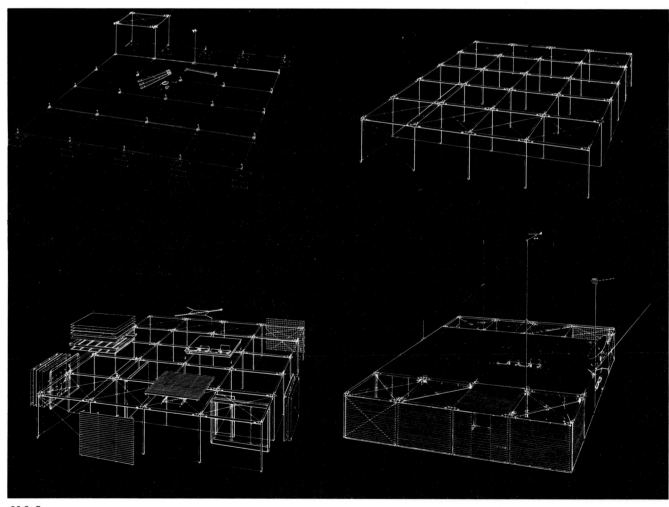

30.2–5.

30.1
Plan: the bays on the south side form a granny flat. 1 Entrance hall; 2 bathroom; 3 bedroom; 4 living room; 5 dining room; 6 kitchen; 7 garage

30.2.
Assembly sequence. Setting out and pouring of concrete pad foundations and ground slab. Columns and spars erected with wind bracing

30.3.
Wind-frame complete. Two opposite corners have vertical wind bracing to ensure rigidity in the vertical plane

30.4.
Cladding and roof panels added

30.5.
The completed house

30.6.
Section through column head detail. 1 Aluminium spar with cutouts; 2 cruciform aluminium member made up from 400 × 100 × 12 mm; 3 76 mm diameter aluminium column; 4 50 × 100 × 10 mm × 80 mm long aluminium angle to take roof panel frame

30.7.
Part plan, part section of column head. 1 Aluminium spar with cutouts; 2 cruciform aluminium member made up from 400 × 100 × 12 mm plate; 3 76 mm diameter aluminium column; 4 bolts with spacers welded to cruciform plate; 5 50 × 100 × 10 mm × 80 mm long aluminium angles

five bays, with a 3.6 m grid to give a variety of living spaces with partitions and using yacht masts as aluminium structural columns on the same grid (Figure 30.1). An interesting aspect of the plan is the variety of inside/outside spaces. Interior modules are covered by solid roof panel comprising metal decking and insulation held down to the deck by marine plywood sheets and all supported by steel angle trays. Some areas such as terraces and garage are covered by fabric canopies, roller reefed to control shading. Other external areas are defined by white variable-pitch aluminium louvres, below which is positioned the cross bracing for wind resistance.

The principle of construction and sequence of assembly (Figures 30.2–30.5), starting with the assembly of columns (masts) and beams (spars) and wind bracing, prior to letting in the roof panels each framed in a steel angle, illustrates Horden's intention to use the elements of yacht technology to produce an interchangeable arrangement of parts which can be easily assembled with unskilled labour – 'like a windsurfing kit for the building industry'.

Structure

The structure is composed of a series of extruded aluminium masts at 3.6 m intervals connected by extruded aluminium spars which form a permanent grid into which a variety of roof and wall panels can be placed. At Woodgreen the roof panels are metal decking, insulation and plywood mounted within a steel frame, but other later developments include g.r.p. panels.

To some extent, the aluminium spars can be considered to be redundant once the roof panels are in place, as these then serve to transfer the load to the aluminium masts. Certainly, the spars then serve no structural purpose (see Winter). However, if the masts can be seen to be permanent bracing to ease the erection process

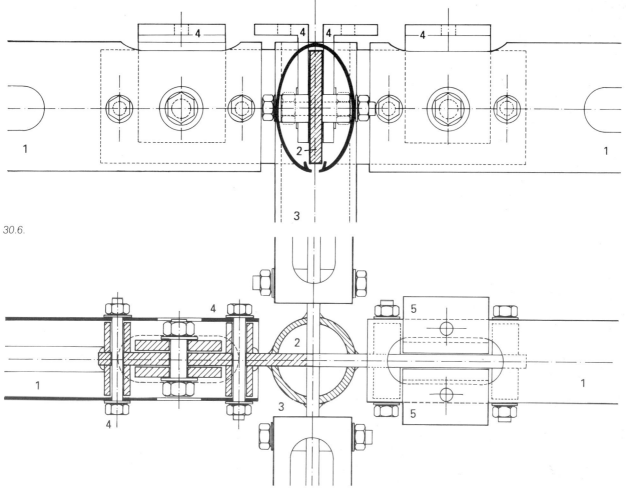

30.6.

30.7.

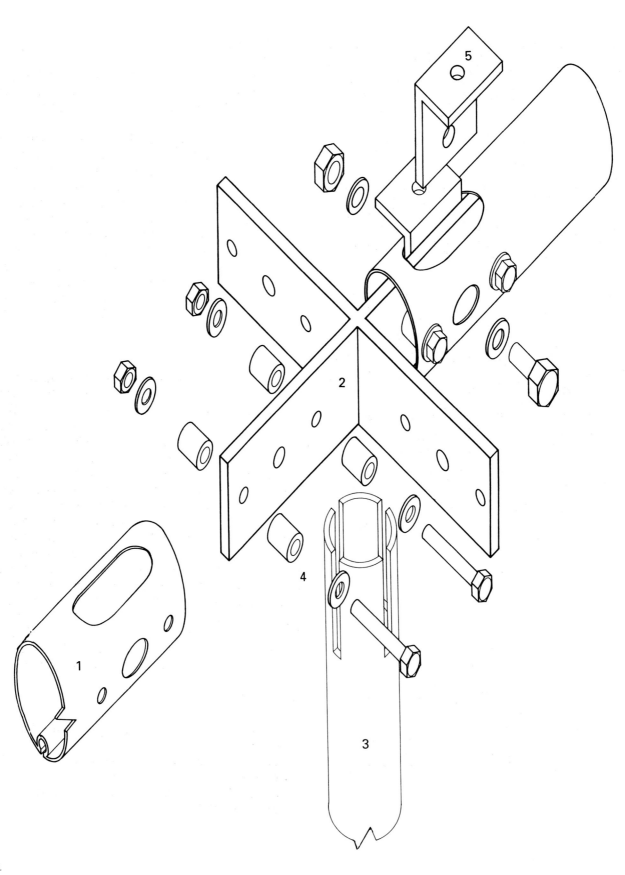

30.8.
Axonometric of column head
assembly. 1 Aluminium spar with
cutouts; 2 cruciform aluminium
member made up from 400 × 100
× 12 mm plate; 3 76 mm diameter
aluminium column; 4 bolts with
spacers welded to cruciform
plate; 5 50 × 100 × 10 mm ×
80 mm long aluminium angles

30.8.

30.9.
Column head assembly showing
roof panel frames resting on
aluminium angles

30.10.
External corner showing spars
fixed to column with aluminium
louvre panel

30.11.
Horizontal section through
column and patio door jamb. 1
76 mm diameter aluminium
column; 2 76 × 76 × 5 mm
aluminium angle; 3 door jamb

30.9.

30.10.

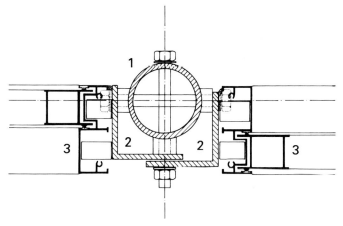

30.11.

and allow interchangeability to the parts, then they are an integral part of the total system. In the house at Woodgreen the spars, painted white and exposed wherever possible, do perform a visual function and can also be used to distribute services through their hollow section.

The details (Figures 30.6–30.8) show the 76 mm diameter × 6 mm thick extruded aluminium mast slotted at its head to receive a stainless steel cross plate 400 mm wide which extends down the hollow centres of the oval-shaped aluminium spars. These are each then fixed with two stainless steel bolts with short stainless spacer tubes welded to the cross plate so that the bolts do not squeeze the spar, and 50 × 100 × 80 mm aluminium angles × 10 mm thick are then also bolted either side of the cross plates and project through pre-cut slots in the top of the spars. These then support the steel angle framing the roof panels (Figure 30.9).

Cladding

The exterior of the house is clad with white aluminium weatherboarding on the sides, mounted onto a cladding unit 3572 mm long × 2400 mm high (Figure 30.10). The front and back elevations have sliding patio doors extending the full 2.4 m floor-to-ceiling dimensions. These glazed doors are fixed to the aluminium tubular masts using 76 × 76 × 6 mm steel angles (Figure 30.11).

Although the house can be admired as an example of clip-together detailing, some of this seems a little crude in comparison to what might have been possible in boat design. To some extent this can be explained by the requirement to self-build, and must have been affected by the cost of the component parts, aluminium masts, stainless steel plates, etc. Even so, it does represent an elegant example of interchangeable component assembly, and with its extensive use of adjustable louvres can be compared to Chris Clarke's Bridge House in Brisbane (Case Study 5). Both architects would have been influenced by Craig Elwood and the Mies tradition.

References

Anon., 'Yacht haven', *Building Design Practice Profile*, 15 March 1985.

Horden, R., 'Yacht-House', *Architecture d'Aujourd'hui*, No. 239, June 1985, pp. 1–47.

Winter, J., 'Ship to shore', *Architects' Journal*, 24 July 1985, pp. 36–50.

31

Victoria Plaza Canopy, London
Architects
Heery Architects & Engineers Ltd

General

When commissioned by Salomon Brothers International Ltd to transform an existing atrium into a dealing room Heery Architects & Engineers Ltd, together with Anthony Hunt Associates, were faced with an unusual problem. The solution was to insert a suspended services canopy which would control the environment below, transforming it from a dead space into the nerve-centre for the whole building. This new roof thus divides the height of the atrium the top of which can be seen from the two floors of offices above.

The 30 × 40 m atrium was ringed by four levels of office space and split down the centre by a two-storey high link block. The whole office block had been constructed above the railway tracks at Victoria Station and consequently the loading points were severely restricted. The brief requirements also added further complexity to the project: the client stated that the dealing room had to be operational by the 'Big Bang' in 1986, only 14 months away when Heery were commissioned. Second, the structure to be inserted was to be fully demountable, since the building would have to be reinstated when Salomon's lease ran out.

Structure

By removing the link block the atrium became one uninterrupted space. This also freed the building of 134 tonnes, which dictated the limits within which the new structure had to lie (Figure 31.1). The side walls of the atrium had not been designed to carry any further load and could not be used for support.

Having established the three loading points, the design was originally based on one mast rising off each

31.2.

of these points from which a Vierendeel box truss (fabricated by Tubeworkers Ltd) could be suspended. Each span is picked up by three pairs of 40 mm diameter rods (maximum load in hangers 105 kN) (Figure 31.2). Since the mast location was offset by 3 m from the centre of the span, counterweights equivalent to the weight of the structure plus services of one bay had to be added to the shorter bay to balance out the loads. When, at a later date, in an attempt to reduce the number of visual obstructions in the dealing room one of the (273 mm diameter, 16 mm wall thickness) columns was eliminated the geometry of the suspension rods increased in complexity, since a total of 48 rods had to be anchored to two column heads (Figure 31.3).

The top level of the canopy plane was set by the office floor level and the structural depth of the Vierendeel box truss was coordinated with the 900 mm depth of the

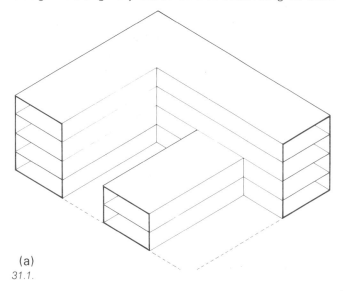

(a)

31.1.

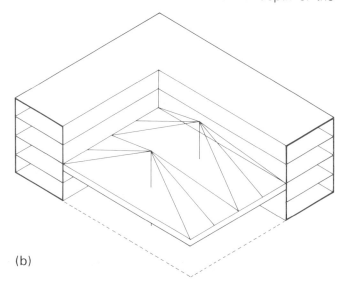

(b)

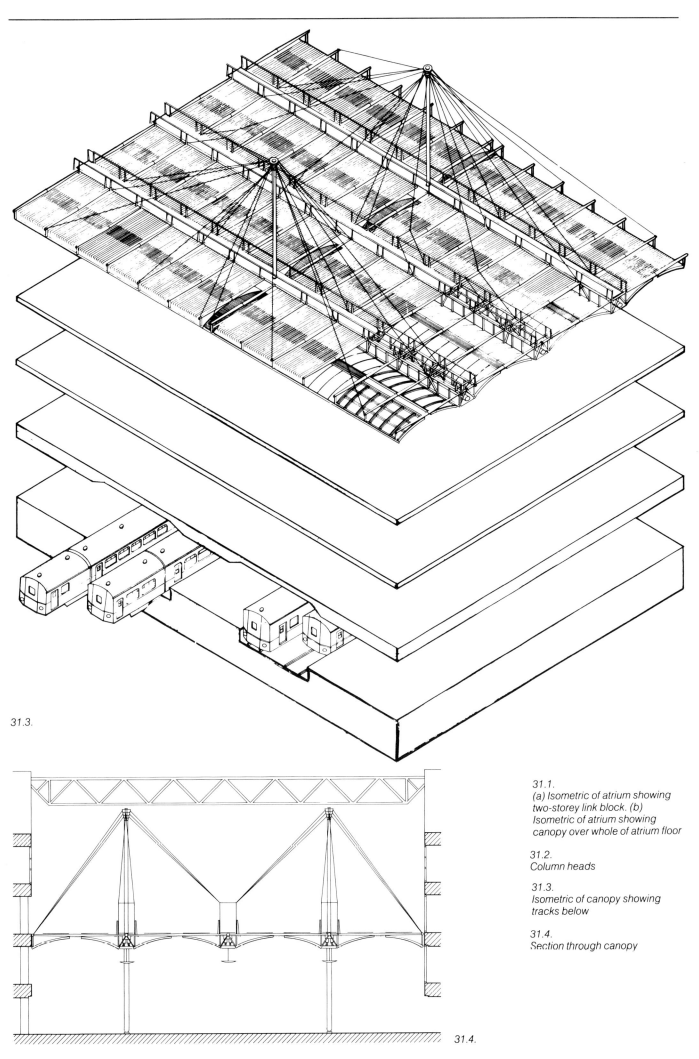

31.3.

31.1.
(a) Isometric of atrium showing
two-storey link block. (b)
Isometric of atrium showing
canopy over whole of atrium floor

31.2.
Column heads

31.3.
Isometric of canopy showing
tracks below

31.4.
Section through canopy

31.4.

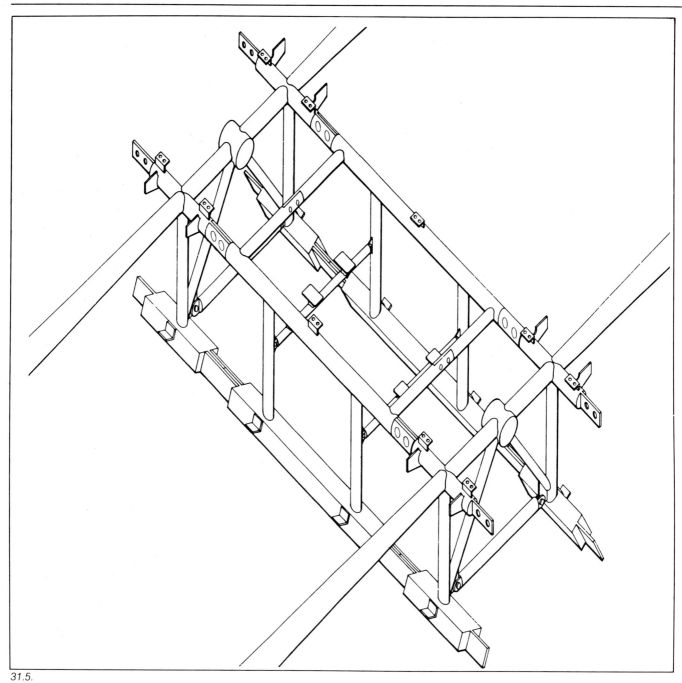

31.5.

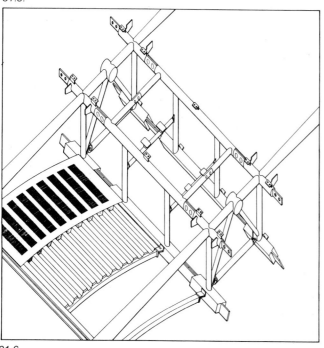

31.6.

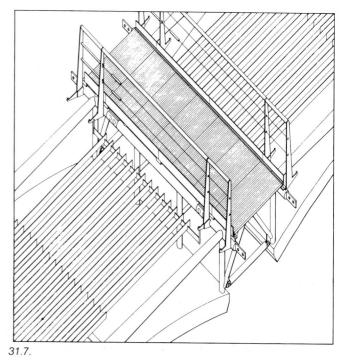

31.7.

31.5.
Isometric of primary structure

31.6.
Isometric of primary structure and
stressed skin

31.7.
Isometric of primary structure
louvres, walkway, kick plates and
handrail

31.8.
Isometric of primary structure and
electrical services

31.9.
Isometric of primary structure and
mechanical services

31.10.
Isometric of primary structure and
water supplies for fan coil units
and sprinklers

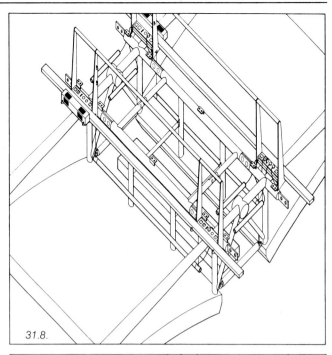

31.8.

cladding spandrel. In this way the canopy does not impinge on the glazed areas of the surrounding offices (Figure 31.4). The maximum depth of structure is required along the box truss 'spines'. The vaulted ceiling rises where this depth is not required, at the same time adding to the visual interest and improving the acoustic qualities of the space below. The 6.3 m long members spanning from spine to spine were designed as double-tapered 'cigar'-shaped circular hollow sections, which makes optimum use of material where the bending moments are greatest . Unfortunately, these had to be abandoned after prototyping led to programming difficulties.

Erection of the canopy within an existing building meant that the size of each component was limited to the physical limits of the access to the site, which was a 1.2 × 3.6 m opening in the cladding, and the weight of each component was limited to that which could be manhandled by a small team of erectors. These constraints dictated that the canopy had to be made up of many small elements. A family of in-line connections was derived to reduce the number of joints which may otherwise have been visually dominant (Figure 31.5). The Vierendeel construction also helped in this respect, since a triangulated truss would also have required joints in the diagonal members.

Diagonal bracing was achieved in the plane of the canopy by using profiled steel panels which were fixed to the secondary steelwork (Figure 31.6) to provide a stressed-skin construction. The requirement for diagonal bracing in an internal structure is minimal, and was quite simply and unobtrusively dealt with.

Due to the severe loading restrictions the weight of the structure had to be kept to a minimum. This meant that much of the tertiary structure (handrails and stanchions, walkways and kickplates) and services (fan coil casings, cable trunking, pipe casings and light fittings) were made of aluminium (Figure 31.7).

Because of the requirement to fully demount the structure at some future date the columns are not anchored at their base. Instead they sit into a pocket at their base and are restrained by the tension structure above (Figure 31.12).

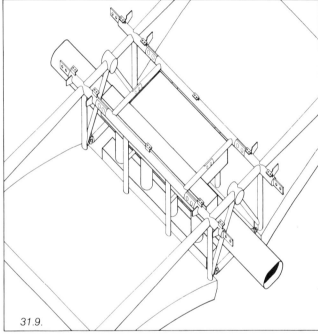

31.9.

Services

All services enter the canopy from the end of each spine and run towards the columns, terminating in the central bays, leaving a clear slot running across the canopy along the column line. Each 3 m bay is subdivided into 500 mm wide units, which provides a framework for the coordination of services (Figures 31.8–31.10). The ser-

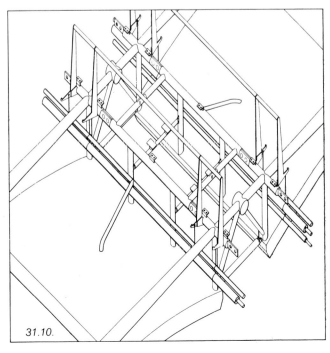

31.10.

31.11.
*General view: note in-line
connectors on structural
members and ball and socket
joint on top half of column*

31.11.

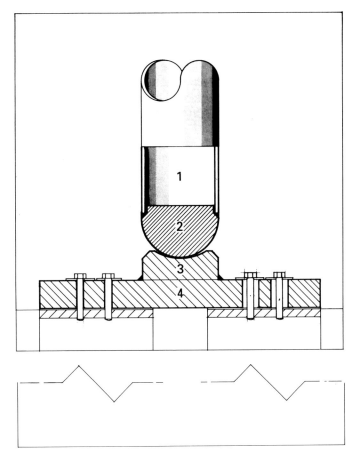

31.12.
*Detail of column base. 1 273 mm
diameter × 16 mm c.h.s.; 2
machined solid steel hemisphere
welded to column; 3 machined
solid steel cup to take column; 4
solid steel base plate spans
expansion joint*

31.12.

vices include: air handling, above- and below-canopy lighting and associated ballast units, communications, pneumatics, sprinklers and general power. Each socket box is punched out with six different socket types giving each electrical service its own dedicated outlet. The below-canopy lighting consists of emergency lighting, uplighters and downlighters. The uplighters were specially designed to reflect light evenly off the vaulted ceiling, mixing halogen and sodium sources to create a different effect in the mornings and evenings. The downlighters were chosen from Siemens range specially developed to eliminate glare on VDU screens.

Acoustic control in a dealing room is potentially a great problem, but the use of perforated ceiling tiles with acoustic backing provided this. Acoustic insulation was also fitted in the troughs of the profiled steel sheet, which were then covered with perforated panels to provide insulation in the case of noise break-out in the canopy space above.

References

Knobel, L., 'Dealing with tradition', *Designers' Journal*, March 1987.
Latham, I., 'Over the top', *Building Design*, 22/29 August 1986.
Thornton, J., 'The lightweight canopy at Victoria Plaza', *Architectural Journal*, 29 October 1986.

Hongkong and Shanghai Bank, Hong Kong
Architects
Foster Associates

32.1.

General

This case study (Figure 32.1) has been included towards the conclusion to this book mainly because it represents the ultimate use of component technology applied to buildings produced to date. Each element of the construction was developed in conjunction with the manufacturers, with claddings from the USA, fire protection of the structure from the UK, staircases from Japan, external sunscoops from West Germany, inner sunscoops from Austria, floor finishes from Finland and refuse disposal from Sweden (Figure 32.2). Each element was designed and developed from scratch in collaboration with the manufacturers. Mock-ups and prototypes were built and tested until their performance and quality met with the architects' approval. In some respects therefore one could regard this building as the ultimate in custom-made component assembly.

One of the factors influencing the architects in their selection of manufacturers was their willingness and ability to manufacture non-standard items. This was

certainly the case in the design of the cladding and curtain wall system, by the cladding contractors Cupples and their parent company H.H. Robertson. The cladding contract for the bank not only represented the largest ever (45 million m^2) but also the most complex in its need to respond to the geometry of the structure and its tolerances, and also to be capable of resisting typhoon conditions.

Cladding panels

The first cladding panels were fitted to a section of the main structure on 23 January 1985 (Figure 32.3). Fire protection to the structure had been achieved using a thin, highly flexible ceramic fibre blanket by Morceau UK, held in position on a stainless steel mesh. A reinforced aluminium foil was wrapped over the completed fire protection to provide a vapour seal and temporary protection prior to fixing the cladding.

The aluminium cladding panels with their extruded edge sections were fixed back through the blanket using cleats onto Unistrut sections attached to the steel frame at the time of applying the 12 mm thick cementicious barrier coating, providing corrosion protection to the structural steelwork (Figure 32.4). Some of the 9 mm joints between the panels were filled with silicone mastic, others were pressure equalized.

Similar aluminium panels were used to clad both the inside and outside of the building. The service modules are also clad using honeycomb-cored aluminium panels. These were produced by Cupples, using purpose-made presses and specially developed robot welders using 4 mm thick plate aluminium with a Duranar PVF^2 finish to produce a large range of individual panels based on a 1200 mm grid. The largest panel covered the joint of the cantilevered truss and the outer hanger (Figure 32.5). Designed and tested to prevent water penetration even under typhoon conditions, great care had to be taken with all panels to ensure that they were located accurately and that all joints were correctly sealed. The weather protection of the complete assembly depends upon the principle of pressure equalization within the joint.

Curtain walling

The great depth of the Bank's offices and Foster's desire for a see-through building on two elevations dictated a fully glazed solution on the Queen's Road side of the elevations to Statue Square. Here the adoption of a curtain walling system spanning between floor levels consisted of a clear-glass outer skin, a cavity containing a venetian blind and an openable inner leaf of tinted

32.1.
General view of Bank in context

32.2.
Chart showing origin of
components

32.3.
First cladding panels to be
erected

32.3.

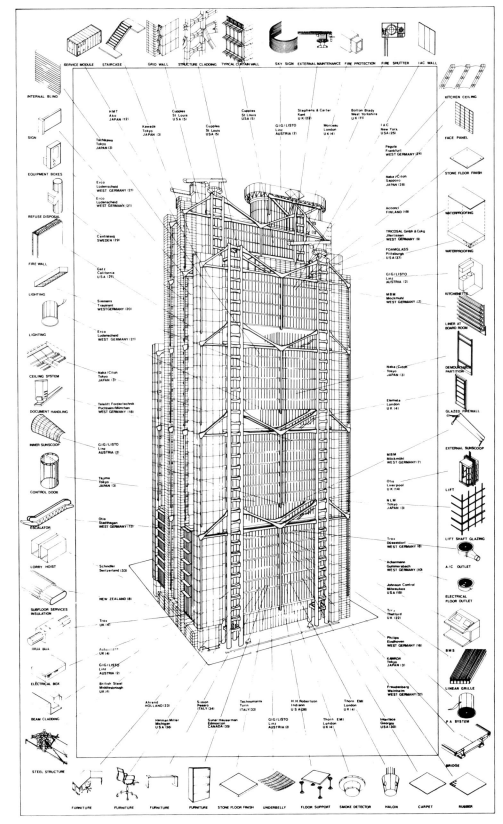

32.2.

32.4.
*Fixing arrangement of cladding
panels. 1 Unistrut fixed to
structural member through fire
blanket; 2 cast cleat; 3 extruded
aluminium edge section; 4
weather seals*

32.5.
*Largest panel being positioned
over joint between truss and
hanger*

glass. Blinds were omitted from the north-facing windows with their splendid views. A *brise soleil* was applied to each of the Bank's facades and it also acts as a walkway for cleaning and maintenance of the facade. At each end of the walkway there are glazed panels that open to form access doors from the interior. These also serve to allow the mandatory 2% of floor area smoke vents (Figure 32.6).

The framing to the curtain walling consists of extruded aluminium vertical mullions with a c.h.s. outer flange and perforated web. These are connected by aluminium castings consisting of an upper and lower spigot which slide into the outer tubes of the mullion. This does most of the structural work, providing a connection capable of accepting vertical movement of +20 to −60 mm. This cast connector is in turn fixed back to the horizontal support rails to the floor slabs by means of T-bracket connectors offering both vertical and horizontal adjustment (Figure 32.7). This casting forms a key to the whole assembly, as it not only supports the ends of the mullions back to the structure, allowing for a large degree of movement, but also provides a connection point for the cast aluminium brackets which support the *brise soleil* and maintenance catwalks. The aluminium brackets were manufactured by a vacuum-evacuated die, and over 4000 brackets were required for the whole building (Figure 32.8). According to Davies:

> This humble component is as finely engineered a piece of metalwork as you'll find in any aerospace factory. The brackets are perforated with round holes that recall Foster's elegant metal furniture designs and the louvres are set at an angle precisely calculated to reduce glare from below, but allow a view down from above. They form a prominent feature of the facade and perhaps for this reason they have been installed over the whole of the north elevation facing the harbour, even though this side of the building rarely receives direct sunlight.

Structural silicone glazing has been used to fix the glass back to the framing members and to form the horizontal joints between glazing. As with the joints between panels, this silicone glazing is visible at ground-floor levels. The glazing system also allows drainage from the fascia at each floor level (Figure 32.9).

The Bank exemplifies the quality of and attention to detailing that is necessary to produce a building of this quality. It is here where the constructional detail becomes an essential feature of design, where at all levels total commitment by the architects towards the buildability of their design ideas would be required. Students of architecture should not underestimate the degree of time

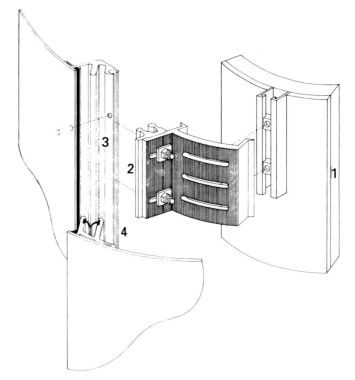

32.4.

32.5.

32.6.
External walkways

32.8.
Exploded isometric of bracket assembly. 1. Cast aluminium walkway support bracket; 2 extruded aluminium fins; 3 aluminium fascia; 4 horizontal glazing frame; 5 extruded aluminium mullion; 6 perimeter steel r.h.s. fixed back to slab; 7 steel bracket; 8 adjustable T-section; 9 cast aluminium bracket with steel spigots to fit cladding mullions

32.7.
Mock-up of bracket

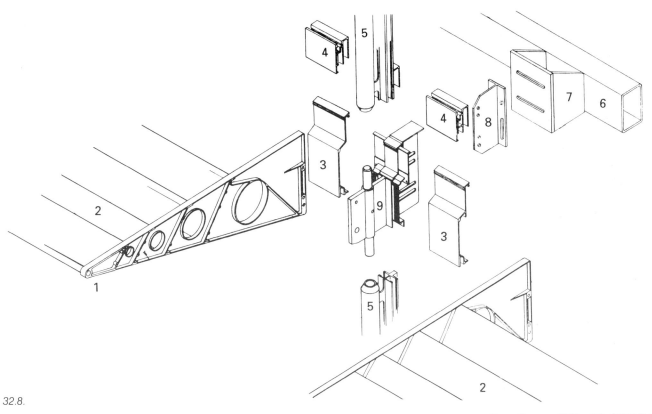

32.8.

32.7.

32.6.

32.9.
Section of glazing cill showing
drainage from fascia at each floor

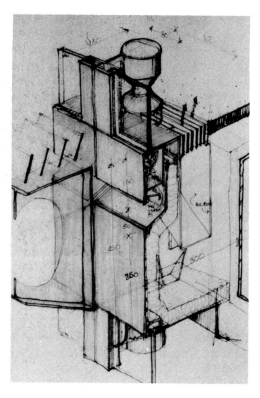

32.9.

and energy this level of commitment would require. It is also interesting to see the ways where elements of one system are re-used in different locations to provide a continuity in the design. For example, mullions from the curtain walling were adapted to form parts of the space frame trusses that support the glazing to the lift lobbies and entrance canopies. In this way, the vocabulary of detailing becomes the language of the design.

References

This building has been widely published throughout the world and we have only here briefly touched on one aspect of the design. For further information the following sources are also useful.

Anon., 'Two engineered solutions', *Architects' Journal*, 22 October 1986, pp. 79–94. This shows a comparison between the construction of the Lloyds Building in London (see Case Study 14) and the Bank, and includes some useful information on the design and development of the structure, cladding and services.

Chaslin, F., *Norman Foster*, Elector Monitor, 1986, pp. 126–154. This summary of the construction includes some excellent early sketches showing the fixing of the cladding to the structure using Unistrut type anchors and the silicone butt jointing in the glazing. There is also an excellent sketch showing the fascia member between the curtain walling and the junction to the floor edge beams. (Similar information is contained in a study of the building in *Architecture d'Ajourd'hui*.)

Davies, C., 'Building the Bank', *Architectural Review*, April 1986, pp. 82–106. In this entire issue dedicated to the Bank, Davies' description of the detail developments is a useful contribution towards understanding the technical nature of the building, with exploded isometrics showing the interfaces between the various components.

Lambot, I., *The New Headquarters for the Hongkong and Shanghai Banking Corporation*, Ian Lambot, Hong Kong, 1985. This is an excellent survey of photographs showing the sequence of assembly of the building from groundworks in 1983 to the official opening on 7 April 1986. As such, it represents the most invaluable and unique guide to students wishing to learn more about the construction not only of this building but also of any building using component technology. Most useful from the point of view of this case study are photographs 72 and 73, showing the location of the steel frame and the fixing of the wall cladding (photographs 62 and 91). There is also an excellent series of photographs on the construction of the suspended flooring with service ducts below. An amusing contrast is shown in the centre page between the hand-tied bamboo scaffolding extensively used throughout the construction and the sophistication of the building elements around it.

Seddon, C., 'Norman Foster's Hong Kong and Shanghai Bank', *Architect (Australia)*, October 1986. This contains a summary of the design construction process, including a description of the sources of building materials and elements used in the Bank, and of the tolerances required for the structure and main components. For example, 'The maximum wind load generating a 4 second oscillation at the top of the building of 300 mm resolves out at 7 mm lateral movement per floor'.

Winter, J., 'Comparing products', *Architects' Journal*, 22 October 1986, pp. 97–102. This article also compares products used at Lloyds and the Bank and gives information on the manufacturers involved.

New Studios and Galleries, Liverpool
Architects
Dave King and Rod McAllister

General

Designed by Dave King and Rod McAllister in association with the Gerald Beech Partnership, the new studio and galleries in Liverpool provide 1500 m^2 of teaching and exhibition space as the major part of the refurbishment of the School of Architecture to accommodate the recent merger with the University's Department of Building Engineering (Figure 33.1).

Structure

The new design spans across the roof of the existing extension to the School of Architecture, an early 1930s Modernist building by Reilly, Budden and Marshal. The lightweight structure, which uses a central arcade of tubular columns, consists of steel beams and purlins supporting a metal-decked roof system over the three-tier open-plan studio and exhibition space. The beams are tapered at their ends and pin jointed to flanged capitals at the column heads (Figure 33.2). Loads are carried down to the foundations mainly through the concrete core and the structure is designed to transmit minimal weight to the existing steel-framed building. Purlins are spaced at 1575 and 2400 mm centres and are carried through to the outer walls, where they continue in the vertical plane to act as cladding posts (Figure 33.3). Junctions between structural members are straightforward and bold in recognition of the fact that they will be exposed internally as well as externally (Figures 33.4–33.6).

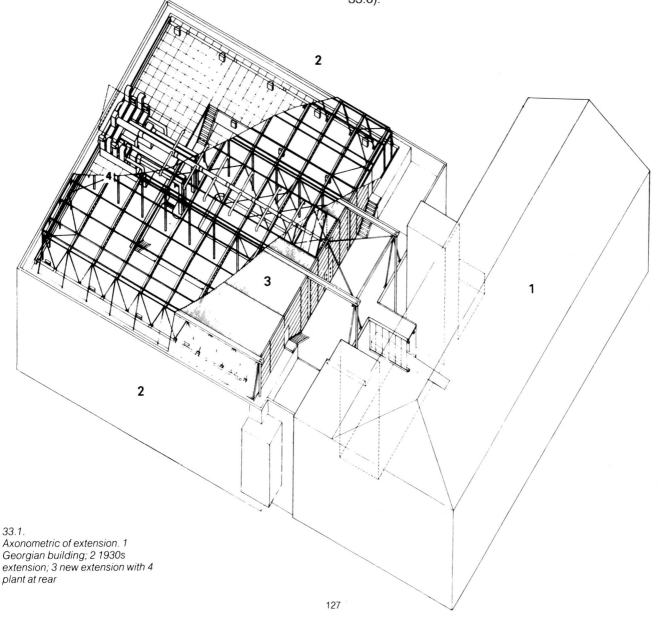

33.1.
*Axonometric of extension. 1
Georgian building; 2 1930s
extension; 3 new extension with 4
plant at rear*

33.2.
Model of central arcade showing
tapered beams pinned to
columns

33.3.
Computer model of central
arcade showing different levels

33.2.

33.3.

33.4.
Steelwork detail showing bracing
to tapered beams

33.5.
Steelwork detail showing bracing
of lower flange of beam to
counteract wind uplift on flat roof

33.6.
Gable wall

The structural engineers for the extension were the local practice of Roy Billington Associates and the steelwork was prefabricated by Roydens of St Helens.

Cladding

The cladding itself is a lightweight 70 mm thick foam sandwich employing microprofile steel sheeting on both inner and outer faces. It is of similar type to that used on Foster Associates' Renault Building at Swindon, being manufactured to fine tolerances and employing a matt silver PVF^2 finish. Jointing is 22 mm butyl rubber gasket in the vertical plane and 8 mm polysulphide pointing horizontally (Figure 33.7).

Unusually for such a building, the cladding system is only on the gable faces, the two sides being glazed (Figures 33.7 and 33.9). It is confined to specifically delineated panels between structural members, and doors, where they occur, do not pierce the cladding itself. The concept is to use cladding as 'lightweight stone' with a strong joint pattern, rather than to 'skin' the building, as is more often the case.

Glazing is a combination of raked patent-glazed outer walls and a central full-length roof light. Although ordinary 6 mm toughened glass was appropriate at the lower level, solar gain necessitated the use of 16 mm three-skin Makrolon on the rooflight. The material, imported from West Germany, gives the appearance of reeded glass and is surprisingly transparent. The effect of bright sun is to reflect a long line of light the full length of the glazing and, therefore, seemingly intensify the light source.

Services

The building's systems are completely integrated with the structure. Electrical installation is concealed within structural members and special light fittings employing a combination of tungsten-halogen fluorescent and discharge lamps give an overall clean white effect.

Mechanical services are exposed, as are internal gutters and rainwater pipes. Another unusual innovation is that the central extract plant room is placed, for demonstration purposes, within the studio space. A specially designed tamperproof control panel constantly monitors the plant operation and gives all relevant zone information at a glance. The services were designed by Henry Gun & Why and Dave Dutton of Liverpool University.

33.4.

33.5.

33.6.

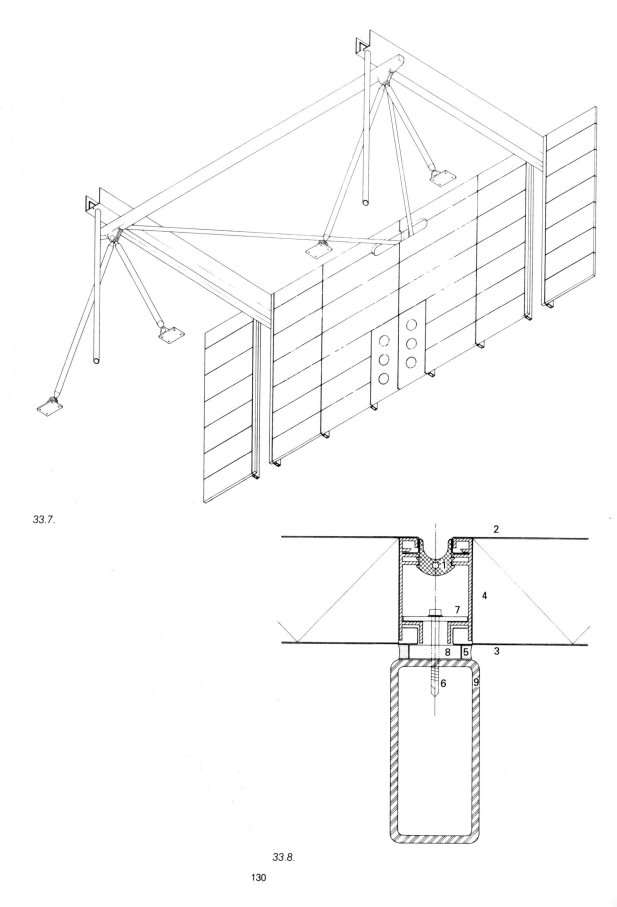

33.7.
Gutter and downpipe detail

33.8.
Cladding fixing detail. 1 22 mm butyl rubber gasket; 2 0.6 mm steel outer skin; 3 0.6 mm steel inner skin; 4 70 mm expanded polystyrene; 5 low-density foam seal; 6 self-tapping screw; 7 3 mm galvanized steel fixing plate; 8 packer; 9 120 × 60 mm r.h.s.

33.7.

33.8.

33.9.
Corner detail. 1 Cladding panels;
2 6 mm toughened glass in raked
patent glazing system; 3 gutter
and downpipe; 4 existing roof of
1930s extension

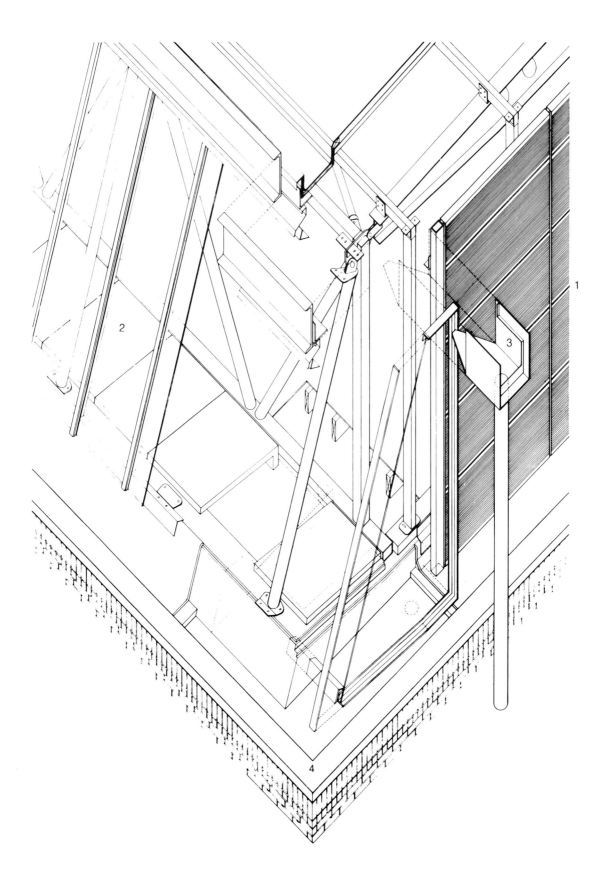

33.9.

Finishes

Finishes are simple and direct. Stainless and galvanized steel are left untreated and the structure is painted throughout with a silicon alkyd aluminium paint which has the property of retaining its sheen. Conventional silver paints tend to chalk quickly. The floor finish throughout is green 'artificial grass', which is carried through to a south-facing terrace.

Conclusion

The design's objective is to present a combination of classical order and technological expression with an exciting special concept... its precise silver cladding, stainless steel rainwater system and sharp triangular rooflight draw more inspiration from recent developments in Switzerland and Italy than from current British Post-modernism. It is intended that the extensive use of exposed services and the direct constructional language will encourage its use as a unique teaching environment.

The project uses a deliberately strong aesthetic to maintain its presence in the context of the school's existing buildings. Its sense of balance and logical juxtaposition of elements are combined with an accurate contemporary style to enhance its rare status as purpose-made 'School Design'.

References

Anon., 'Dave King and Rod McAllister, architects', *Architectural Review*, May 1989, pp. 40–41.

Index of Names

Ahrends, Burton & Koralek, 89
Aldington, Craig & Collinge, 97
Arup Associates, v, 41
Arup, O. & Partners, vi, 34, 46, 55, 61, 92
Asselbergs, T., 66
Barclay, M. Partnership, 78
Barker, T., 63
Beech, G. Partnership, 127
Bell, P. & Partners, xiii, 78
Benthem & Crouwel Architekten, xiii, 5, 7, 31, 34
Bickerdike Allen Partners, 80
Billington, R. Associates, 129
Bloomfield, R., 80
Brock Carmichael Associates, 58
Buchanan, P., 42
Building Design Partnership, 26
Cepezed, 109
Clarke, C., 19, 115
Cohen, M., 109
Cook, P., 34
Cox, P. & Partners, 34
Davies, C., 124
Davis Brody & Associates, 71
Dini, M., 63
Di Stasio & Van Buren, 85
Eekhout, M., 2
Eiffel, G., 2
Elwood, C., 115
Fainsilber, A., 74
Foster, N. & Associates, vi, xi, 2, 74, 76, 87, 101, 107, 122
Gasson, B., 10
Grad Hillier Partnership, 85
Green, E. & Partners, 90
Grimshaw, N., xii
Hampshire CC, Architects' Department, 13
Heery Architects & Engineers, 116
Hopkins, M. & Partners, 92

Horden, R., 21, 69, 112
Hunt, A. Associates, 90, 107, 112
Kalsi, A., 56
Kaplicki, J., 2
Kinch, R., 46
King, D., 127
Law, M., 2
McAllister, R., 127
Murcutt, G., 64
Nixon, D., 2
Palladio, A. di, 3
Paxton, J., v
Peacock, F., 56
Pei, I., 50
Pesman, J., 109
Piano, R., 46, 61
Picardi, G., 26
Property Services Agency, 22
Prouvé, J., xi, 2
Rice, P., Francis & Ritchie, 61, 63, 74
Rodney Experimental Consultants, 60
Rogers, R. & Partners, vi, x, 2, 49, 54, 81, 89
Rohe, L., Mies Van der, 19, 92
Scott Sutherland School of Architecture, 112
Sherry, K., 107
Smithson, A., 64
Steffian & Bradley Associates, 39
Stirling, J., v
Sturn, D., 85
Taut, B., 3
Thamesdown, Architects Department, 107
Wachsmann, K., 2
Whitby, M., 19
White, D., 13
Wilkinson, C., Architects, 2, 46
Wilson, G., 22

Acknowledgements

During the preparation of this book we were both very busy in private practice, thus without the constant prodding from our research assistant, Rebecca Cavell, this project could not have been completed. Thanks must also go to our typist, Marylynn Fyvie-Gauld, for her willing smiles and late-night stints on the word processor and the additional help received from Debi Wallace. Thanks also to Jackie and family for their continuous support.

Many colleagues have also offered helpful advice with the various case studies, and in particular we would like to thank Mike Stacey for his collaboration on a number of articles, including the *AJ Focus* series on 'Cladding and Curtain Walling', on which the Introduction to this book is based. Our thanks also to Chris Wilkinson, Jim Eyre, Mick Eekhout, Michael Cohen, Tony Hunt, Spencer de Grey, John Silver, John Thornton and Mark Goldstein. Kind assistance was also provided by Shirley McPherson at the *Architects' Journal* and Pauline Shirley at Ove Arup and Partners by giving us access to their photographic libraries and by Alan Ogg for drawings from his own book. Our thanks also go to the various students and colleagues who helped us with the preparation of the drawings, especially Kim Ng, Lucas Murphy, Manfred Huber, Christian Huber and Jerry Metcalfe.

Photographic credits

Ahrends Burton & Koralek, 24.1
Arup Associates, 11.2, 11.4, 11.6, 11.7
Asselbergs, T., 18.1, 18.5, 18.10
Atelier Piano, 12.5
Bailey, R.P., 28.2
Baitz, O., 22.1, 22.4, 22.5, 22.6, 23.6
Bell & Partners, 21.1, 21.2, 21.3, 21.4, 21.5, 21.6, 21.7, 21.8
Benthem Crouwel Architekten BNA, 2.7
Bower, D., 25.9
Boyd, R., 15.8
Brock Carmichael Associates, 15.7

Brookes, A.J., Intro 3, 1.4, 1.6, 2.3, 2.6 5.1, 5.6, 5.7, 9.1, 9.2, 9.10, 9.11, 9.12(a), 9.12(b) 12.9, 12.10, 13.2, 14.3, 14.6(a), 18.9, 29.2 29.3, 29.4
Bryant, R., Intro 1, 16.1, 16.5, 26.2, 26.7, 31.2, 31.11
Charles, M., 2.1, 14.1
Childs, N., 21.7
Clarke, C., 5.2
Cook, P., 4.3, 4.4, 4.5, 4.7, 6.2, 6.5, 6.11, 14.5, 24.4
De Backer & Associates, 11.5
Eekhout, M., 1.1
Foster Associates, Pref. 2, 27.1, 27.2, 27.3, 27.4, 27.5, 27.6, 27.7, 27.8, 27.9, 32.2, 32.4, 32.8, 32.9
Future Systems, Pref. 1
Gibson, K., 3.1, 3.2, 3.5
Grad Hillier Partnership, 23.1
Grech, C., 8.1, 8.3, 8.4, 8.5, 14.6(b), 25.1, 25.5
Hannay, P., 12.8
Horden, R., 30.2, 30.3, 30.4, 30.5, 30.9
Hoyt, W/Esto., 19.2
Integration AP, Intro 4
King D/McAlister R., 33.1, 33.2, 33.3, 33.4, 33.5, 33.6, 33.7, 33.8, 33.9
Kirkwood, K., 30.10
Lambot, I., 32.1, 32.5, 32.6
McKenna, S., 5.2
Michael Hopkins & Partners, 25.2
Mills, J. Photography Ltd, 15.1
Nye, J., 32.3, 32.7
Ogg, A., 9.3, 9.4, 9.5, 9.6, 9.7, 9.8, 9.9
Picardi, G., 7.2, 7.3, 7.4, 7.5, 7.6, 7.7, 7.8, 7.9, 7.10
Richard Rogers & Partners, 14.4, 14.7, 14.8
Sharp, D., 1.3
Stoller, E . Esto., 13.1
Studio 70, 28.28.3
Theodorov, S., 6.6
Vanden Bosche J., 20.2, 20.4
Vanderwarker, P., 10.1
Wilson, G., 6.3
Young, J., 14.2
Ove Arup & Partners, 12.1, 12.5, 12.7, 16.1, 16.5, 22.1, 22.4, 22.5, 22.6

CONNECTIONS
Studies in
Building Assembly

1

Bari Football Stadium
Architects:
Renzo Piano Building Workshop

1.1

General

When the city of Bari was selected as one of the twelve hosts for the 1990 World Cup Football Championships, the city fathers took the opportunity of commissioning a brand new stadium as the centrepiece of a Sports City in a greenfield location on the outskirts of their town (Figure 1.1).

The architectural inspiration for the stadium came from the imposing Castel del Monte (1240) sited at the summit of a hillock in the otherwise featureless Apulian landscape (Figure 1.2). This uncompromisingly geometric castle, consisting of an octagonal keep with precise octagonal towers at each corner, casts its influence over the surrounding landscape.

The sunken pitch and the gently sloping crater of the surrounding landscape enclose the first tier of seating and reduce the apparent bulk of the stadium (Figure 1.3). The remaining tiers of seating are supported on a concrete shell, suspended from thin rectangular piers. The stadium appears to hover over the pitch (Figures 1.3 and 1.4). A lightweight steel and fabric canopy reverses the curvature of the concrete shell to complete the clam-shell image.

1.2

Structure: concrete

Two major determinants influenced the layout of the stadium. The first was in response to regulations set down by FIFA as a consequence of the Heysel Stadium tragedy. The major implications of these rules require the elimination of standing accommodation and, most importantly, quick and easily identifiable evacuation of the stadium.

1.1
General view

1.2
Aerial view of Castel del
Monte

1.3
Renzo Piano sketch

1.4
Section through stands.
1 Pitch level; 2 changing
rooms; 3 terrace seating; 4 in
situ reinforced concrete
columns; 5 circulation area;
6 precast radial segment
units; 7 access to upper
stand; 8 in situ extension to
precast radial segments; 9 in
situ reinforced concrete
principal annular beam;
10 precast concrete seating
tiers; 11 cantilever canopy

transition block; 12 principal
cantilever box section arch
beam at halfway line;
13 profile of canopy at ends
of stadium; 14 maintenance
access walkway with
floodlighting

1.5
Plan of stadium showing
geometry. Solid arcs 190 m
radii drawn from corners of
pitch. Dotted lines show
centres and common radii for
end and side geometry.
1 Lower tier of seating;
2 raised tier of seating;
3 canopy; 4 90 m arcs;
5 centres of stadium
geometry

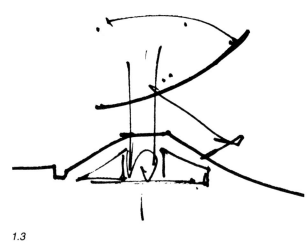

1.3

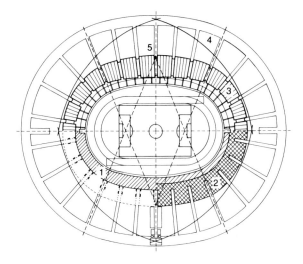

1.5

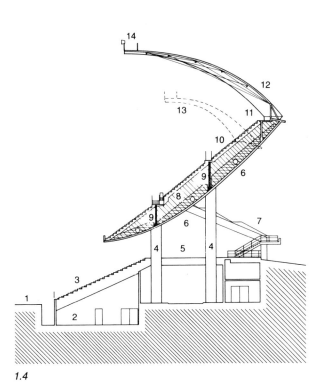

1.4

The second determining factor was the geometry
dictated by adequate sightlines and viewing
distances. According to recent recommendations
the limiting viewing distance for football stadia is
190 m. The resulting arcs drawn from the corners of
the pitch determine the maximum plan size of the
seating area (Figure 1.5). Splitting the
accommodation into two tiers with the upper
overhanging the lower and increasing the number of

seats around the half-way line of the pitch improves
viewing distances generally.

The concrete shell is divided into 26 petals, each
supported on four 1 m by 1.8 m in situ concrete
columns. These columns have been designed to
resist seismic loadings without the need for cross
bracing which would have compromised the visual
clarity of the structure. Two sets of annular beams,
cast in situ, span between the columns, forming an
armature from which the ten shell segments that
make up each petal are hung (Figure 1.4).

Each segment is made up of three inverted
T-shaped precast concrete sections whose curved
underside forms the external soffit of the ribbed
shell. These segments were precast in concrete
moulds on site (Figure 1.6). The web of each section
is sized to provide adequate stiffness to allow the
precast unit to be handled on site. An in situ
concrete extension to the precast web (Figures 1.4
and 1.7) stitches the three precast sections together
and to the two annular beams. Precast concrete
sections span across the webs to support the
seating. In situ concrete beams at each end of the
segments complete the concrete structure.

The articulated clear zone in between each of the
26 petals is dedicated to access stairs for the two
adjacent petals of seating. Although originally
planned to be made of steel these stairs are built of
concrete to resemble a lowered section of the
precast segments in imitation of a spaceship loading
door.

1.6
T-shaped precast concrete sections

1.7
Precast units assembled to form separate petals

1.8
Steel reinforcement bars around high strength threaded bars.

1.9
Transition block bolted to threaded bars

1.6

1.8

1.7

1.9

Structure: Steel

A lightweight canopy of cantilevered steelwork tops the concrete bowl. Each petal supports two curved, tapered, box section, high grade steel arms whose lengths vary according to the geometry of the stadium (Figure 1.4). The steel arms are connected to the concrete shell via steel transition blocks cast into the *in situ* concrete (Figure 1.9). Twelve prestressed, high strength, threaded bars are bolted at one end to a steel anchor block embedded in the concrete and at the other end to the transition block which acts as a baseplate to the steel canopy arms. The threaded bars are lapped with reinforcement bars in the concrete (Figures 1.8 and 1.10). All the bending moments from the canopy are transferred into the concrete by the reinforcement adjacent to the twelve threaded bars. One significant reason for using a transition block which is small relative to the

steel canopy arms is that its size allows it to be placed, levelled and set in concrete (Figure 1.11) with greater ease and accuracy than the enormous steel arms which would be suspended from a crane (Figure 1.12).

A U-shaped steel truss spans between the front edges of the cantilevered arms. The truss forms an access walkway and a support for the floodlighting. Between the steel arms are three arched tubular steel beams. A PTFE-coated, glass-fibre, woven fabric is stretched over this structure and fixed at its edges only. Threaded bars connect the membrane's clamped edges to the supporting steelwork and allow the fabric to be prestressed up to 5 kN per metre width of fabric. Cables stretched over the fabric prevent uplift. The fabric has a 13% translucency. The same type of roof membrane is stretched over a different secondary structure spanning over the gap between each petal.

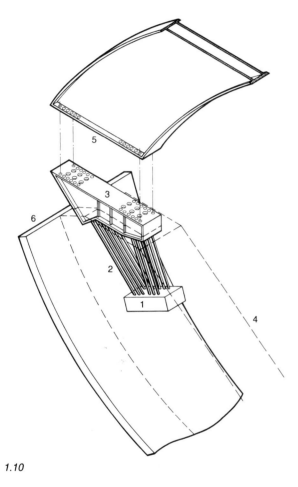

1.10

1.11

1.12

Services

All the facilities necessary for players and public are located along the radiating access corridors within the crater base. The slot between the two tiers of seating allows a free flow of air across the arena which helps to provide a measure of cooling during the summer months.

The translucent fabric canopy transmits a proportion of natural light at the same time cutting down on shadow intensity. The continuous platform allows infinite flexibility for the location of the floodlighting. The 264 floodlights provide a minimum vertical illuminance on the football pitch of 1800 lx towards the main camera position and 1500 lx towards the secondary positions.

Credits

Client: Commune di Bari
Structural and lighting engineers: Ove Arup and Partners International.
Foundation and specialist concrete engineers: Studio Vitone, Bari Contracting Consortium: Bari-90.
Roof steelwork contractor: Petitpierre Sud, Bari.
Fabric roof contractor: Koit Hi-tex GmbH, Germany.

References

Rice, P. Lenczner A. Carfrae T., Sedgwick, 'The San Nicola Stadium, Bari', *Arups Journal*, Autumn 1990, pp. 3–8.

Vercelloni, M., 'Le Nuovo Stadio di Bari', *Edizioni L'Archivolto*, Milan 1990.

Ranzani, E., 'Stadio di calcio e atletica leggera, Bari' *Domus*, May 1990, pp. 33–39.

Castellano, A. 'Poetry and Geometry for Bari', *l'Arca*, November 1987 pp. 80–85.

2

Bercy Charenton Shopping Centre, Paris
Architects:
Renzo Piano Building Workshop

General

In 1987 the client, GRC (P. Emin and J. Renault), previously responsible for the Centre Usine in Nantes by the Richard Rogers Partnership, commissioned Renzo Piano to modify an existing design for 100 000 m² of shopping and parking on the eastern outskirts of Paris (Charenton) adjacent to the junction of the Paris Périphérique and A4 Autoroute. Renzo Piano's involvement came at a late stage, six months before the building permit was due to expire, with a brief to provide a flagship for the redevelopment of the site on the edge of a development zone (Figure 2.1).

The architect's intent was to create a sculptural form determined by the line of the adjacent intersection of flyovers which would be visually understandable from the major ring road (Figure 2.2). It was an early intention to provide a precise form using standardized stainless steel panels for the building envelope.

The challenge to design a curvilinear form in three dimensions using flat sheets established the main constructional theme which separates the cladding from the environmental functions of the wall: drainage, waterproofing, insulation, light transmission, all of which occur below the 'cosmetic' cladding skin.

Structure

The predetermined concrete frame, set out on an 8 m grid, was used to organize the laminated timber beams on a diagonal geometry that addresses the corner site.

The complex curvilinear shape is simplified by the use of a standard curved profile that is displaced

2.2

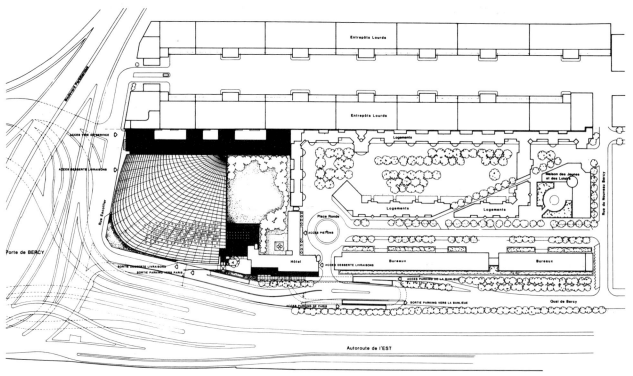

2.1

2.1
Location plan

2.2
View of west corner

2.3
Internal view of trussed beam

2.4
Geometry of curved external
profile

2.5
Double hinged bracket.
1 Doubled 500 × 210 mm
laminated timber beam;
2 steel pivot plate; 3 steel
end plates; 4 150 × 80 mm
laminated timber purlins

2.3

horizontally and vertically to generate the desired bubble shape (Figure 2.4).

The curved laminated timber beams, typically 500 mm deep by 210 mm wide, span diagonally across two 8 m bays. The beams spanning the three-bay wide central mall span approximately 33 m and are trussed to cope with this extended span (Figure 2.3). In the top compression boom the timber beams are doubled and the tension is accommodated by steel tie rods held off the timber members by tubular steel struts. The nodes formed at the junction between rods and struts are located on the 8 m grid points as a reminder of the theoretical column locations.

The doubling up of the laminated beam extends over the shorter span between columns where they are visible, including at the exposed edge perimeter where they meet the ground. Elsewhere they are single beams.

A double hinged bracket (Figure 2.5) allows the 80 × 150 mm laminated timber purlin to span across beams and follow the building curved profile. The angle of the fixing can thus be adjusted at the point of bolting to allow the purlins to always span between the shortest distance between two points in space.

The use of laminated timber beams in this building develops a theme evident in earlier projects.

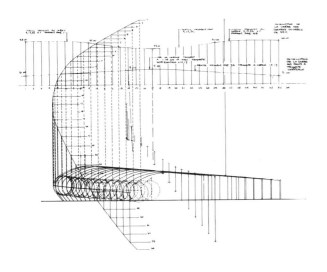

2.4

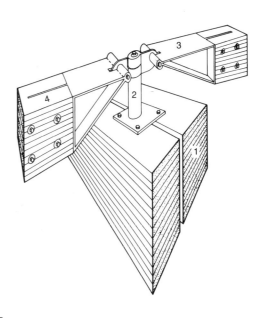

2.5

2.6
View of laminated timber
beams and purlins with
unwrought battens. Vertical
steel bars to support cladding
rails are shown fixed to the
purlins

2.7
Typical bay of ten panels.
1 Meridian tiles; 2 tapered
stainless steel panels

2.8
Cross section through
meridian tile. 1 Axis of
meridian tile

2.9
Cross section though
cladding fixing. 1 Stainless
steel tile; 2 PVC fixing clips;
3 fixing rail; 4 adjustable
bracket; 5 support bar; 6 PVC
weather proofing membrane;
7 50 mm polyurethane
insulation; 8 12 mm plywood/
chipboard; 9 timber batten;
10 laminated timber purlin

Cladding

Unwrought timbers span between the laminated purlins (Figure 2.6) to support a weatherproof skin or *peau étanche* consisting of a deck of 22 mm tongued and grooved chipboard on to which a polyethylene vapour barrier, 50 mm polyurethane insulation and PVC weatherproof membrane by Alkorplan are placed. Where the curve of the wall is most pronounced, 12 mm plywood is used instead of chipboard to achieve the required radius of 6.1 m.

From this weatherproof skin, and fixed at intervals to the purlins, 3000 short vertical bars (Figures 2.6 and 2.9) with adjustable fixings protrude through the PVC membrane to support the tubular steel cladding rails. The sleeve of the upstand is heat welded to the PVC. In this way the cladding rails are separated by a distance of 450 mm from the PVC skin (Figure 2.9).

Where, in plan, the building's curve is tightest, at a radius of 35.5 m, the fixing rails are curved, in other areas where the curve is produced at a larger radius of 275 m the use of straight rails was possible.

The stainless steel (Grade F11) panels are clipped to the cladding rails using special PVC fixing clips (Figure 2.9). The stainless steel surface has a brushed finish to reduce reflection and any apparent distortion of the skin.

Each 300 mm wide stainless steel panel or tile is slightly tapered and varies in length between 800 mm and 2000 mm depending upon its position on the building. They are fixed in bays of ten tiles between a recessed tile known as the "meridian" (Figure 2.7) which forms the basis for setting out the facade and acts to articulate the direction and layout of the cladding like a deep joint (Figures 2.8–2.10).

In this way, 27 000 tiles with 40 different types were used to form the 13 000 m² of the shell.

The position of the fixing rails was plotted on the waterproof PVC skin by site surveyors. The meridian tiles were fixed first to define the panels of the tiles between and to ensure the meridians themselves ran in continuous lines. Despite this, and the use of computers to predict the exact

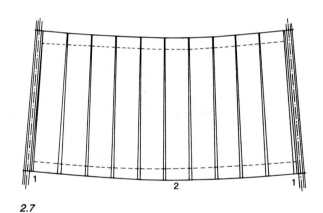

2.7

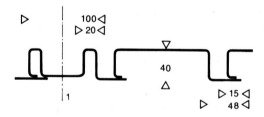

2.8

2.6

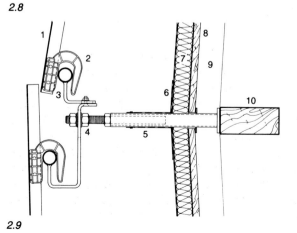

2.9

2.10
*Detail of elevation showing
perforated stainless steel
cladding panel*

location of the tiles, their fixing was very labour intensive to achieve a satisfactory visual location. It was eventually necessary for fixing operatives to climb into the space between the underside of the tiles and the deck and to receive verbal instructions as to their precise adjustment. Even the most precise technology is thus dependent upon visual rather than theoretical criteria.

Rooflights and smoke vents

Circular acrylic rooflights allow natural light to percolate through the building (Figure 2.3). The stainless steel cladding runs, unbroken, over the rooflights but here the tiles are perforated by a 50% mesh of small holes allowing light to diffuse through to the mall.

Similarly, rectangular smoke vents, which open automatically in the case of fire, are installed above the mall and perforated tiles also run above the roof vents.

A gutter is formed in the waterproof membrane, hidden beneath the stainless steel panels. This gutter is located at the point where the tangent to the curved envelope is vertical.

Comment

Although achieving a difficult marriage between the shell and the interior space of the shopping centre, and despite the banality of the predetermined main concrete structure, this organic solution for a building envelope incorporating a metal skin and laminated timber structure follows a logical development from early building forms produced by Renzo Piano as well as providing a cladding prototype for the Kansai Air Terminal.

We have already mentioned the laminated timber beams at the Prometeo Opera. Similarly one could refer to the IBM Travelling Exhibition where polycarbonate panels were fixed to laminated timber trusses (see Brookes & Grech *The Building Envelope*, Case Study 12) or even to the experience of a rainscreen panel demonstrated by Renzo Piano's design of the brick cladding at the Ircam Building in Paris. The main contribution of this case study is the example of separating out the function of elements of the building skin, taking advantage of modern materials achieving a unique form related to the brief and conditions of the site.

2.10

Credits

Client: G.R.C. Emin, Jean Renault
Engineer (structural frame): JL Sarf
Engineer (external envelope): Ove Arup and Partners
Bureau d'étude: Otra

References

Davies, C., 'Piano Quartet', *Architectural Review*, October 1989, pp. 70–73.

Dawson, S., 'Case Study: Piano's Paris Cladding', *AJ Focus*, March 1990, pp. 21–23.

Ellis, C., 'French Connection', *Architectural Review*, July 1991, pp. 59–63.

Melvin J., 'Bercy Beaucoup', *Building Design (supplement)*, April 1990 pp. 12–19.

Menard, J. P., 'Piano à Bercy' *l'Architecture d'Aujourdhui*, June 1990, pp. 162–166.

Miotto, L., Renzo Piano, exhibition catalogue, Editions du Centre Georges Pompidou, 1987.

3

Billingsgate Market Refurbishment, London

Architects: Richard Rogers Partnership

3.1

General

Old Billingsgate Fish Market (Figure 3.1), designed by Sir Horace Jones and built between 1874–1877 is located a little way upstream from Jones' other landmark, Tower Bridge. As City Architect and Surveyor from 1864 to 1887, Jones was also responsible for Smithfield and Leadenhall Markets. Old Billingsgate operated as a fish market for over 100 years until the fish market moved to new premises on the Isle of Dogs. After Citicorp Investment Bank purchased the old Market in 1985 they commissioned the Richard Rogers Partnership to convert it into a state-of-the art trading house. The Grade II listing of this building meant that a sensitive conversion would have to acknowledge the importance of the basement vaults, external walls, roof and supporting structure.

Refurbishment

Although the external works consisted of extensive restoration, the greatest interventions were internal. Most of the original structure has been retained, in an effort to return the basic building to its original 1877 form. This was roughly square in plan (Figures 3.2 and 3.3) with a large Market Hall occupying the greater part of the ground floor. Two rows of cast-iron Doric columns run down the centre of the Market Hall (Figures 3.4 and 3.5) and support the Haddock Gallery. Beneath the Market Hall is a brick-vaulted basement.

The most obvious elements of the internal refurbishment are the mezzanines added to the Market Hall, together with the careful integration of services within the original shell.

3.1
*River elevation with Lloyds
Building in the background*

3.2
Ground floor plan

3.3
Mezzanine plan

3.4
North–south section

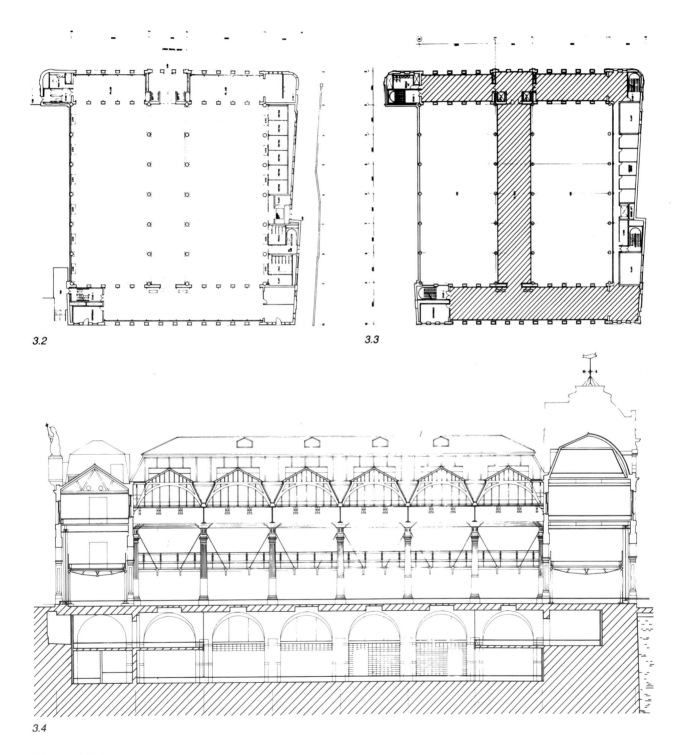

3.2

3.3

3.4

Mezzanines

The mezzanines occupy an H-shape on plan (Figure 3.3) and provide an extra 1000 m² of work space. The north and south galleries running along the perimeter of the building are supported from below on steel columns. The central run is suspended from diagonal steel hangers attached to

145

3.5

the underside of the strengthened Haddock Gallery (Figures 3.4 and 3.5). As the existing mass concrete fill of the Haddock Gallery floor was being broken out to expose the old plated wrought iron beams which were to have supported the mezzanines, it was discovered that many of these beams had deteriorated to such an extent that any residual strength left in them would have to be ignored. New reinforced concrete beams were cast around these old beams (Figure 3.7). This work was carried out from above without disturbing the soffit below, in fact the existing jack arch plates were used as permanent shuttering. At this stage a bolt box installed around the existing beam could be cast into

the concrete. The bolt box consists of a bottom plate to which four 85 mm diameter steel sleeves are welded (Figure 3.6). These sleeves allow 700 mm long bolts to be threaded through the newly cast concrete, clamping the hanger bracket on the bottom face and the spreader plate on the top surface of the new reinforced concrete beam. Once the assembly was completed the sleeves were filled with a cementitious grout which fire protects the bolts. Steel rods, 60 mm in diameter, with cast fork end connectors at each end, link the mezzanines to the hanger brackets. The connectors on the mezzanines are curiously organic in shape (Figure 3.8), introducing gradual curves between members.

3.6
Exploded isometric of beam bolt box, hanger bracket and existing steel.
1 Existing plated wrought iron beam; 2 20 mm thick steel spreader plate; 3 bolt box consisting of 12 mm thick steel lower plate with upstands; 4 85 mm diameter sleeves with 12 mm thick wall; 5 40 mm thick steel plate to concrete hanger bracket; 6 700 mm long bolt

3.7
Detail of connection.
1 Existing plated wrought iron beam; 2 20 mm thick steel spreader plate; 3 bolt box consisting of 12 mm thick steel lower plate with upstands; 4 85 mm diameter sleeves with 12 mm thick wall, showing grout nipple; 5 new reinforced concrete beam; 6 existing jack arch plate; 7 hanger bracket

3.8
Exploded isometric of mezzanine perimeter beam.
1 193 mm diameter, 10 mm thick circular hollow section; 2 cast-steel saddle bracket, welded around the perimeter; 3 168 mm diameter, 10 mm thick circular hollow section with cast steel connector, welded around the perimeter; 4 cast-steel saddle bracket connecting bottom boom to top boom

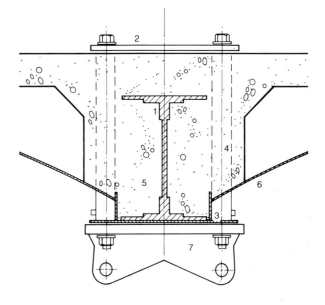

3.7

However, the architects have then designed a notched perimeter to these castings, so that, even with a 10 mm fillet weld and a 1.7 mm thick coating of intumescent paint the outline of the casting remains distinct and sharp. A family of similar organic castings is used at the junctions between the members making up the trusses that span

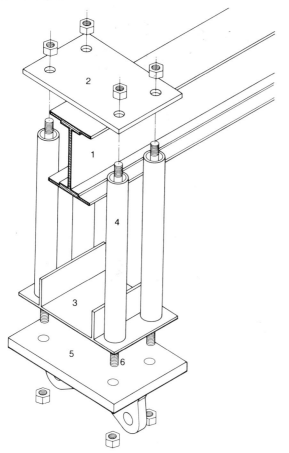

3.6

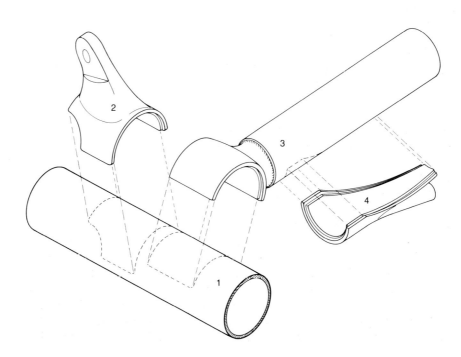

3.8

across the undersides of the mezzanines at 3.46 m centres. A lightweight reinforced concrete deck spans across the trusses and supports a raised service floor. The open mezzanines are designed to be demountable and relocatable.

Roof

The roof over the Market Hall is supported on timber arches at 550 mm centres. These rest on wrought-iron lattice trusses spanning 18.6 m at 6.9 m centres onto the cast-iron columns. These timber arches had deteriorated to such an extent that 75% of them had to be replaced. The Market Hall and Haddock Gallery are spaces to be used principally by employees working at VDU screens so it is important to provide controlled, glare free lighting appropriate for such machines. The natural lighting to these spaces is modulated by the use of prismatic polycarbonate sheets incorporated into the Market Hall roof lights. These sheets avoid the glare associated with direct sunlight, since a process of internal reflection and refraction produces an even, diffuse light.

Services

The existing building did not allow for one large centralized plant room, so a number of smaller, more readily integrated 'invisible' plant rooms were distributed around the building. Because the refurbished Market is fully air-conditioned, fifteen separate air handling volumes were devised, each served by local plant. For example twelve specially designed units (Figure 3.9). recycle the air in the dealing space, accepting recirculated air at high level and discharging the conditioned air into the 450 mm deep underfloor plenum void.

A tank room, housing water and services storage tanks was built 7 m into the Thames underneath the existing jetty.

Artificial lighting to the Main Hall is provided by specially designed fluorescent fittings that give both downlighting and uplighting which highlights the newly refurbished roof trusses.

Costs

The total cost of the refurbishment was £26m, giving a square metre cost of £2892.

3.9

Credits

Client: Citicorp Investment Bank Ltd
Structural, mechanical and electrical engineers: Ove Arup and Partners
Quantity surveyors: Hanscomb Partnership
Acoustic engineers: Arup Acoustics
Management contractor: Taylor Woodrow Management Contracting Ltd

References

Smith, R., and Wattridge, I., 'Billingsgate Fish Market Refurbishment', *The Arup Journal*, Vol 24, No 2, Summer 1989, pp. 2–7.
Moore, R., 'From Fish to Finance', *Architectural Review*, October 1989, vol 1112, pp. 50-58.
Dietsch, D., 'Changing Markets', *Architectural Record*, September 1989, pp. 73–77.
Cruickshank, D., 'Billingsgate Market', *Architectural Review*, April 1988, Vol 1094, pp. 38–42.
Powell, K., 'From Fish to Finance', *RIBA Journal*, August 1989, pp. 31–34.

4

Bracken House, London
Architects:
Michael Hopkins and Partners

4.1

General

Bracken House in the City of London was originally designed by Albert Richardson in 1955, based on Guarino Guarini's seventeenth century Palazzo Carignano in Turin. These new headquarters for the *Financial Times* broke the mould of the established horizontal organization of publishing and printing houses by sandwiching the printing works between two wings of offices (Figure 4.3).

In 1987 the *Financial Times* moved to their new building in docklands designed by Nicholas Grimshaw (see Case Study 10, p. 42) and sold the property to the Japanese Developers Obayashi who commissioned Michael Hopkins to carry out the redevelopment of this listed building.

Hopkins has retained the distinctive north and south wings of the original building which face Cannon Street and Queen Victoria Street respectively (Figures 4.1 and 4.2). These have been upgraded as cellular offices. The original printing works have been demolished and replaced with an

oval office building set around a central atrium (Figure 4.4). The form and construction of the curved glazed facades developed by John Pringle and Bill Dunster form the major part of this case study.

Perhaps inspired by Peter Ellis' 1864 Oriel Chambers in Liverpool the design of the curtain walling incorporates an external structural frame in cast gunmetal with deep drawn bronze spandrel panels separating suspended frameless double glazing (Figure 4.5).

The choice of gunmetal (a material more frequently used for casting sculptures) and Hollington Stone (a highly textured but structurally weak material) provide continuity with the richness of the materials chosen for Richardson's original building. The architects also considered the use of aluminium bronze which although stronger than gunmetal would not have patinated so well with age. The challenge for the architects was to use these materials in a structurally honest manner.

4.1
General view from north

4.2
Site plan.
1 Central hall; 2 office space;
3 gallery; 4 lifts; 5 stairs;
6 Friday Street;
7 Cannon Street;
8 Queen Victoria Street

4.3
Diagrammatic representation
of existing building

4.4
Diagrammatic representation
of redeveloped building.

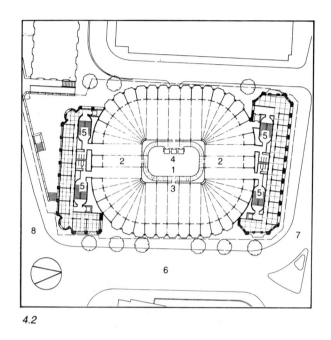

4.2

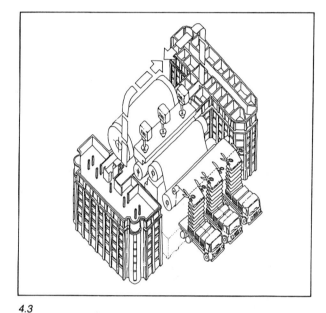

4.3

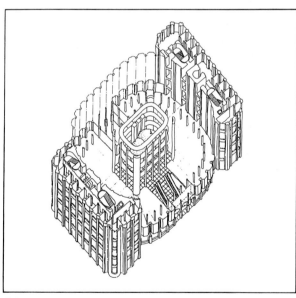

4.4

Internal structure

The reinforced concrete beams that radiate from the central atrium span 13.2 m to the main ring of internal columns and, at a reduced depth, project a further 3.6 m to the loadbearing external wall. Since this is a non-fire protected facade the structure has been calculated so that in the event of a fire and consequent loss of the facade the cantilevered floor would still maintain its integrity under reduced loading safety factors.

External structure

The key to the construction of the external wall are the connection brackets (Figures 4.5–4.8) which are fixed back to the floor slab providing a bearing to the columns and support for the clamping plates used to fix the glass. These brackets were cast in two pieces using gunmetal by Sweetmore of Stoke on Trent. The same company was responsible for casting the columns and the large castings at ground level where the columns are gathered together to transfer the loads to the loadbearing stone plinths.

The nature of the hidden process of metal casting is to an extent unpredictable and thus careful quality control and testing for internal defects is essential. In 1851 at Paxton's Crystal Palace, the castings were weighed to ensure no voids were present.

Nowadays more scientific methods are used such as X-ray and ultrasound. At Bracken House however, the lead content in the casting alloy made it difficult to use X-ray methods and the size of some of the castings was too big to apply ultrasound testing. It was therefore necessary to load-test some elements. This requirement for testing illustrates the importance of agreeing a high specification with the fabricator (see East Croydon Station (BSA), Case Study 8).

4.5
Completed bay assembly

4.6
Principal bay window components.
1 Gunmetal air supply/return spandrel cowling; 2 gunmetal transom clamp-plate assembly; 3 clear sealed double glazed unit; 4 external planar bracket; 5 retractable motorized internal blinds; 6 gunmetal inter-bay panel; 7 openable insulated double glazed smoke vent; 8 gunmetal column;

9 gunmetal column bracket; 10 precast reinforced concrete beam; 11 in situ concrete slab.

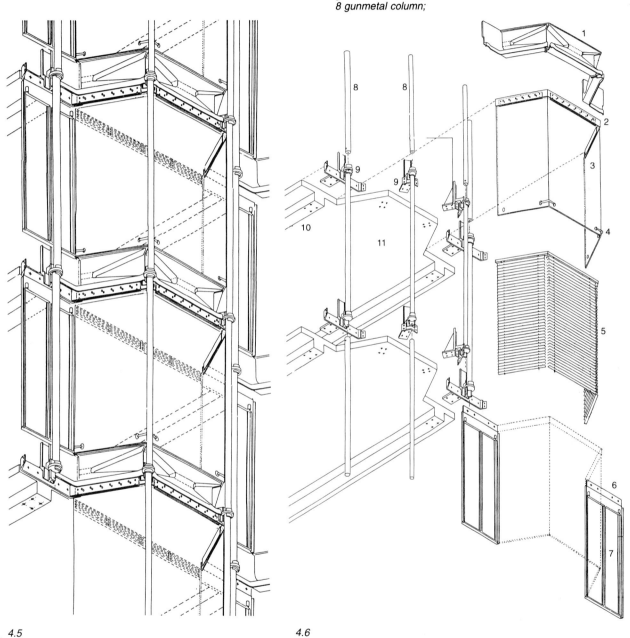

4.5

4.6

The storey-height solid gunmetal columns fit neatly into the support brackets (Figures 4.7 and 4.8). Metal collars at the head and base of each column lock them in place. The large, forked gunmetal casting picks up the loads from these columns and transfers them via the stone plinths to the piled foundations (Figures 4.9 and 4.10). The eccentric load on the bracket is balanced by tensioned tie rods attached at their top to the rear of

the casting and anchored at the other end to the concrete foundations.

Hollington Stone had been used on the facade of the original building. This relatively soft stone has been used by Hopkins, once again to provide continuity between the new and the old. In designing these stone plinths the designers have accepted the limitations of this material, hence they are larger than would be the case if other materials had been

151

4.7
Slab to column bracket at
external angle (toned area
denotes steel portion of
composite bracket)

4.8
Slab to column bracket at
internal angle (toned area
denotes steel portion of
composite bracket)

used. It is this honesty to the nature of materials that has come to characterize the product of this practice.

Glazing

In between each bay of this external framework of columns projects an oriel window made up of three clear, sealed double glazed units independently supported at the head using a clamp plate assembly clearly derived from the Faber Dumas building (see Brookes, *Concepts in Cladding*).

The double glazed units step back into single glazing where they are clamped and where they overlap the gun metal spandrel panel below. The side panes are fixed to the central pane by curved external brackets with planar fittings at their ends. These angled flanking panes provide a stuctural depth to the bays with which to resist the wind loading on the central pane. Retractable motorized venetian blinds are provided inside the glazing.

Cladding

The gunmetal inter-bay panels incorporate small bronze doors which open to provide smoke ventilation. The insulated gunmetal spandrel panels to the air supply and return ducts below the glazing were deep drawn by the subcontractor MBM (Germany) who were the subcontractors responsible for the whole cladding package. This company which specializes in special projects were also responsible for the glazing at the Crescent Wing at the Sainsbury Centre (see p24) and the external sunscoops at the Hong kong and Shanghai Bank (see Brookes and Grech, *The Building Envelope*, 1990, p. 122).

Credits

Client: Obayashi Europe BV
Structural engineers: Ove Arup and Partners
Services engineers: Ove Arup and Partners
Quantity surveyors: Northcroft Neighbour and Nicholson
Main contractor: Trollope and Colls Construction Limited

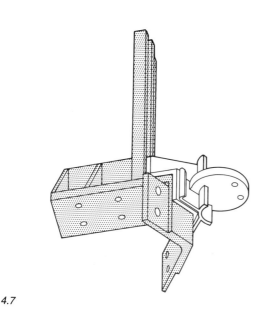

4.7

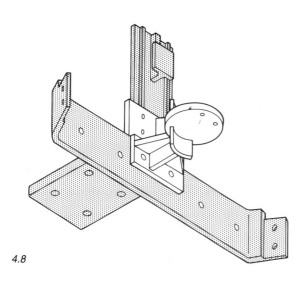

4.8

4.9
Exploded explanatory
diagram of base bracket
casting

4.10
Exploded explanatory
diagram of base bracket and
stone plinth assembly.

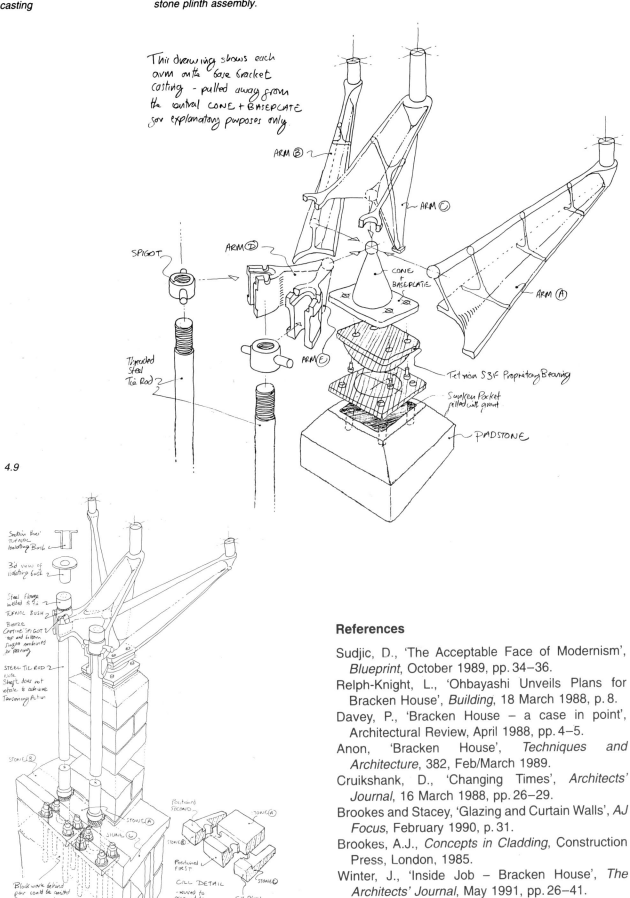

This drawing shows each
arm on the base bracket
casting – pulled away from
the central CONE + BASEPLATE
for explanatory purposes only.

ARM (B)

ARM (C)

SPIGOT

ARM (D)

CONE
+
BASEPLATE

ARM (A)

Threaded
Steel
Tie Rod

ARM (E)

Tetrion S3F Proprietary Bearing

Sunken Pocket
filled with grout

PADSTONE

4.9

Section thru'
TUFNOL
Isolating Bush

3d view of
Isolating Bush

Steel Flange
welded to tie

TUFNOL BUSH

Bronze
Captive SPIGOT
Top and bottom
Surface machined
for bearing

STEEL TIE ROD
Note
Shaft does not
rotate to achieve
Tensioning Action

STONE (B)

STONE (A)

STONE (C)

STONE (D)

Positioned
SECOND

STONE (A)

STONE (B)

Positioned
FIRST

STONE (C)

CILL DETAIL
- raised to
accomodate
Tie Rod Detail

STONE (D)

Cill Placed
after Bracket
positioned and
Tie Rods
tensioned.

Blockwork behind
pier could be omitted
to give access to
Tie Rod holding down bolts
for adjustment // inspection
- Access by lifting Raised Floor Tile

4.10

References

Sudjic, D., 'The Acceptable Face of Modernism', *Blueprint*, October 1989, pp. 34–36.

Relph-Knight, L., 'Ohbayashi Unveils Plans for Bracken House', *Building*, 18 March 1988, p. 8.

Davey, P., 'Bracken House – a case in point', Architectural Review, April 1988, pp. 4–5.

Anon, 'Bracken House', *Techniques and Architecture*, 382, Feb/March 1989.

Cruikshank, D., 'Changing Times', *Architects' Journal*, 16 March 1988, pp. 26–29.

Brookes and Stacey, 'Glazing and Curtain Walls', *AJ Focus*, February 1990, p. 31.

Brookes, A.J., *Concepts in Cladding*, Construction Press, London, 1985.

Winter, J., 'Inside Job – Bracken House', *The Architects' Journal*, May 1991, pp. 26–41.

Hodgkinson, P., 'Gothic phoenix classic support', *Architectural Review*, May 1992, pp. 26–39.

5

Church at Buseno, Switzerland
Architects:
Mario Campi and Franco Pessina

5.1

General

Located at an altitude of 1000 m above sea level in the Calanca Valley near Bellinzona this chapel acts as a powerful reference point for visiting pilgrims (Figure 5.1). The analogy with the lighthouse-type is a recurring theme which underlies the chapel's form (Figure 5.2).

Although dedicated to Our Lady of Fatima, it is the ambiguity of the symbolism implied in the chapel's morphology that underpins its ecumenical objectives. The architects claim that the simplicity of the rational shapes satisfies the functional requirements of the brief and at the same time allows the building to dematerialize thus achieving a spirituality that reinforces the concept of worship. The long gestation period during which the design was developed and discussed with the bishop responsible for the chapel's commission enhanced the symbolism of the finished product.

The cupola, as well as taking up the canonic

5.2

reference, is brought up to date by the inclusion of a real light source at its apex, so that eventually a shaft of light originating from the centre of the chapel will project vertically upwards to the clouds above. Even though this beacon has not yet been installed, the users of the chapel have already nicknamed it the 'Atomic Chapel'.

5.1
General view

5.2
Architect's sketch

5.3
(a) East elevation;
(b) transverse section;
(c) south elevation;
(d) longitudinal section

5.4
Plan

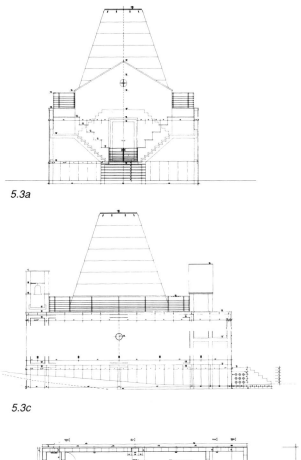

5.3a

5.3c

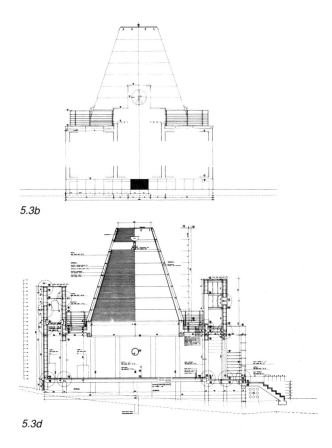

5.3b

5.3d

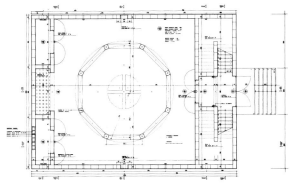

5.4

The eight internal columns (Figure 5.4) are derived from the date 8 September (Feast of Our Lady of Victories) being one of the major feast days in the calender of Marian devotion.

Structure

The architects' belief that 'it is a mistake to mime' leads not only to the oblique references to historicism mentioned earlier but also to a conviction that materials should be used honestly and appropriately. Therefore there is no obligation to respect the vernacular by using indigenous materials. A building must reflect contemporary building technology, and if this means that regular maintenance, in the form of repainting, say, is necessary, then the public ought to be ready to accept that. 'If we are nowadays accustomed to the

The pedimented front, again another classical element, is reinterpreted to relate to the pitched roofs of the vernacular.

The accentuated external staircase to the top of the building, as well as affording visitors a measure of comfort in experiencing the building, even when the interior is shut, also alludes to the biblical walls of Babylon.

5.5.
(a) Section through cupola.
(b) Detail at apex of cupola.
1 double glazed rooflight;
2 6 mm steel skin; 3 anti-
insect wire mesh;
4 ventilation louvres;
5 perforated metal lining;
6 thermal and acoustic
insulation.   (c) Detail of joint.
1 M12 connecting bolt;
2 neoprene isolating tape;
3 perforated metal lining;
4 6 mm steel skin overlapping
ring below.

(d) Detail of fixing at cupola
base. 1 M16 anchor bolt cast
into concrete; 2 concrete
upstand; 3 perforated metal
lining;
4 thermal and acoustic
insulation; 5 6 mm steel skin.

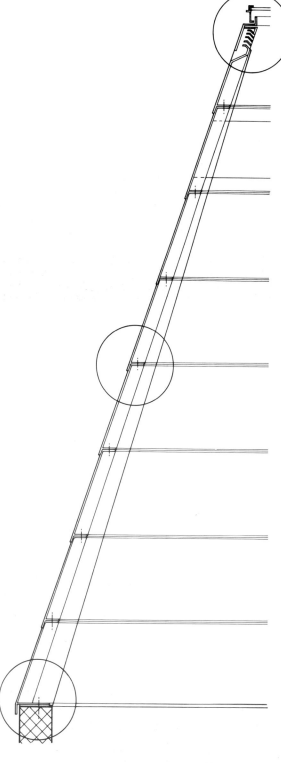

5.5a

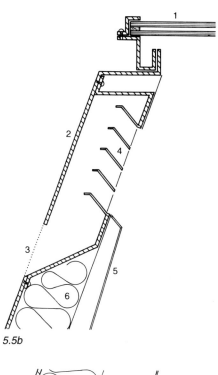

5.5b

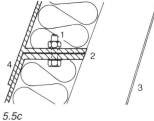

5.5c

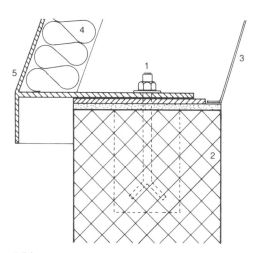

5.5d

5.6
*Delivery of components by
helicopter*

5.7
*Detail of roof perimeter.
1 Precast concrete paving;
2 concrete fill; 3 waterproof
membrane; 4 concrete roof
slab; 5 water spout;
6 styrofoam joint; 7 external
render; 8 internal render;
9 Durisol concrete blocks.*

idea that a car needs regular maintenance, why should a building be so different?' argue the designers.

When the site was chosen there was no serviceable road leading to it, just a rough track. This constraint lead to the solution where as many as possible of the building components were prefabricated so that they could be transported to site by helicopter (Figure 5.6). The size of prefabricated components was therefore determined by the payload of the helicopter, in this case 800 kg.

The main body of the chapel is of loadbearing reinforced Durisol concrete blocks built off a concrete base (Figures 5.3a–d). The eight reinforced concrete columns define a central space and support a concrete ring beam on which the cupola is supported. This cupola is built up of eight prefabricated sheet steel ring sections that interlock simply (Figures 5.5a–d). The fact that the cupola is prefabricated has meant that components could be adjusted off site before final erection ensuring that on-site tolerances could be kept to an absolute minimum. Due to their size and weight the bottom two rings had to be split into two halves for delivery to site. The cupola is then lined internally with fibreglass thermal insulation. A perforated metal sheet forms the internal skin of the cupola. This construction also provides excellent acoustics to the space below.

The roof is designed to drain water directly out to the perimeter of the *in situ* concrete roof (Figure 5.7). A secondary system is provided to minimize the effect of frost shattering caused by moisture trapped within the roof construction.

5.6

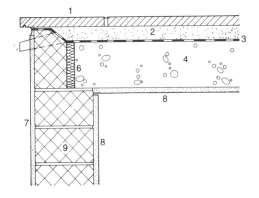

5.7

Services

The chapel currently lacks electrical power and is not heated. A system of natural ventilation has been provided to eliminate the problems of condensation. Perforated concrete blocks at the base level allow fresh air in, it is then drawn through the main chapel space and up the cupola by means of the stack effect, then out through weather-tight slots at the apex of the cupola.

Cost

The fact that a large part of the materials and labour that have gone into this building have been donated by the local community makes it impossible to estimate its cost. The architects also waived their fees for this job.

References

Gazzaniga, L., 'Chiesa di Nostra Signora di Fatima, Buseno'. *Domus*, March 1989, pp. 29–35.

Anon, 'Mario Campi e Franco Pessina', *Abitare*, November 1990, p. 189.

Buchanan, P., 'Swiss Essentialists', *Architectural Review*, January 1991, pp. 19–22.

6

Crescent Wing, Norwich
Architects:
Foster Associates

General

The Crescent Wing is a part-subterranean extension to the Sainsbury Centre for Visual Arts, at the University of East Anglia at Norwich (Figure 6.2). The four principal additional facilities provided are the Reserve Collection Display, the Lower Gallery, the Conservation Suite of rooms and the Art Transit Room (Figure 6.3).

The Lower Gallery extends out underneath the grassed forecourt at the east end of the Sainsbury Centre (Figure 6.4). By digging into the natural slope of the site, a vast crescent of glass, angled to be flush with the landscape, creates an internal circulation route with a magnificent prospect to the lake beyond (Figure 6.1).

The gently descending public access ramp, the rooflights and the angled glazing are the only visible traces of the new building.

Structure

The Crescent Wing understates its own structure in deference to the forceful structural logic of the

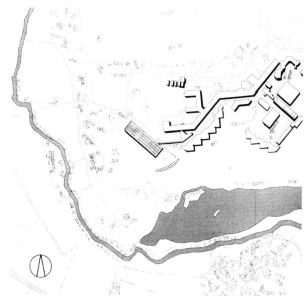

6.2

adjacent Centre. The sloping site allowed for a cut and fill insertion into the landscape. A waterproof concrete retaining wall approximately 300 mm thick forms the external perimeter (Figure 6.3). The whole

6.1

158

6.1
General view from across lake

6.2
Site plan.
1 Sainsbury Centre for the Visual Arts; 2 Crescent Wing; 3 lake; 4 Sir Denys Lasdun Buildings

6.3
Floor plan.
1 External public ramp down from Sainsbury Centre; 2 reception; 3 lower gallery; 4 reserve collection display; 5 toilets; 6 service zone: photography studio, conservation laboratory, packing area, research room, seminar rooms, workshops; 7 workshops; 8 plant and stores

6.4
Bird's-eye view of Crescent Wing

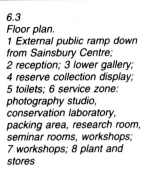

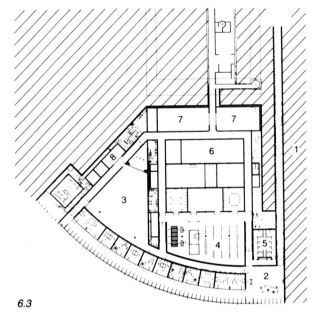

6.3

is built on a conrete base which sits on a gravel pad. The roof slab which varies in thickness between 250 and 325 mm is supported on a combination of columns and loadbearing walls.

Glazing

The crescent of sloping glazing forming the major visual element is a sophisticated pressure plate, double-glazed cladding system, supplied by Metallbau Gmbh (MBM fabricated the external sun scoop for the Hong Kong and Shanghai Bank). Each trapezoidal double-glazed panel is 4.2 m × 1.2 m inclined at 37.5° to the horizontal. The 12 mm thick toughened outer sheet is separated from the inner sheet of toughened, laminated (2 × 8 mm) glass by a 12 mm sealed space. The glazing achieves the 3.2 W/m2°C U-value required by the performance specification. The overall average U value for the extension is 0.4 W/m²°C . The outer sheet of glass is fritted to provide a total solar shading coefficient over long and short wavelengths of 0.53. The proportion of opaque fritted dots varies from 5% at the base of each glazed panel to 95% at the top in such a way that the overall average of opaque area is 50% of the whole.

The carrier rail is made up of extruded aluminium sections which when assembled form elegant radiused rhomboid ribs (Figure 6.6). The finish to

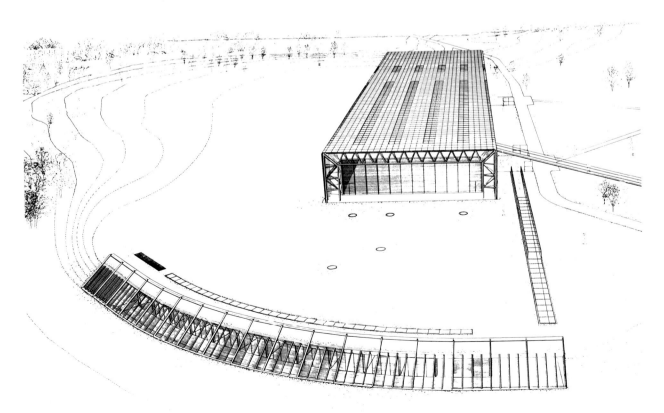

6.4

6.5
Section through extruded
aluminium handrail

6.6
Sections through mullions.
1 Extruded aluminium cover
trim; 2 extruded aluminium
pressure plate; 3 2 mm thick
Itart PVC thermal barrier;
4 silicone gasket; 5 outer
sheet of fritted 12 mm
toughened glass; 6 inner
sheet of 18 mm laminated
glass; 7 silicone gasket with
flap seal; 8 extruded
aluminium carrier rail

6.7
Section through circular roof
light. 1 Concrete upstand;
2 Halfen anchor; 3 hot dip
galvanized steel plate ring;
4 perforated strainer; 5 drain
medium; 6 Erisco Bauder
composite insulated
waterproof membrane;
7 shot-blasted stainless steel
cover trim; 8 silicone seal;
9 30 mm laminated glass with
non-slip surface treatment;
10 10 mm laminated glass;

11 aluminium trim; 12 steel
grout plate; 13 clamp plate;
14 Sealant

these aluminium items, both internally and externally is natural silver anodizing. The outer section of every fourth upright is increased to provide sufficient strength to be extended beyond the roof line to form a balustrade supporting an extruded aluminium handrail running along the top of the crescent (Figure 6.5). At an overall sectional width of 337 mm this extrusion is comparable to the stair extrusions at Sir Richard Rogers' Lloyds Building, London. (For more information see Brookes and Grech (1990) *The Building Envelope*, pp. 54–57). A 2 mm thick Itart PVC thermal barrier isolates the male and female components of the carrier rail, eliminating any cold bridging. The PVC barrier was cycle tested specifically for this application to prove that condensation would not form within the aluminium sections. The internal silicone gasket is formed with an extended flap which laps over the junction between the two aluminium components to form an internal gutter along which any condensation can drain.

Incorporated within the glazed crescent are emergency exit doors and air intake louvres. the two full-height, double-glazed, top hung doors are activated by a push-bar mechanism which breaks an electrical circuit releasing a constantly pressurized cylinder which elevates the door (Figure 6.9).

The fresh air intake duct is hidden behind two major bays of weather louvres. The 37.5° incline of the louvre panel lead to the testing and development of specially extruded, aerodynamically profiled blades that provide noise reduction criteria of NR35 at 1 m for an air volume flow rate per square metre of 1.5 m³/s against a static pressure of 25 Pa.

Rooflights

In addition to the lighting slot that follows the curve of the crescent there are five circular rooflights that sit flush with the grassed surface. These rooflights are strategically located to provide natural lighting to the conservation and study areas below.

One of the major design criteria for these elements of glazing was that they should not provide a weak link in the building's security. Hence the rooflights are sealed and designed to take massive vehicle loadings.

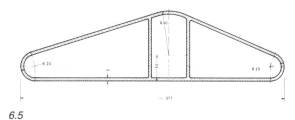

6.5

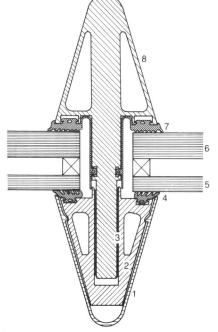

6.6

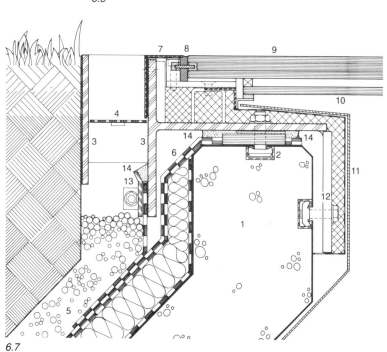

6.7

6.8
Conservation laboratory with
rooflight

6.9
Cross-section through gallery
and office

The outer element of each double glazed unit is laminated from three sheets of 10 mm thick glass (Figure 6.7), the top surface of which has a silkscreen applied non-slip textured coating which is then baked onto the glass. The reduced radius of the middle glass layer creates a groove into which a metal tongue can be inserted to lock the glass in place. Additional security is provided by a complex arrangement of elements that are hidden behind a minimal stainless steel cover trim.

A single-element, spun aluminium, parabolic reflector is fitted into the oculus below the glazing.

6.8

This reflector, based on the theory of the parabolic reflectors employed in commonplace artificial downlighters, focuses the natural daylight into a pool of light onto the working surface directly below the rooflight (Figure 6.8). The parabolic reflector also reduces glare when viewed obliquely.

The finished reflectors are 980 mm high, with diameters of 1600 mm at the base, reducing to 750 mm at the top. A 3 m diameter, 6 mm thick aluminium sheet is spun around a computer-generated parabolic mould. The spinning was carried out in Newcastle, the reflectors were then sent to Thetford (just a few miles from Norwich) for hand polishing. Electropolishing of the reflectors was carried out in Birmingham, following this they were then transported to Scotland for anodizing before being installed in Norwich.

The users' acclaim is some measure of the success of the rooflights in providing concentrated natural light, as well as an awareness of the outside world beyond these subterranean confines. The sensation of being part of the larger world beyond is enhanced when the lawn above is mowed.

Services

Within the Crescent Wing is a suite of plant rooms, completely independent of the Sainsbury Centre. All

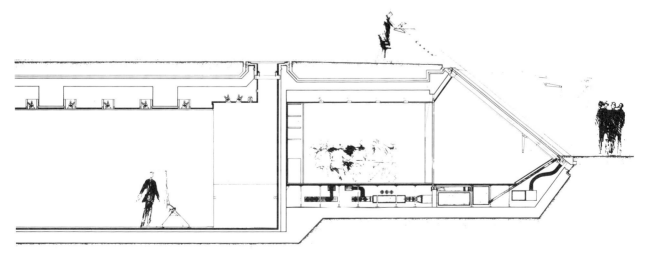

6.9

the art-spaces are fully air conditioned. Heating and cooling but no humidity control is provided to the office spaces.

The curatorial staff can use the light slot to suffuse the curved gallery wall with light, or to block it out with louvre blinds to achieve very low light levels. The ceiling to the gallery has one of the first wholly recessed but fully flexible display lighting systems ever used.

Costs

The Crescent Wing reached practical completion in November 1990 and was opened to the public in April 1991. The specialized nature of this building renders cost comparisons, even with similar building types, of little value. The generous patronage of Sir Robert, Lady Sainsbury and their son David has ensured that this is one of the finest art galleries in the world.

Credits

Client: Sir Robert and Lady Sainsbury and the University of East Anglia.
Structural engineers: YRM Anthony Hunt Associates.
Quantity surveyor: Henry Riley & Son
Services engineer: J. Roger Preston
Museum and lighting consultant: George Sexton Associates.
Acoustic consultant: Acoustic Design Ltd.

7

David Mellor Cutlery Factory, Sheffield
Architects: Michael Hopkins and Partners

7.1

General

This truly modern and elegant factory (Figure 7.1) was designed by Michael Hopkins and Partners (project team Michael Hopkins, John Pringle, Bill Dunster, Neno Kezic) for David Mellor in Hathersage in the heart of the Peak District, about 20 miles west of Sheffield. Completed in 1988 it represents an unusual circumstance of a client wishing to involve himself in the building process to the extent of manufacturing and sourcing many of the building elements.

It also represents the high degree of engineering skill carried out by Whitby and Bird (project team Mark Whitby and Mark Lovell) to achieve the effect of this floating roof balanced over a stone drum related to the circular form of the concrete slab of a redundant gasometer. Mellor obtained permission to build the workshop on this rural site largely because

it made use of the existing foundations and also because the walls were to be faced with local stone detailed in a traditional manner.

The building was built to an extremely tight budget since the usually costly ground works were largely in place, moreover the client had a cheap source of stone and was willing to fabricate and erect much of the building himself.

Structure

The original design by the engineers envisaged steel columns outside the enclosing wall with radial roof trusses running through a strip of glazing above the wall in this way exposing the structure.

The existing 25 m diameter base of the gasometer, capable of taking the weight of water equivalent to the volume enclosed by a three-storey building was extended by 915 mm by casting a new

7.1
General view

7.2
Section through factory.
1 Central rooflight; 2 lead
covered roof panels; 3 steel
roof truss; 4 stone wall;
5 new concrete slab;
6 existing concrete slab

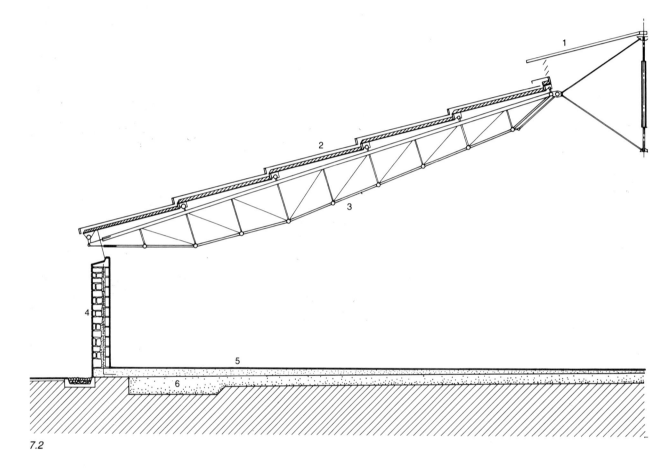

7.2

slab 390 mm thick of approximately 27 m diameter over the old one (Figure 7.2). The additional area of slab cantilevered beyond the existing base.

The loadbearing conditions of the subsoil around the edge (previously an old drain culvert) were suspect and the idea of exterior columns with their requirement for additional foundations and possible interference with traffic around the building was therefore abandoned. Consequently the shallow pitched roof is supported directly off a loadbearing masonry drum approximately 2.5 m high. Built without buttresses, the walls are 450 mm thick with an outer face of 150 mm split stone from a local quarry, and 140 mm blockwork internally with concrete infill between the two. These walls were constructed to a remarkable tolerance of ±2 mm to allow a precise fit of the steel roof structure (Figure 7.3).

Roof

Although originally anticipated as a steel roof using Patera-type panels (see Brookes, A.J., *Concepts in Cladding*, 1985, p. 90), eventually lead brought from Ireland was used because its association with traditional detailing also meant that it could be easily crafted to the required segmental shapes.

Twenty-four 12 m long tubular steel trusses radiate out from a 4.8 m diameter central rooflight that floods the workspace below with natural light. The roof trusses, consisting of one top chord and two bottom chords are shaped to follow the bending moments therein. The concentric purlins are graduated from 60 mm diameter at the centre to 114 mm diameter at the periphery but the latter was considered to be visually too heavy so the last purlin is propped to reduce its dimension.

7.3
Sections through perimeter wall. 1 Prefabricated plywood roof panel; 2 76.1 mm diameter top chord of truss; 3 two no. 33.7 mm diameter bottom chords; 4 pre-cast concrete padstone; 5 100 mm insulating concrete bock; 6 waterproof concrete fill; 7 15 mm rough-cast render; 8 reinforced concrete floor slab; 9 rough stone wall; 10 12 mm steel bars;

11 60 mm diameter solid perimeter ring tie beam; 12 88.9 mm diameter circular hollow section purlin.

7.4
Detail of panel fixing. 1 Code 5 lead sheeting; 2 underfelt; 3 plywood skin; 4 ventilation route; 5 60 mm insulation quilt; 6 vapour barrier; 7 treated softwood joists; 8 plywood soffit; 9 steel spacer between purlin and roof truss; 10 steel purlin; 11 mild steel hook plate.

7.5
Roof plan and reflected ceiling plan showing petal bracing.

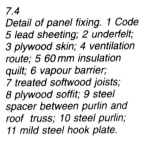

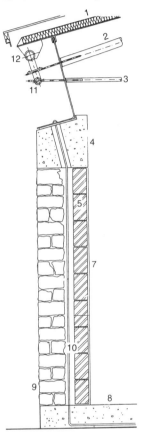
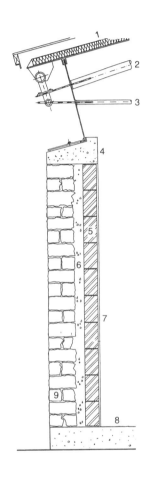

7.3

The roof covering is formed from five tiers of lead covered panels that hook onto the steel purlins and lap over the tier below (compare this method of fixing with that of the cladding panels of the Bercy Shopping Centre on page 6). The side joints between panels are standard rolled lead joints, those at the top and bottom are simply lapped. Each panel is formed as a hollow birch plywood box open at its top and bottom edges which link up to provide a continuous ventilation route from eaves to lantern (Figure 7.4). This through ventilation ensures that condensation and consequent corrosion is greatly reduced.

The 480 panels forming the roof were made by David Mellor to give different tapering sizes. The Code 5 lead sheeting used is 600 mm wide and overlapped at its edges. To allow for cutting and overlapping, 70% more lead was required than the cover dimension.

The decision to form the roof using lead sheeting, meant that the anticipated weight of the lead roof was 15 tons, the roof structure weighing an additional 17 tons. A major structural dilemma was how to avoid transferring lateral loads to the masonry walls which are typically weak in bending. The solution was to resolve lateral thrust by an adjustable tubular steel tension ring connecting the lower ends of the roof trusses making the roof an

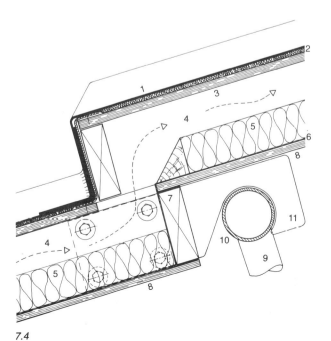

7.4

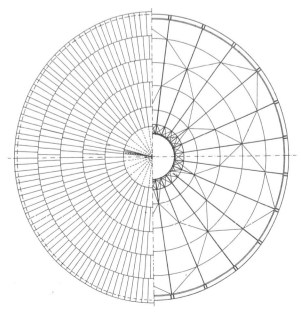

7.5

*Detail of bent steel plate,
truss end, and perimeter tie
junction. 1 60 mm diameter
solid perimeter ring tie bar;
2 88.9 mm diameter circular
hollow section purlin; 3 steel
plate; 4 76.1 mm diameter
circular hollow section top*

*chord; 5 two no. 33.7 mm
diameter circular hollow
section bottom chords;
6 6 mm clear glass; 7 precast
concrete padstone; 8 12 mm
diameter steel reinforcing
bars.*

*Internal view of steel plate
and truss junction*

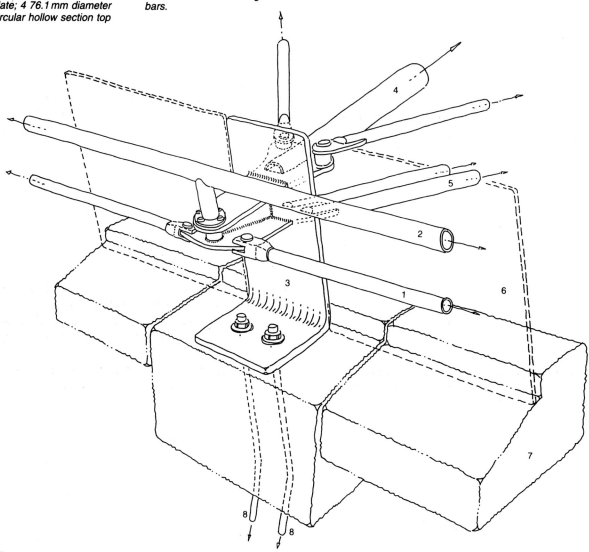

7.6

7.7

independent element exerting no outward thrust to the walls. The roof construction sits on a series of 12 mm thick bent steel plates fixed to padstones at the head of the wall (Figures 7.6 and 7.7)

Several options were suggested for this means of taking up both lateral loading and thermal movement including roller bearers and rubber bushes but it was this simple bent plate of grade 50C steel which allows the desired flexibility and achieves such a minimalist feel to this element.

Roof bracing

It was realized that the main problem of a roof of this type is twist as for example at the Victorian glass house in the Keeble Museum, Glasgow, where the small glass segments add to the stiffness. At the David Mellor factory the first idea was to take out rotational twist at quarter points. This was later changed to perimeter stiffeners but in order to achieve greater constructional elegance the petal form of roof bracing was devised by Whitby & Bird, firstly in the form of eight petals but later reduced to six petals so that each petal could occur at a node (Figure 7.5).

Costs

The approximate total cost of this building was £400 000 giving a square metre cost of around £700.

Conclusion

This excellent design responds to its site and the client's requirements beyond a casual reinterpretation of nineteenth century industrial construction. It demonstrates how a building with a utilitarian function and responding to pragmatic needs can offer opportunities for a high level of innovative design given an enthusiastic talented design team and a commitment to the design by the client.

Credits

Client and builder: David Mellor Design
Structural engineers: Whitby & Bird

References

Cruikshank, D., 'Rounded Design', *Architects' Journal*, 14 September 1988, pp. 26–30.

Murta, K., 'Design at the Cutting Edge', *RIBA Journal*, Vol. 95, No. 10, October 1988, pp. 40–45.

Anon, 'Werkstatte bei Sheffield', *Der Baumeiste*, Vol. 86, No. 3, March 1989, pp. 30–35.

8

East Croydon Station
Architects:
Brookes Stacey Randall Fursdon

8.1

General

This building was designed in 1990 to serve approximately 10 million passengers a year commuting to and from Central London to Gatwick Airport and the South East of England. The new station floor replaces and upgrades the existing bridges, the superstructure of the new station spans 55 m and transfers the new loadings down to existing brick abutments on either side of six busy railway tracks (Figure 8.1). This minimizes the disruption to the railway, allows for the differential movement in the existing bridges over which it spans and creates a column-free interior. Suspended below the masted external steel structure is a highly glazed envelope which provides a sophisticated shelter. The specially developed glazing support system achieves maximum transparency whilst meeting the robust demands of a railway station. Retail and Ticket Office accommodation is in the form of freestanding table structures located adjacent to the glazed perimeter walls. Glass fins connect the internal accommodation to the glazing mullions. The station provides a major transport interchange between trains, buses, pedestrians and taxis, under the cover of generous canopies.

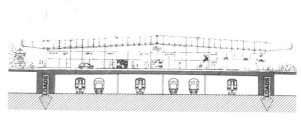

8.2

Structure

The 179 tonne structure completed in May 1991 consists of four double masts erected on to the existing abutments with tie bars between column bases to accommodate the horizontal forces from the structure. The tie bars are buried within the depth of the new floor slab. The masts support tubular latticed box girders over the 55 m clear span (Figure 8.2). During erection the latticed box girders were centrally supported by a jacking tower. On completion of the erection, the tensions in the roof

8.1
General view of station
from George Street

8.2
Cross-section showing
structural concept

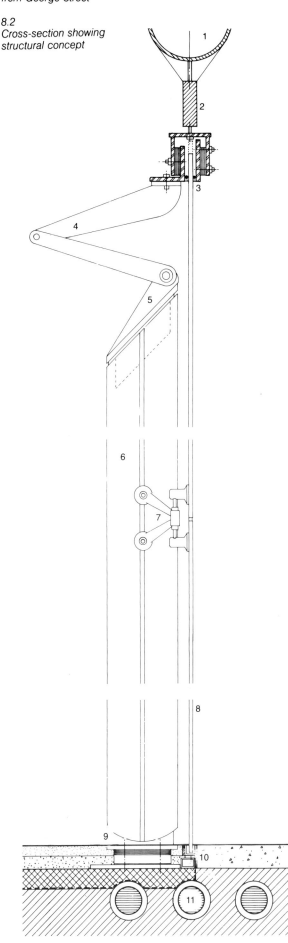

8.3

8.3
Section through wall glazing
assembly. 1 244x16 mm
circular hollow section bottom
boom of main truss;
2 intermediate rigid support;
3 sliding head channel
arrangement; 4 stainless steel
scissor arm assembly;
5 stainless steel head casting;
6 extruded aliminium mullion;
7 cast stainless steel bracket
with Planar fittings; 8 12 mm
toughened glass; 9 stainless-
steel base casting; 10 base
glazing channel; 11 100 mm
diameter Macalloy tension
rods

8.4
Stainless steel castings and
aluminium mast extrusion for
wall glazing

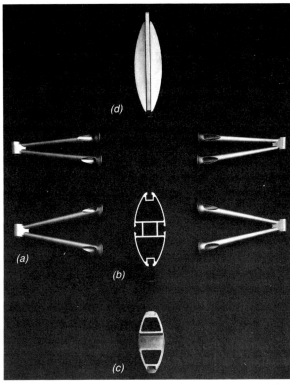

8.4

tie bars were equalized and the jacks progressively lowered. The tension in the tie bars was continually monitored using strain-gauges.

Glazing system

The glazing system, using planar fittings, aims to maximize the potential of the toughened glass and the extruded aluminium supporting structure. The specially extruded aluminium mast supports the glazing assembly and resists wind loads (Figure 8.3). Each 2.99 m × 2.08 m pane of 12 mm clear toughened glass is supported at only four points. Deflection of the glass is limited to a fraction of one over 112 of the span by the use of inboard stainless steel cast brackets (Figure 8.4a) which effectively reduce the glass spans. The form of the extruded mast is elliptical (b) to achieve an elegant and rigid structural form with minimum profile. This extrusion is held at its base (c) and head (d) by stainless steel castings also designed especially for the project. The articulated mast head assembly accommodates the vertical and differential movement between the structure and vertical

8.5
Detail of wall glazing
assembly

8.7
Corner connecting bracket to
wall glazing

8.8
Roof glazing hung beneath
steel structure

8.6
Glazing assembly under test

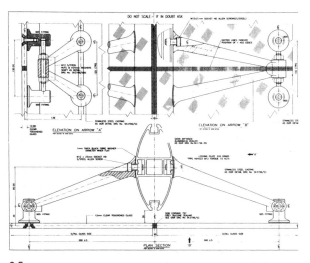

8.5

8.6

8.7

cladding and also allows for tolerance in assembly. This detail resolves the interface between longspan structures and their associated curtain walling and is similar in principle to the mullion details at Stansted Airport and the Renault Parts Distribution Centre.

The extruded aluminium mast at East Croydon Station is also designed to receive extruded silicone gaskets acting as closure pieces at the wall junctions and the groove to the rear of the extrusion has been designed to carry door tracks and signage and to receive internal glazing. This economical solution is flexible and provides an elegantly articulated alternative to the standard curtain walling box section (Figures 8.5 and 8.6).

The 10 mm clear toughened roof glazing is suspended below stainless-steel twin-armed castings (Figure 8.8). In this case, 902 Mark 2 Planar fittings are used, but are reversed from the normal mode of operation demonstrated by the 905 fittings to the wall glazing. Of particular interest on this project are the stainless-steel castings specially produced by means of a lost wax process for this project by BSA. The roof castings enable the

8.8

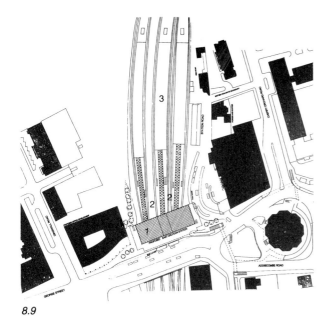

8.9

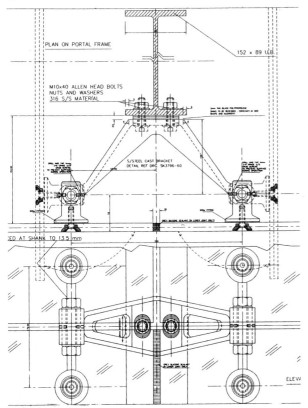

8.10

similar horizontal 'V' castings which are then fixed to the side channels in the extruded aluminium mullions. The corner detail is achieved without the use of the vertical mullion by means of a connecting bracket (Figure 8.7).

Ramps

The Ramps are conceived as an extended canopy where the roof is held above the glazed wall with a space between to allow ventilation to the ramp area. The 152 × 89 mm joists form a series of portals, which are assembled perpendicular to the ramp. This, together with the different angles at which each ramp intersects with the station building, links the platforms to the main building in the manner of a gangplank between ship and quay (Figure 8.9).

The upper areas of glazing are openable into the ramp, supported by 905 fittings which pivot on purpose designed castings (Figure 8.10). This enables the glazing which is inaccessible for cleaning from the platforms to be easily maintained.

Credits

Client: British Railways Board – Network South-East
Structural engineer: Anthony Hunt Associates/YRM
Civil engineer: British Rail Regional Civil Engineers
Quantity surveyors: Hanscomb
Main contractor: Trafalgar House Construction Ltd
Glazing subcontractor: Briggs Amasco Curtain Walling Ltd
Main Steelwork subcontractor: Blight and White Ltd

References

Anon 'Croydon Canopy', *Architectural Review*, December 1989, pp. 84–87.

Berrien, V., 'L'aluminium au service de la transparence', *Le Moniteur*, May 1991, p. 125.

Brookes, A.J., Stacey, M., 'The Role of the Die', *Building Design*, 30 November 1990.

Brookes, A.J., Stacey, M., 'Glazing and Curtain Walling', *Architects' Journal*, Focus, February 1990, p. 32–37.

G.H. Taylor, 'On the Right Track', *Steel Construction Today*, July 1991.

underhung glass to be fixed to the structure via mild steel bosses. Tolerances between the steelwork and the glazing are accommodated within the fixing points in the castings. The wall glazing is fixed to

9

338 Euston Road, London
Architects:
Sheppard Robson

9.1

General

338 Euston Road is the sixteen storey office building (Figures 9.1 and 9.2) that counterbalances the Euston Tower at the end of the massive 1960s office development that stretches from John Soane's church on Marylebone Road to Hampstead Road.

When the British Land Company purchased the freehold of the tower in 1987, they commissioned Sheppard Robson to carry out a feasibility study into the building's potential future use. At this stage total demolition and rebuilding was still an option. Analysis of the building revealed that the narrow plan and limited floor to floor height would require a major services reorganization if the building was to operate as a viable office. The existing floor to floor height of 3.2 m meant that there would not be a

9.2

9.1
General view of refurbished tower

9.2
General view of original tower

9.3
Cross-section through original tower

9.4
Cross-section through refurbished tower

9.5
Plan of typical floor. Doted line shows extent of original floor plate

9.6
Exploded isometric of box bracket assembly. 1 Existing concrete column; 2 existing floor slab notched out; 3 box bracket; 4 suspension rod; 5 steel platform

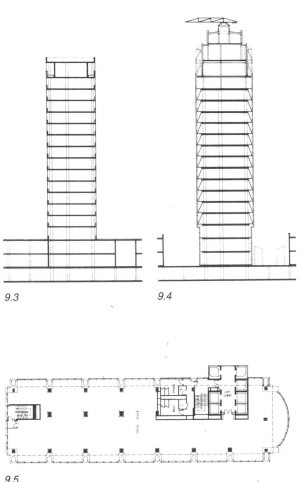

9.3

9.4

9.5

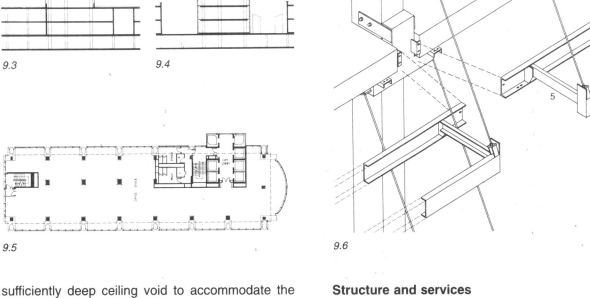

9.6

sufficiently deep ceiling void to accommodate the increased services hardware required by the modern information technology-supported office.

Together with structural and mechanical engineers Ove Arup and Partners the architects devised a strategy of retaining the existing building skeleton, upgrading it by adding a clip-on service wall to the perimeter of the building.

Unlike the lightweight, fast track office buildings erected in the 1980s, this building incorporated many of the denser materials associated with traditional construction. It is surprising to learn that by stripping out floor screeds, half-height perimeter blockwork walls and the massive double storey height rooftop plant room, replacing them with a structure composed of lightweight materials allowed an increase of 20% to the nett lettable floor area. (Figures 9.3–9.5).

Structure and services

Once the building had been stripped back to the concrete frame notches were cut out of the perimeter of the floor slab at every column base. A box bracket (Figure 9.6) made up of steel plates was bolted to each column, these brackets extend below the slab to provide fixing points for the suspension rods that support the outer ends of the steel platforms that form the extension to the floor below. The inner edge of these platforms is bolted back to the box brackets. Suspension rods 1.5 m apart allow space for the vertical routing of ductwork (Figure 9.6). The horizontal services distribution routes are suspended from the newly provided steel platforms which, being of a greatly reduced depth to the adjacent concrete slabs provide the necessary space around the whole perimeter of the building.

*Cut-away isometric showing
cladding and services.
1 Existing concrete column;
2 existing floor slab notched
out; 3 box bracket;
4 suspension rod; 5 steel
platform; 6 supply duct;
7 extract duct; 8 variable air
volume control box; 9 bellmouth return air duct; 10 stick
system cladding to projecting
boxes*

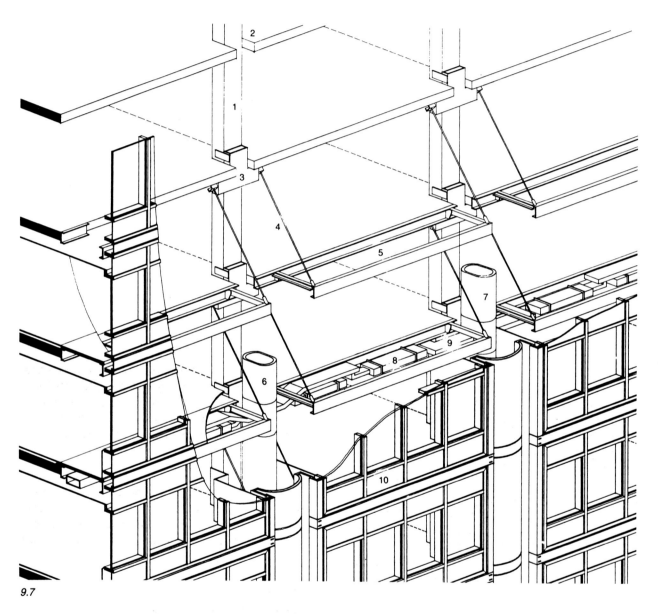

9.7

Supply air ducts branch off the main vertical duct to variable air volume control boxes which feed into the perimeter of the office space servicing a 4 m deep perimeter zone. The benefit of the narrow plan configuration is that the central zone can easily be served by a duct running between the two service cores. The ceiling void is treated as an air-return plenum. A bellmouth duct at the perimeter of the office feeds straight into the vertical air-return duct. Supply and return air ducts alternate down each of the long elevations of the building, and are linked to the rooftop plant room.

Cladding

The project team (Ken O'Callaghan, Frank Ling and Mark Dillon) working intensely over a twelve month period with cladding subcontractors Chamebel utilized a combination of cladding types which relate to an intricate hierarchy of spaces and details.

The broad expanses of flat panels visible at the top and corners express the limits of the former building. This is a rainscreen type system of 3 mm thick polyester powder-coated aluminium sheet fixed back to the structure through a sealed butyl sheet waterproofing system.

9.8

Exploded isometric of lift shaft corner cladding. 1 Double glazed unit; 2 extruded aluminium corner mullion; 3 horizontally slotted steel plate attached to mullion; 4 vertically slotted steel plate; 5 steel connector bracket; 6 Macalloy threaded steel bar; 7 machined steel fork connector; 8 steel circular hollow section

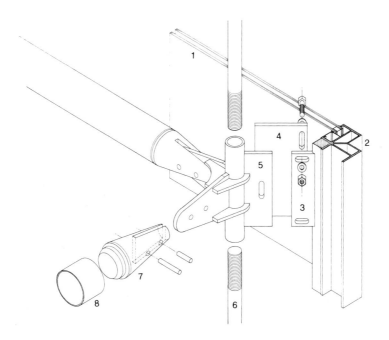

9.8

The additional area, treated as projecting bays, along the east and west elevations, with the articulated vertical services in between, are clad in a conventional stick system. The north/south axis of the building, recognized as a worst case orientation for heat gain reasons means that the low E coating to the double glazed units is essential. Provision has been left for the tenants to install their own blinds should this prove necessary.

A system of extruded aluminium casings was developed to express the new external suspension structure. This feature is most visible at the top of the bays. The vertical trusses at the corners of the buildings are in fact decorative, there is no structure within.

Lifts

Two additional wallclimber lifts project from the eastern elevation. These are enclosed in a glazed envelope made up from a stick system into which the double glazed panels are shuffled. In an attempt to prevent the corner structure from providing too much of a visual obstruction this corner is supported from a Macalloy steel bar suspended from the roof structure (Figure 9.8). Horizontal rods lock into the suspension rod restraining it at each floor. The suspension structure is a critical interface between steelwork and cladding subcontractors. Potential problems were avoided by designing a detail that allowed a wide variation in tolerance, the use of steel plates slotted vertically and horizontally permitted site adjustments in two directions.

Costs

Sheppard Robson were appointed in July 1987. Work started on site in October 1988 and was completed in December 1990. The cladding cost averages out at approximately £450 per square metre.

Credits

Client: The British Land Company.
Structural and mechanical engineers: Ove Arup and Partners.
Quantity surveyors: Gleeds.
Management contractors: Mowlem Management Ltd.
Steelwork subcontractor: HCG.
Cladding subcontractor: Chamebel Ltd.

References

Anon., 'Euston Cladding', *Building Design Supplement*, March 1991, pp. VI–VII.

10

Financial Times Building, London
Architects: Nicholas Grimshaw and Partners

10.1

10.1
External view of printing hall
glazing

10.2
North south section. 1 East
India Dock Road; 2 press
hall; 3 spine plant room;
4 offices and publishing
rooms; 5 car park

10.3.
Circular connecting 'dinner
plate' glass fixing

10.4.
Glass fixing plate assembly.
1 12 mm thick toughened
glass pane, 2 x 2 m; 2 black
silicone joint; 3 220 mm
diameter stainless-steel fixing
plate; 4 Pilkington Planar
fixing; 5 M20 stainless-steel
bolt, nut and washer;
6 110 mm diameter turned

mild-steel boss with 10 mm
thick spade plates to take
suspension rod assembly;
7 suspension rod assembly
for 18 mm Macalloy
suspension rod; 8 75x16 mm
mild-steel glazing arm welded
to mild-steel boss

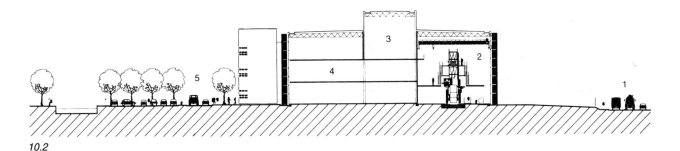

10.2

General

Located in East London, adjacent to the Blackwall
Tunnel approach, this new printing works for the
Financial Times was built in the remarkably short
time from start on site in February 1987 to
installation and fitting out in June 1988. The
introduction of new technology into the newspaper
industry has removed the need for the editorial and
production departments to be close to one another.
Hence the location of this printing works close to the
East India Dock Road one of the main arterial roads
leading out of the City. The rectangular building
planned on a 6 m grid consists of a press hall 96 m
long by 18 m wide separated from office areas of
similar dimensions by a 12 m wide service zone
(Figure 10.2). At one end of the building is the paper
storage and at the other the dispatch bays.

Glazing

It is the glass skin that forms the sides of the building
which dramatically exposes the printing press to the
road. (Figure 10.1) The glazing 96×16 m is formed
by 2 m square panes of 12 mm thick glass bolted at
their corners to a circular patch plate known as the
'dinner plate' (Figure 10.3). Each 'dinner plate' has
four adjustable bolt connectors which mate with predrilled holes in the corners of the four adjacent
sheets of glass (Figure 10.4). Butt joints between
the glass are sealed with black silicone. Although at
the time of design this size of glass pane was the
maximum possible using the Pilkington Planar fixing
technology, spans of larger glass panes have
subsequently been achieved by using brackets
which project well inboard of the glass edge (see
East Croydon Station, Case Study 8). The 'dinner
plates' are supported by fabricated steel outriggers

10.3

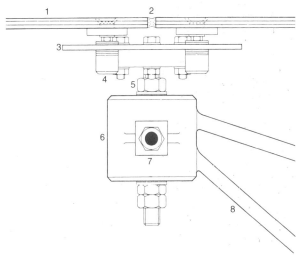

10.4

177

10.5
Corner of solid clad ends of
main block

10.6
1 Fabricated steel column;
2 fabricated steel wind
restraint glazing arm;
3 suspension rod assembly;
4 12 mm thick toughened
glass panes

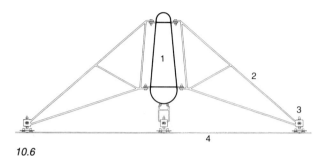

10.6

10.5

projecting from the main steel columns at 6 m
centres (Figure 10.6). These columns are often
mistakenly identified as aluminium sections. In fact
they are formed by two half-round steel sections of
differing diameters linked by flat plates. From these
the fabricated steel arms allow fixings for the glass.
The vertical loads are taken by tension rods
extending up and over the head of the column. Thus
the outriggers at first appear to be holding up the
glass but in fact primarily offer wind restraint.

Cladding

The solid ends of the building comprise vacuum
formed panels of Superform aluminium finished with
grey Duranar PVF2 (Figure 10.5). Superform panels
were originally used at the Sainsbury Centre at the
University of East Anglia but were later replaced due
to corrosion and moisture retention in the phenolic
foam core. At the Financial Times Building the
architect and subcontractor were able to extend the
existing technology by developing fully formed
cladding panels of the commercial grade S083 SBF
aluminium alloy. The panels are fixed back onto
silver-anodized extruded-aluminium cladding rails
(Figure 10.7).The horizontal joints every 2 m (Figure
10.8), are emphasized by projecting rails with
slotted holes, these rails serve to conceal the
collected rainwater and drain it through the system
to ground level.

Conclusion

It could be said that the technical language of this
building is quite ordinary in comparison with many
other Grimshaw designs. However, as John Winter
has remarked, 'to find the ordinary done so well is a
lasting pleasure'. Within the fast time-scale set by
the client it may not have been possible to develop

10.7
Cut away axonometric of cladding assembly. 1 Vertical extruded aluminium cladding rail; 2 vacuum formed aluminium panels; 3 horizontal extruded aluminium channel with projecting cladding rail

10.8
Vertical and horizontal joints between solid and ventilation louvre panels

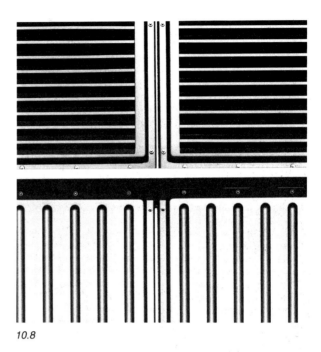

10.8

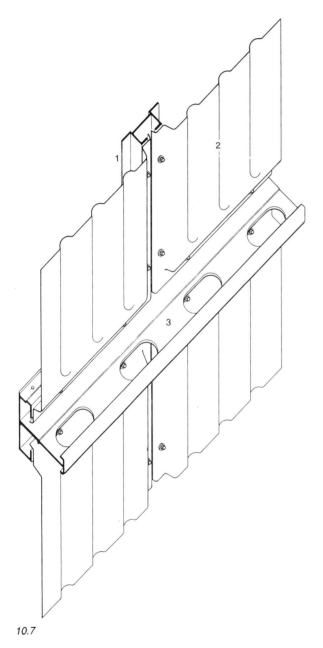

10.7

using planar fittings at 2 m centres is well within the limits of suspended glazing technology. Despite this the building exists for many architects as an example of the vanguard of current technology and 'High Tech' design.

Credits

Client: Financial Times
Structural engineers: J Robinson & Sons
Interiors: Robinson Design Partnership
Service engineers: Cundall Johnston & Partners
Quantity surveyors: Smerdon & Jones
Management contractors: Bovis Construction Ltd

References

John Winter, 'Glass Wall in Blackwall', *Architectural Review*, 1101, Nov 1988, pp. 42–49.

Hugh Aldersey-Williams, 'A Sign of the Times', *Blueprint*, Nov 1988, pp. 60–62.

Anon, 'Zeitungsdruckerei in London', *Baumeister*, July 1989, pp. 74–89.

Stacey, M., 'Maximum Vision', *AJ Focus*, October 1988.

David Jenkins, 'Financial Times Print Works', *Architecture in Detail* 1991.

Brookes, A.J., Stacey, M., 'Product Review', *AJ Focus*, March 1990.

an innovative constructional method. The direct fixing of the panels using steel self tapping screws to vertical aluminium cladding rails is very reminiscent of their detail at the Herman Miller Extension in Chippenham (see Brookes, *Concepts in Cladding*) with the exception that in this case the joints arc open and not gasket sealed. The aluminium-clad staircases are separated and curved in the manner that Grimshaw previously used at Queen's Drive Nottingham. Also, the means of fixing the glass

Finland Lion Lighthouse, Baltic Sea
Architects:
Esko Lehesmaa

11.1

11.2

11.3

11.4

General

If one excludes the Colossus of Rhodes, then probably the first lighthouse to be constructed wholly of metal was built in Swansea in 1804. It no longer exists. The oldest metal lighthouse still in use is thought to be Maryport in Cumberland dating from 1834. The Baltic Sea also has a long history of metal lighhouses: in 1886 the firm of Henri Lepaute of Paris built an iron lighthouse for Valassaaret in the Gulf of Bothnia off the Finnish West Coast. It has some features in common with the Tour d'Eiffel, which the same firm constructed in Paris three years later.

In the Baltic Sea, after the Second World War, lightships began to be replaced by lighthouses standing on the submerged shoals. Here the solid ice can be up to 1.8 m and pack ice several metres thick, the forces against these structures is

11.1
General view

11.2
Reinforced steelwork cage for caisson base

11.3
Floated caisson towed out to sea

11.4
Caisson being sunk

11.5
Location map

11.6
Elevation of lighthouse.
1 Helicopter landing pad;
2 halogen light; 3 wind driven generator; 4 passive radar reflectors; 5 concrete filled skirt, over articulated joint; 6 access hatch; 7 steel shaft; 8 concrete stem; 9 concrete caisson; 10 sea bed

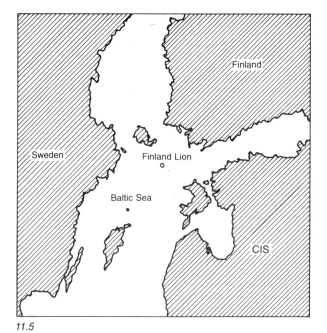

11.5

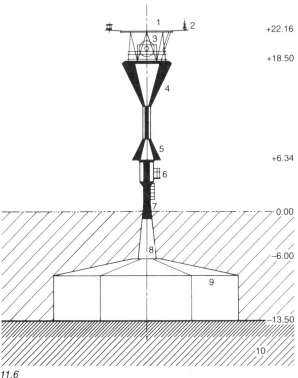

11.6

To make the ice-resisting foot slimmer, some lighhouses were built of steel. However, they became so light that the passing ice made them vibrate so violently that they collapsed. Finally, in the mid-1970s, Professor Mauri Määttänen of the Oulu University developed a structure combining a rigid, caisson-supported foundation with a lightweight steel lighthouse tower.

The Lion of Finland Lighthouse (Figure 11.1) completed in 1987 is the largest of such lighthouses to be built so far. It is the first to be encountered on arriving at the Finnish waters of the Baltic Sea (Figure 11.5).

Structure

The hexagonal caisson base is 24 m wide across its diagonal and 7.5 m high, made from 800 m³ of concrete and 150 tonnes of steel reinforcement, the four chambers making up this base have a total capacity of 2000 m³. The hollow concrete caisson was cast in dry dock, floated by virtue of its own buoyancy, and towed out to sea (Figures 11.2 and 11.3). There it was sunk (Figure 11.4) by flooding the chambers with approximately 1250 m³ of wet sand, which anchors the base to the 13.5 m deep shoal (Figure 11.6). This mass of ballast gives the lighthouse a minimum metacentric height (height of centre of gravity above the base) of 0.12 m which ensures that with this degree of stability it will not overturn. Projecting from this concrete base is a 6 m high conical steel stem with a lower diameter of 2.6 m reducing to 0.9 m at its top. It is this slim pillar of steel that allows the lighthouse to slice through the pack ice. The visible part of the lighthouse is made from 65 tons of steel.

At the vertical section of the stem the steel is 13 mm thick, increasing to 40 mm at the conical section. The steel is coated with an epoxy paint that has been developed for use on ice-breakers because it is abrasion resistant. However, the problems associated with ice abrasion and temperature variation are minimal when compared with the forces due to ice movement against the lighthouse stem (Figure 11.10).

At about 6 m above sea level is an articulated joint that acts as a huge shock absorber to prevent vibration being transmitted to the upper part of the structure (Figures 11.7 and 11.8). This joint consists of six 5 m long elastic columns, that support the

enormous. In Finland these lighthouses were built of steel reinforced concrete until the 1970s. The theory behind these structures was tested and improved when wind-driven pack ice knocked down some of these concrete towers.

11.7 and 11.8
1 7mm thick vulcanized
rubber seal; 2 5m long
elastic columns; 3 shock
absorber; 4 concrete ballast;
5 floor grating; 6 steel shaft

11.9
Steel bars with vulcanized
rubber sheath

11.10
The Kemi II lighthouse shown
slicing through the pack ice.

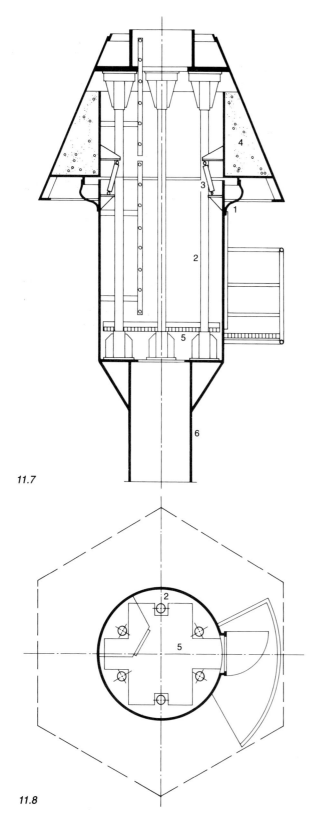

11.7

11.8

11.9

11.10

lighthouse above. Each column is made up of a bundle of steel bars vulcanized together with rubber (Figure 11.9). The arrangement is such that it ensures that when bent, the bars remain parallel and keep the tower vertical. Heavy-duty shock absorbers at the top of these columns together with the concrete mass of the helicopter landing pad, used to tune superstructure natural vibration modes, reduce the resonance-borne vibration so that the tower swings only very slightly. The six columns are enclosed in a sheet-steel accessible enclosure. The Finland Lion Lighthouse is currently the largest application of this technology.

The joint between top and bottom sections of the lighthouse is sealed by a large 7mm thick vulcanized rubber bellows that runs around the stem, underneath a protective steel skirt. It seems that this detail is the greatest problem that the keepers of such vibration-isolated lighthouse structures have to contend with. Constant wave action causes this seal to deteriorate, needing replacement every 3 months or so.

The total structure is 36.2 m high with the top 22.2 m projecting above the sea surface. The construction is calculated to withstand 26 MN of pack ice force, of which 18 MN is directed to the concrete caisson. The steel superstructure is designed to withstand 3.2 MN of dynamic ice forces and 49 kN of wind force. The prevailing wind is from the south-west and can muster waves of up to 14 m in height. The ambient temperature varies between $-35°C$ and $+26°C$.

Services

The halogen light of 23 000 Cd, which flashes every 12 seconds, has a range of 14.6 nautical miles. Radar reflectors are passive. A 150 W wind-driven generator and storage batteries provide power for lights and racon transmitter.

Costs

At a cost of 4.2 million Marks (FIM1987) this lighthouse worked out at less than half the cost of an equivalent traditional all-concrete lighthouse.

Credits

Technical design: Mauri Määttänen, Lujari Engineers
Concrete structure design: Lauri Pitkälä Engineers
Contractor: Suomen Merityö Oy
Instrumentation: National Board of Navigation

References

Anon, 'Suomen Leijona Faro nel Mar Baltico', *Domus*, March 1990, No. 714, pp. 74–79.
Anon, *Arkkitehti* (Helsinki), April 1989.
Anon, *Detail Serie* (Munich), June 1990.

12

Glass Music Hall, Amsterdam
Architects: Pieter Zaanen in association with Mick Eekhout

12.1

General

The renovation of one of Amsterdam's earliest modern buildings, H. P. Berlage's Exchange of 1899, has provided the city with a glass music hall that builds on its modernist pedigree.

The three large halls, formerly used as merchants' exchanges, have been converted by Pieter Zaanen to an exhibition hall, concert hall and rehearsal room. Zaanen, an architect specializing in adaptive use of old buildings, has trained under such Modern Masters as Frank Lloyd Wright, Le Corbusier and Gerrit Rietveld.

The conversion of the former shipping exchange

12.1
General view

12.2
Ground floor plan of
Berlage's Exchange. 1 Aga
hall; 2 Wang hall

12.3
Aerial perspective of music
hall

12.4
Section through music hall.
1 Concrete base; 2 cruciform
steel columns; 3 cross
bracing to columns; 4 space
frame roof structure;
5 external columns supporting
curved glass wall; 6 8 mm
fully tempered suspended
glass; 7 vertical truss of guy
rods on cross bars

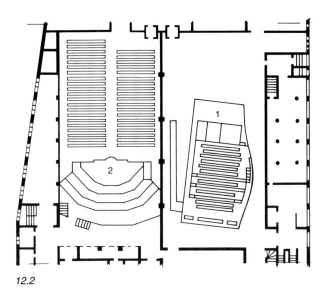

12.2

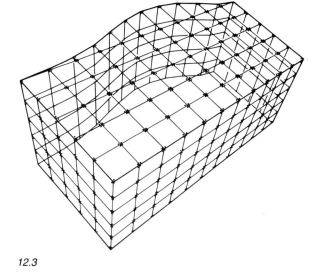

12.3

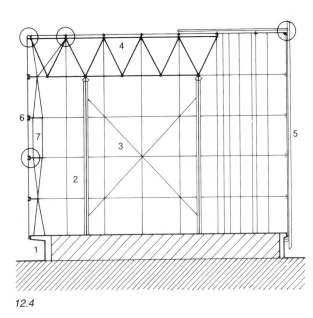

12.4

into a 600 seat concert hall was largely achieved by hanging fabric banners, increasing the acoustic absorption, thus reducing the reverberation time. The rehearsal space proved more complex. The brief required the integrity of Berlage's hall to be preserved, yet prevent noise from reaching the surrounding offices. The solution chosen by Zaanen was a totally glazed box within the hall (Figures 12.1 and 12.2). The 8 mm glass used provides the necessary sound reduction. Structural designer Mick Eekhout was appointed to design and build this acoustic envelope.

Structure

The glass box, 9 m high, 21.6 m long and 13 m at its widest was originally designed as a rectangle, the introduction of a bulging side wall, the 'cello belly', reduces flutter echoes (Figure 12.3).

Six internal cruciform columns support a rectangular space frame from which 8 mm grey tinted fully tempered glass sheets are hung on the three straight sides (Figure 12.4). These three walls are built as true curtain walls; the glass panels are suspended one under the other, the topmost panel carrying the dead weight of all the lower panels. Hence the upper bolt holes take the greatest load. Each 1.8 m square glass panel is suspended from two 20 mm diameter bolts 100× 100 mm in from each corner. The connecting brackets are built up of four solid cylindrical blocks, connected by diagonal strips (Figures 12.5–12.7). A perpendicular stud

welded to the crossing point of the diagonals is connected to the two tensile bars inside the glass face. A stainless steel Allen-type countersunk high-tensile bolt clamps the glass to the solid blocks at each corner of the bracket. The external face of these three walls presents a totally flush surface. Although full wind loads were not taken into account on this project, the counterspanning guy rods are necessary due to pressures caused by the air-conditioning system, and visitors pressing against the lower panels. For a similar external system, it is thought that the rods would be increased from 10 to

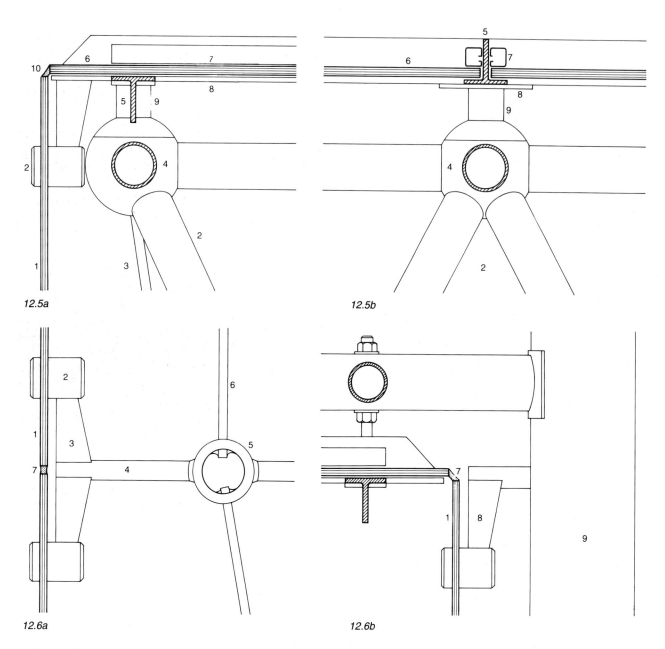

12.5
(a) Eaves detail at suspended wall. (b) Roof glazing. 18 mm tinted tempered glass; 2 space frame structure; 3 guy rod; 4 spherical space frame node; 5 50 × 50 × 6 mm T-section; 6 roof glazing; 7 20 × 20 mm steel glazing bead; 8 80 × 80 mm base plate; 9 hub spacer; 10 silicone sealant

12.6
(a) Suspended wall detail. (b) Eaves detail at curved wall. 1 8 mm tinted tempered glass; 2 metal stud stabilizer; 3 X-bracket; 4 cross bar spacer; 5 guy rod connector ring; 6 guy rod; 7 silicone sealant; 8 shaped metal bracket; 9 External column

12.5a

12.5b

12.6a

12.6b

16 mm diameter and the glass thickness would increase to 12 mm.

The safety of the fully tempered glass is equal to similar installations in shop windows or squash courts. During installation, one of the upper panels was shattered by one of the installation crew. The lower panels, which had already been fixed, were unaffected. Progressive collapse did not follow, thus proving the designer's 'square chainline' theory as an extra safety mechanism: the dead weight of the panels below the shattered pane were taken by the

adjacent panels.

The curved wall is dealt with using a completely different system. The use of clear glass and an external structure further highlight the nature of this wall. Thirteen tubular steel external columns rise from the concrete base, brackets attached directly to these columns support each panel of glass (Figures 12.4 and 12.6). The roof glazing is simply supported on T-section glazing bars that span from the space-frame nodes (Figures 12.5 and 12.8).

12.7

12.7
X-bracket showing support
studs which stabilize the
corners of the four glass
panels

12.8
Internal view

12.8

Conclusion

An unfortunate consequence of the increasing complexity of the practice of architecture has been the move away from general practice towards specialization. A reaction to this process is the multidisciplinary practice where architects, engineers and quantity surveyors working in close proximity can share their experience to create better informed and highly integrated buildings. Encouraging as this exchange of information may seem, its impact can be lost when there is a lack of similar exchange between architect and contractor. Performance specifications which encourage a pooling of knowledge between designer and specialist subcontractor go some way to remedy this problem.

Mick Eekhout, as architect, structural engineer, product designer, manufacturer and specialist contractor has managed to integrate all these processes under the umbrella of Octatube Space Structures. Combining quality control, economy and continuous feedback he manages to advance the development of product technology and create exciting structures.

Credits

Client: Dutch Philharmonic Orchestra
Structural designer: Mick Eekhout
Acoustic engineer: Bureau Peutz
Contractors: Octatube Space Structures bv.

References

Anon, 'Glass Music Box', *AJ Focus*, February 1990, pp. 21–23.

Lewers, T., 'Music in Glass: Acoustic Revelation', *Architects' Journal*, 27 March 1991, pp. 51–53.

Metz, T, 'Cultural Exchange', *Architectural Record*, September 1990, pp. 81–87.

Eekhout, M., *Product Development in Glass Structures*, 010 Publishers, Rotterdam, 1990.

13

Hotel Saint James, Bordeaux
Architect:
Jean Nouvel

13.1

General

If art generally imitates life, then in France at least, architecture imitates restauration. The combination of chef cuisinière client with a strong interest in contemporary art and an architect whose main hobby is gastronomy has produced a reinterpretation of a standard favourite. The form and flavour of the hotel is strongly influenced by the tobacco drying sheds in the region. The new dish is not to everyone's taste (Figure 13.1): this is a deliberate ploy on the client's part in wishing not to compromise a strong design by pandering to wealthy bourgeois expectations. Although the inhabitants of Bordeaux tend to favour the traditional, music festivals or art shows at Bordeaux's famous Modern Art Museum draw many visitors who appreciate the Saint James Hotel.

Jean Marie Amat's existing four-star restaurant was sited on a ridge overlooking the Garonne valley, the extension consisting of new restaurant and eighteen bedrooms steps down the hill to make the most of this panoramic view. The rooms are accommodated in three detached rectangular pavilions (Figure 13.2) which capitalize on their isolation by making use of floor to ceiling windows to enjoy the views. Spartan interiors and elevated beds concentrate one's attention on the landscape beyond (Figure 13.6). The grounds immediately in front of the restaurant have been planted with vines which will produce the future house wine.

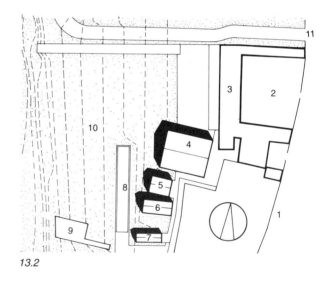

13.2

Structure

The desire not to obscure the view by bulky structural elements led to a frame made up of many closely spaced but slender columns. Steel rectangular hollow sections 100 mm by 50 mm at 3.6 m centres form the basis of the 1.8 m planning grid (Figure 13.3). The mullions of the double-glazed full-height sliding windows are, when closed, hidden behind the columns. These columns support 360 mm deep steel universal beams at first floor level, reducing to 180 mm at second floor level, partly due to the reduced loading and partly due to

13.1
General view

13.2
Site plan. 1 Place Camille
Hostiens; 2 courtyard;
3 existing building; 4 new
restaurant (building B);
5 bedrooms (building C);
6 bedrooms (building D);
7 bedrooms (building E);
8 swimming pool; 9 squash
court; 10 vineyard; 11 access
to parking

13.3
Floor plans. 1 Building E;
2 building D; 3 building D;
4 building C; 5 building C;
6 building C; 7 building B

13.4
Cross-section through
building B. 1 Restaurant;
2 bedrooms; 3 electrically
operated grilles

13.5
Detail of cruciform bracket.
(a) Front elevation. 1 Grille
frame; 2 bracket; 3 fixings. (b)
Section. 1 Grille frame;
2 bracket; 3 fixings; 4 cladding
face

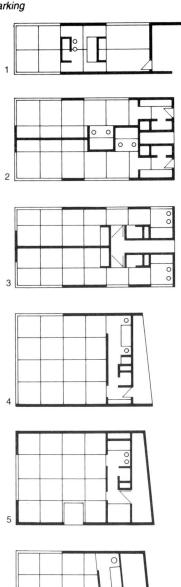

13.3

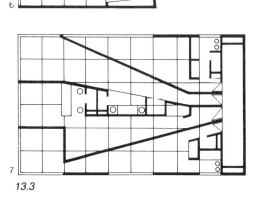

13.4

13.5a   **13.5b**

the fact that this floor is relieved by being suspended
from the roof structure (Figure 13.4).

Concrete floor slabs and service cores stiffen the
building frame. The columns are concrete filled to
help structurally and to build up the structure's fire
resistance.

Cladding

The striking rusty exterior skin is a cosmetic trellis
wrapping around the walls and roof of the pavilions.
The weather-proofing is achieved by the use of
Heronville cladding which consists of 80 mm of
rockwool insulation on either side of which are fixed
factory-painted flat metal cladding sheets.

Cruciform steel brackets project off the steel
frame and support the 1.8 m square metal grilles
approximately 300 mm off the Heronville cladding
(Figure 13.5). The grilles resemble industrial floor
grating and are made of 'rustol' steel which has
been left unprimed and unfinished to rust and add
character to these barn-like structures. This double
skin approach is justifiable in the hot humid

13.6
View from bedroom

13.6

summers of Bordeaux. The sun screen casts shade on the main bulk of the building, the air gap allows a cooling breeze to disperse the heat generated. The band of grilles in front of the bedroom windows (Figure 13.6) are hinged and elevated by hefty electrically operated jacks activated from a control panel by the bedside. This form of overcladding unifies the facades, and it is only when the grilles are elevated that the windows are defined.

Programme

The deadline for the opening of the new hotel was set by the June opening date of the 1989 Vin Expo in Bordeaux. Although the client approached Jean Nouvel in 1987 and initial studies were commenced in November of that year, access to site was gained in September 1988. Construction could not start until sufficient finances were available in February 1989. The 1900 m^2 of hotel (including car parking areas) was completed in a hectic six-month construction period which led to much on-site design and resolution of problems. In fact, the finishing touches to some of the rooms were added as guests were finishing off their dinners in the adjacent restaurant.

The estimated cost of the hotel was 5800 FF/m^2 at 1989 prices.

Credits

Client: J. M. Amat
Landscape architect: Yves Brunier

References

De Giorgi, M., Boissière, O, 'Ampliaments Hôtel Saint James, Bouliac-Bordeaux', *Domus*, April 1990 No.715, pp. 29–37.

McGuire, P., 'Nouvel Cuisine', *Architectural Review*, August 1990, pp. 44–48.

Ivry, B., Nouvel, J., 'Nouvel Hotel', *Architectural Record*, September 1990, pp. 98–102.

Colin, C., 'Emballé c'est Rouillé', *Le Moniteur Architecture*, November 1989, No. 6, pp. 32–36.

14

Imagination, London
Architects:
Herron Associates

14.1

14.1
General view of atrium

14.2
Section. 1 Entrance; 2 atrium;
3 rear block; 4 gallery

14.3
Typical floor plan. 1 Atrium;
2 front block; 3 rear block

14.4
Roof plan

General

In line with his long held views expressed in the once influential *Archigram* magazine, and appropriately close to the Architectural Association where he has taught for the last 23 years, Ron Herron has 'tuned up' an uninspiring Edwardian school to provide the design and communications consultants, Imagination Ltd, with a dramatic new office environment in Bloomsbury (Figure 14.1).

A previously narrow, gloomy lightwell separates a curving six-storey block of office accommodation on Store Street from a five-storey block to the rear. Following its transformation into a light bright atrium, with lightweight bridges leaping askew across it, this space has now become the focus of the extensive refurbishment (Figures 14.2–14.4).

Canopies

Although almost invisible externally the most important elements of the new work are the translucent white fabric canopies that span across the 7 m wide atrium and the rooftop gallery of the south block. The architects had originally considered glazed roofs over these spaces but the awkward geometry would have led to a cumbersome structure. The advantage of a tensioned fabric canopy is that it adapts more easily to unorthodox geometries.

Steel frames span across the atrium and gallery to form the canopy support structure (Figure 14.5). Glazed screen assemblies fixed to the upright verendeel trusses define the limits of the gallery space. Tapered sloping verendeel trusses complete the structural frames. Structural steel members have been given a powder-coated paint finish. Suspended in between the trusses are stainless-steel 'push-up' struts with umbrella heads (Figure 14.6). The spokes of the umbrella spread the forces across the surface of the fabric. The connection between hub and strut is a form of ball and socket joint that rocks, allowing the fabric to find its own position under tension. As the support rods to these 'push-ups' are tensioned they rise and stretch the fabric. The fabric should be restressed periodically.

The 590 m² membrane is a PVC coated scrim of 820g/m² weight. It is lacquer coated to reduce ultraviolet deterioration and has a translucency of

14.2

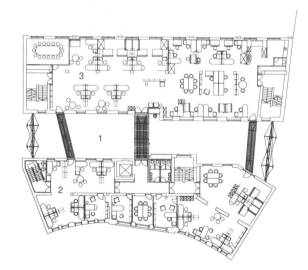

14.3

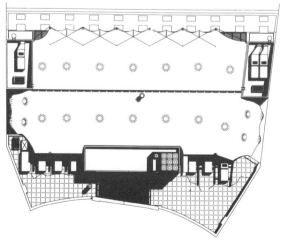

14.4

14.5
Cut-away isometric of
canopies. 1 Atrium; 2 rooftop
gallery

14.6
Compression umbrella.
157.2 mm diameter 4.9 mm
thick steel strut; 2 retaining
springs; 3 12 no. 10 mm thick
alloy spokes; 4 pultrusion
capping

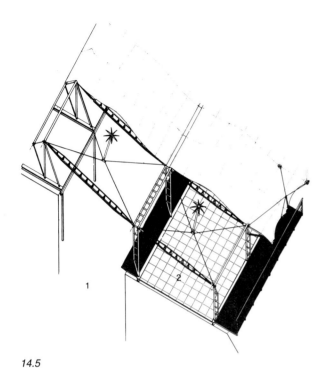

14.5

about 15%. The fabric also has a fifteen year
guarantee. The atrium canopy is independent of the
gallery canopy and can be replaced separately.

Both canopies together took just two days to erect.
Each canopy is made up of panels cut from
computer generated templates. A specially
fabricated white fibreglass gutter pipe runs between
the two sections of canopy (Figure 14.7). Run off
water at the perimeter drains into existing gutters.

The fabric is clamped at its perimeter (Figure
14.8). Long stainless steel tensioning bolts screw
into 25 mm diameter aluminium bars that are
threaded through pockets along the perimeter of the
fabric. These bars spread tension evenly along the
fabric. Where at its edges the fabric runs over
perimeter steelwork they are separated by 0.25 mm
thick PTFE film pads that reduce friction and assist
the tensioning up of the fabric. The lightwell canopy
returns vertically downwards at the ends to the
notional eaves level.

Services

The office and atrium spaces are naturally
ventilated. Obvious but not obtrusive ventilation
shafts extract air from the atrium and adjacent
offices. Raised floors provide a means of coping
with cableways. There are generally no suspended
ceilings. Money has been wisely spent and

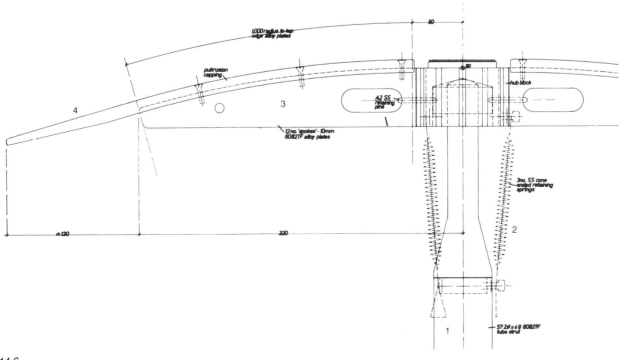

14.6

14.7
Detail of canopy gutter.
1 150 mm diameter white
fibreglass gutter-pipe; 2 3 mm
PVC bellows boot; 3 PVC
retaining collar; 4 stainless
steel clamping collar;
5 double skin pressed metal
gutter with 12 mm foam
insulation; 6 perforated
stainless-steel gutter cover;
7 bar nut hooked into
receptacle; 8 stainless steel
tensioning screw; 9 seal flap;

10 89 mm diameter x 4 mm
circular hollow section,
powder-coated white;
11 34 mm diameter x 3.2 mm
circular hollow section;
12 12 mm diameter, 160 mm
long stainless steel hangers
at 2 m centres

14.8
Detail of gallery eaves.
1 Glazed screen assembly;
2 aluminium closing pressing;
3 12 mm diameter stainless
steel bars; 4 stainless steel
swivel captive mounting pins;
5 liner membrane; 6 30 x
0.25 mm PTFE film; 7 25 mm
diameter aluminium bar in
fabric pocket edge; 8 main
roof membrane; 9 strut

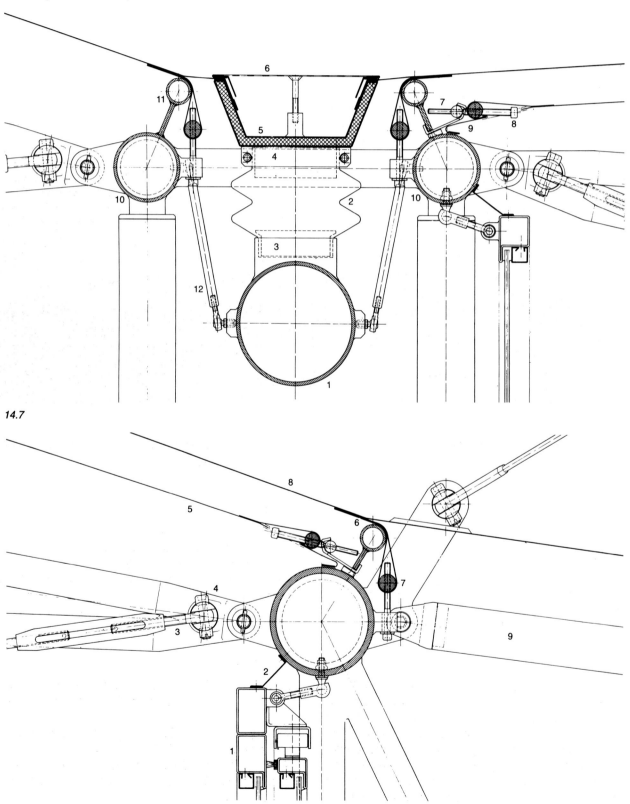

14.7

14.8

14.9

concentrated where it is most appropriate, in the public spaces.

Spotlights in the atrium pick out salient architectural elements.

Costs

Work started on site in August 1988 and the client moved into Staffordshire House at Midnight on 14 August 1989. The total cost of the refurbishment was £4.5 million and added approximately 600 m² of floor space to the building.

Conclusion

The canopies featured in this refurbishment deserve comparison with the vault used at the Hamburg Museum of Local History. Both of these structures apply different technological solutions to enclose totally diverse spaces (Figure 14.9). Each response seems thoroughly appropriate to its location. The sensitive use of appropriate technology should convince the most ardent sceptics that a

technology-led architecture does not necessarily result in sterility.

Credits

Client: Imagination Ltd
Structural engineer: Buro Happold
Quantity surveyor: Boyden & Co
Mechanical and electrical consultants: Buro Happold
Main contractor: R. M. Douglas Construction

References

Allford, D., 'Maturity and Innocence in Herron's Imagination', *Architecture Today* No. 2, October 1989, pp. 36–43.

Pawley, M., 'Store Street Snowline', *Architectural Review*, January 1990, pp. 40-46.

Anon., 'Working Details, Canopy Structure', *The Architects' Journal*, 11 April 1990, Vol. 191, No. 15, pp. 56-59.

15

Interflora Pavilion, Genoa
Architects:
Alessandro Savioli and Valeria Lelli

15.1

General

In April 1991 the sixth International Flower Exhibition was held in Genoa. This major international event, held quinquennially, attracts many thousands of visitors and brings both prestige and revenue to the host city. Interflora, as befits an organization with international stature was allocated a prime site immediately adjacent to the main entrance, in the shadow of Pier Luigi Nervi's prominent Exhibition Building.

The client's brief required a visitors' meeting place which would provide shelter from the elements under a clearly identifiable structure which would be a relaxing and joyful experience. The temporary nature of the exhibition meant that the designers were allowed only a very limited budget to satisfy the brief.

The designers addressed the problem by creating a lightweight remountable pavilion formed by a double row of inclined steel posts supporting a vault

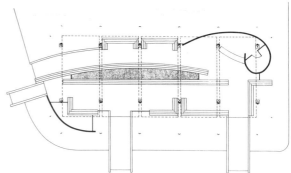

15.2

of teflon-coated fabric sheets stretched over laminated timber arches (Figures 15.1 and 15.9).

A free form layout of benches are arranged around a large central flower bed generating a fluid circulation pattern for the visitors and contrasts with the formal geometry of the structure (Figure 15.2). A limited range of materials and a subtle palette of colours are used to enhance the fine detailing.

15.1
General view

15.2
Plan

15.3
Detail of steel post.
1 Reinforcing mesh; 2 200 mm
thick concrete platform;
3 steel base-plate; 4 140 mm
diameter steel post; 5 70 mm
diameter horizontal bar
supporting laminated timber
arch; 6 saddle joint; 7 33 mm
diameter steel strut;
8 laminated pine arch;
9 Teflon coated fabric;
10 restraining cables;
11 Interflora logo; 12 tension
cable end fixing

15.4
Timber arch and saddle
connector

15.5
Exploded isometric of saddle
connector. 1 70 mm diameter
circular hollow section;
2 20 mm external diameter
sleeve welded to 7 mm
upright plate; 3 8 mm thick
U-shaped saddle bracket;
4 160 mm long M10 bolt; 5 M8
self-tapping screws; 6 250 mm
× 50 mm laminated pine arch

15.4

15.3

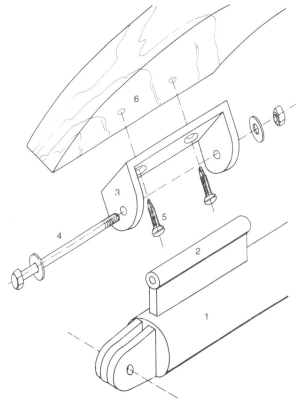

15.5

197

15.6
First goalpost being erected

15.7
First vault being installed

15.8
Structure completed

15.6

15.7

15.8

Structure

A 20 m × 10 m, 200 mm thick concrete base provides a level surface and anchor points for posts and cables. Each 140 mm diameter post is braced at its head by three steel cables (Figure 15.3). The six pairs of inclined steel posts are spaced at 3.5 m intervals. A 70 mm horizontal steel member connects adjacent posts and supports one end of a section of roof vault (Figures 15.4 and 15.5). A rotating saddle joint connects the vault to the structure. This type of joint, with its inherent self-adjustment, ensures that the angle of bearing need not be determined with any great precision; the process of erection will create the optimum bearing. This is doubly appropriate since the extent of overhang, and therefore the angle of inclination, is different on each elevation. The vault is made up of a series of arched laminated pine beams, tied by steel cables to prevent the arc from flattening out.

Erection

Once the simple concrete base had been poured and allowed to cure for a couple of days, the erection of the steel could commence. Pairs of steel posts were pinned at thier bases, connected together by the horizontal steel members, lifted into place (Figure 15.6), and located by means of a simple timber template that set out their final angle of inclination, then fastened in place by means of three anchor cables. Fine tuning of the position of the post was achieved by means of adjusting the anchor cables. Once three sets of goalposts had been erected down each side of the pavilion the two intermediate horizontal members were added (Figure 15.7), completing the structure on that side of the pavilion. Each bay of the vault was then assembled on the ground, covered with the teflon coated fabric, and lifted into place to sit on the saddle bearings (Figure 15.8).

15.9
Computer generated image of
pavilion

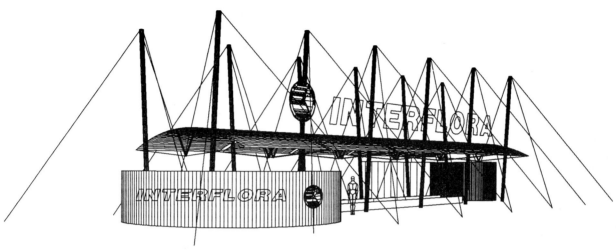

15.9

Rapid erection of the pavilion structure over a two day period was facilitated by an enthusiastic team. The small contractor responsible for all aspects of the pavilion derived much pride and satisfaction in both the production and the erection of the beautifully crafted building. The lifting gear was quite conveniently loaned from the adjacent yacht marina.

Costs

The total cost of the pavilion was approximately £42 500 since the overall surface area of the plot was 500 m², this gives a square metre cost of £85. The pavilion provides a covered area of 250 m².

Credits

Client: Interflora
Main contractor and timber construction: Giovanni Giorgi
Steelwork subcontractor: Angelo Zucchelli
Lighting: Sgarbi Impianti

References

Anon., *l'Arca*, October 1991, p. 103.

16

Kindergarten, Lausanne
Architect: Rodolphe Luscher

16.1

General

Rodolphe Luscher has been described as attempting to create a new architectural language using contemporary technical means (Figure 16.1). He is interested in classical architecture, although stressing that this in no way involves the search for classical origins. Through his architecture he hopes to have a positive influence on the changing way of life for the users.

In this kindergarten in the Parc de Valency, Lausanne, Luscher and his collaborators, Sandra Rouvinez, Pascal Schmidt and Rudolf Zoss have achieved all these objectives.

16.2

Structure

Built in 1988 as a result of a competition held in 1983 the building incorporates the unusual combination of lightweight steel-framed pavilions set in between *in situ* concrete cores (Figure16.2). It is this steel frame which forms the major spaces of this building (Figure16.3).

Set out on a planning grid of 2.7 m the school is divided into four pavilions, each separated by a one-bay wide concrete core (Figures16.4 and 16.5). Each core is dedicated to services and vertical circulation. The steel structure of the three-bay pavilion consists of 121 mm diameter circular hollow section columns with lattice trusses spanning parallel to the cores (Figure16.6). The concrete floor slab spans the 2.7 m between trusses and braces the structure in a horizontal plane. The concrete cores form the main external elements as they

16.3

16.1
General view from the east

16.2
In situ *concrete cores*

16.3
Hall, doubles up as dining
and assembly space with
stair core behind

16.4
East–west section

16.5
Ground floor plan. 1 Main
entrance; 2 entrance hall;
3 kitchen; 4 laundry; 5 nursery;
6 dining/assembly space;
7 lavatories; 8 group rooms;
9 external sandpit; 10 staff
room; 12 stair cores;
13 terrace

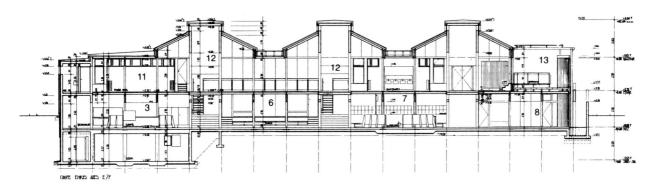

16.4

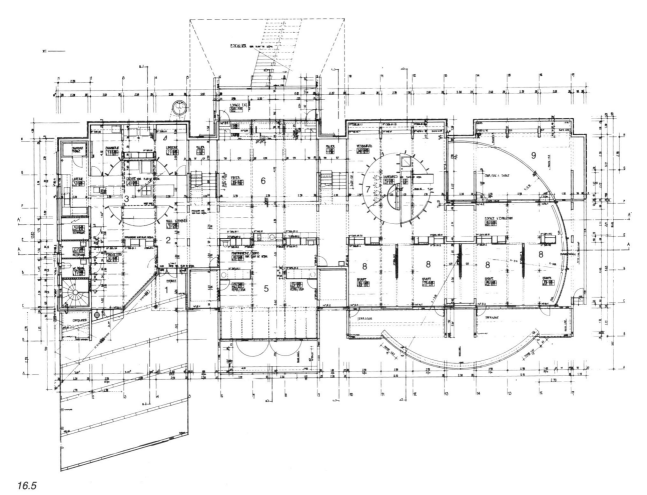

16.5

project beyond the adjacent pavilions. The roof
slope to the ridge at the cores reverses the
anticipated dominance of the pavilion over the core.
It is this device which gives the impression that there
are in fact only three pavilions.

In the same way that Aldo Van Eyck developed a
language of two-way spanning prefabricated
systems at the Amsterdam Orphanage (1958),
Luscher here makes extensive use of a series of
prefabricated components. The kit of components is

16.6
*Cut-away axonometric
showing structural principle*

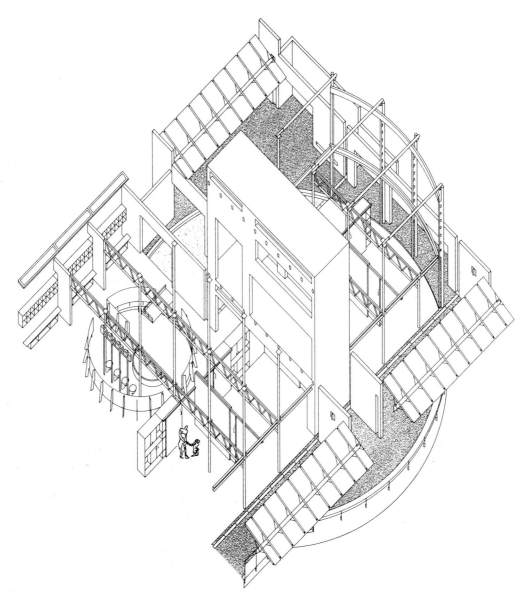

16.6

accentuated by the use of vivid primary colours, and further contrasted by the juxtaposition of partitions and ducts in an unfinished state. The exposed structure and services are used to explain the building, define the various elements, and assist the occupants, consisting of up to 80 children plus teachers and staff, to be more inquisitive about their surroundings.

The objective of providing a sense of exploration and personal development has also influenced the plan form and organization. By positioning the kitchens next to the main entrance and screening the lavatories without the use of closed doors, the younger children arrive at the school and by observing others, the 2- and 3-year-olds discover how to use the cloakrooms and lavatories. As Luscher himself reports, 'the way one group encounters the next reinforces the desire to grow up to join the privileged school-age children on the upper floor and share the secret ladder to the attic galleries on the roof'.

The current forms which relate to the plan grid increase this complex play between open spaces and protective niches to further encourage exploration.

16.7
Corner detail of cladding.
1 120 mm diameter steel
column; 2 15 mm sterling
board; 3 0.2 mm vapour
barrier; 4 60 mm rockwool
insulation; 5 80 × 40 mm
main timber stud; 6 Sisalcraft
wind barrier; 7 40 mm
rockwool insulation;
8 ventilation gap; 9 48 ×
24 mm vertical and horizontal
batten framework; 10 support
panelling; 11 0.7 mm zinc-
titane membrane;
12 50/25 mm stainless-steel
cladding; 13 drainage
channel; 14 double-glazed
timber framed window

Cladding

Externally the park elevation consists of the main light steel framed pavilions disappearing in favour of 'houses' growing around the concrete towers. The stainless steel cladding wraps around the building forming an integral whole (Figure 16.7), at the same time allowing separately articulated volumes to break down the scale. Perhaps for the same reason the giant steps leading to the main entrance form an external play area from the park. Positioned on an *in situ* concrete base the building appears to grow from the sloping ground. On the back elevation the articulation is achieved by the circular structure and drum-like units containing the staffroom and toilets.

It is this interesting debate between heavy and light forms of construction which make Luscher's work interesting. Whilst demonstrating a commitment to detailing and construction he uses this as a means towards an improved environment and intriguing spatial form 'drawn full of hope'.

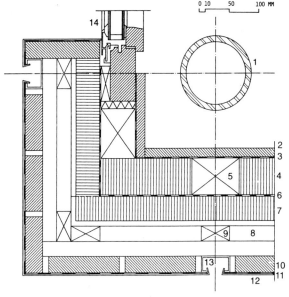

16.7

Conclusion

An independent sociological survey of the kindergarten concluded that the teachers, moving from a more conventional building with their established working routines, found the openness of the planning difficult to cope with and use to advantage. They also noted that the building was successful in stimulating the children, the organization of spaces and the expressed technology acting as an effective teaching tool.

Credits

Client: City of Lausanne
Structural engineer: W. Birchmeier
Mechanical engineer: R. Fazan
Electrical engineer: Betelec

References

Brookes A.J., Stacey, M., 'Rudolphe Luscher in La Faye', *Architectural Review*, March 1989, pp. 58–63.

Blundell Jones, P., 'Kindergarten Contrasts', *Architectural Review*, September 1991, pp. 48–53.

Anon, *Portraits D'Architecture Vaudoise 1985–1988*, Editions Payot Lausanne, 1989.

Anon, *Detail*, June 1991.

Anon, 'Lausanne', *Architecture Today*, November 1990, p. 16.

Museum of Local History, Hamburg
Architects:
Von Gerkan, Marg and Partner

17.1

17.1
View along vault

17.2
Section through courtyard

17.3
Plan of museum

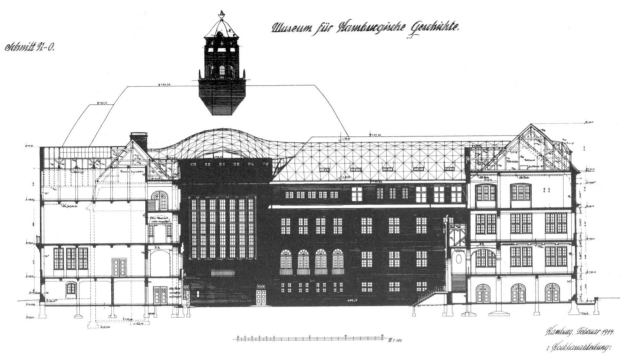

Museum für Hamburgische Geschichte.

Schnitt N-O.

Hamburg, Februar 1914.

17.2

General

The Hamburg Museum of Local History, designed by Fritz Schumacher in 1913 is a large four-storey building in the North German vernacular tradition. It is organized around an L-shaped courtyard previously open to the skies. Although Schumacher did consider providing a glass roof over the courtyard, this was not provided until 1988 for the celebrations of the eighth centenary of the founding of the Port of Hamburg. The new lightweight glazed skin provides shelter for exhibits and functions that take place in this space (Figures 17.1 and 17.2).

Glazed canopy

This innovative structure satisfied the three basic requirements that the historic fabric should not be substantially altered, that the roof should be non-directional, and that the enveloping structure should not dominate the courtyard. By a happy coincidence the consulting engineer, Jürgen Schlaich had been researching a glass and steel shell structure with the roofing contractor Helmut Fischer when contacted

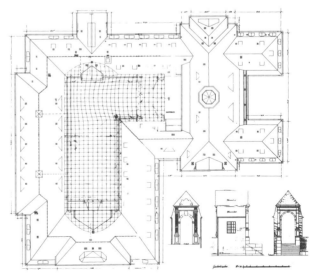

17.3

by the architect Volkwin Marg. The structure is made up of a web of steel glazing bars which when bolted together and tensioned up lock to form a structurally stable shell. The two vaults (13 m and 17 m wide) intersect to form a shallow dome (Figures 17.3 and 17.4).

17.4
Isometric of vault. 1 Vaults, tension cables not shown for clarity; 2 dome at crossing; 3 tension cables; 4 fan bracing; 5 anchor points

17.5
Fan of tension rods

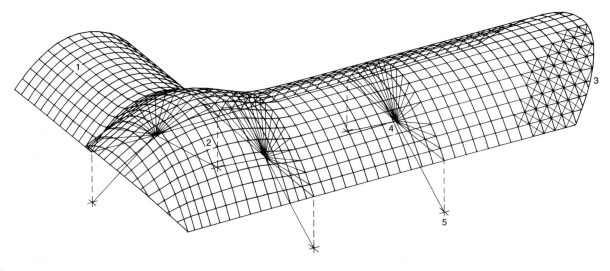

17.4

Computer analysis of the structure determined the optimum geometry of the vault and the consequent lengths of all the glazing bars to ensure that loads are uniformly distributed throughout the shell. Scaffolding was erected to provide temporary support for the glazing bars. Each 60 mm wide by 40 mm deep glazing bar is approximately 1.7 m long and forms one side of each rectangular pane.

At their intersection point the glazing bars are bolted together (Figure 17.6), this bolt also picks up three circular steel plates which clamp the two sets of paired steel tension cables which run diagonally across each panel. It is these cables, which when tensioned provide the lateral bracing that gives the shell its stability. A deep, extruded neoprene gasket provides the seating for the glass panes. The glass used is laminated from a top layer of 6 mm silver grey glass, a central plastic membrane and a lower layer of 6 mm float glass. A 140 mm diameter circular steel fixing plate bolted to the intersection provides a sufficiently large pressure plate to restrain the four corners of the adjacent panes.

Between the glazing bars and the neoprene gasket is a T-shaped aluminium spacer which also protects two heating cables that run along the glazing bars. These cables are installed to melt any snow lying on the roof which may produce excessive snow loading.

17.5

The tension cables are loosely held by the circular plates until erection is completed, when the central node bolts are tightened in a predetermined sequence to lock the shell into shape.

The perimeter of the glass shell is supported on a continuous rigid universal beam (Figure 17.1) which

17.6.
Exploded isometric of glazing intersection. 1 Dome-head nut; 2 140 mm diameter steel plate; 3 12 mm laminated glass; 4 neoprene gasket; 5 steel spacer; 6 M12 threaded central shaft; 7 M12 bolts; 8 40 × 60 mm steel glazing bars; 9 8 × 90 mm diameter steel plate; 10 10 × 90 mm diameter steel plate; 11 steel cables; 12 12 × *90 mm diameter steel plate; 13 heating cables*

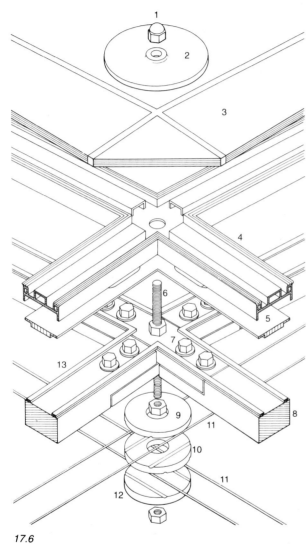

17.6

the dome where the surface follows a double curve. Here, the engineers introduced fans of steel tension rods to stabilize the structure (Figures 17.1 and 17.5). The fixing of these rods to the vault was easily achieved, more problematic was the means of fixing the two anchor cables to the existing structure.

Costs

The plan area of the courtyard is approximately 900 m², the total area of glass roof is approximately 1000 m². A total cost of DM 3.45 million gives an approximate square metre cost of £1200.

The total weight of the basic structure is approximately 50 tonnes. Approximately 2.4 km of glazing bars and 6 km of steel cable were used in the shell construction.

The design and planning period was three months, followed by a construction period of a further three months.

Credits

Client: Verein der Freunde des Museums fur Hamburgische Geschichte e.V.
Structural engineer: Buro Prof Schlaich Bergermann and Partner
Roofing contractor: Helmut Fischer GmbH

References

Baus, U., 'An goldener Ketten. . .', *Deutsche Bauzeiting*, 7 July 1990, pp. 32–39.
Magnano Lampugnani, V., 'Copertura vetrata della corte del Museo di Storia della Citta, Amburgo', *Domus*, September 1990, No. 719, pp. 38–43.
Zimmerman A., 'Vague de Verre', *Techniques + Architecture*, September 1990, No. 391, pp. 122–124.
Anon, 'Over the Top', *AJ Focus*, April 1991, pp. 15–19.

is supported at intervals off brackets that are fixed back to the concrete floor of the museum attic. Lead flashings seal the penetration points through the pantiled roof. The voids between universal beam and roof provide natural ventilation.

Once erected it was found that there was excessive movement in the vault at the perimeter of

18.5

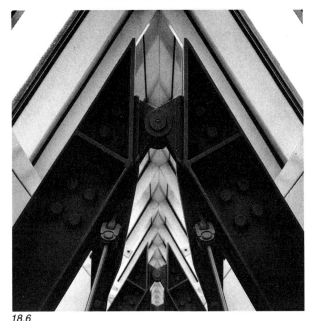

18.6

18.7

18.8

18.5
Library

18.6
Apex pin connection

18.7
Base pin connection

18.8
Prefabricated turret
installation

Costs

The Schloss Guttesaue project was completed in 1989 at a total cost of DM 44.9 million, giving a square metre cost of DM 15 478.

Conclusion

Mario Botta once said that we ought to regard the past as 'a friend'. At Schloss Gottesaue Barbara Jakubeit has found a worthy ally to fight the battle against the literal conservationists who would rather preserve historic buildings at all costs. In as much as this intervention takes hints from the original building existing on the site, it is comparable to Michael Hopkins' refurbishment of Bracken House. Among the large number of buildings remodelled or reconstructed phoenix-like from the neglected ruins of once great buildings are a fair sprinkling of museums. With Carlo Scarpa's subtle incisions at the Castel Grande in Verona at one end of the spectrum and the bold bludgeoning of Hans Döllgast at the Alte Pinakothek in Munich at the other, the two extremes are well defined. The middle ground is taken up by such competent examples as Schloss Gottesaue.

Credits

Design and project Leader: Barbara Jakubeit
Design team: Horst Stüven, Helmut Knecht, Godehard Sicheneder
Client: Land Baden-Württemberg
Structural engineer: Ingenieurgruppe Bauen, Karlsruhe

References

Bloomfield, R., 'Renaissance', *Architecture Today*, September 1990, No. 11, pp. 28–35.

Peters, P., 'Schloss Gottesaue in Karlsruhe', *Baumeister*, June 1990, pp. 30–39.

Rumpf, P., 'Schlossmusik', *Bauwelt*, 11 May 1990, pp. 908–917.

Stock, W., 'Schloss Gottesaue', *Stahl und Form*, 26 October 1990, pp. 1–16.

Baus, U., 'Neuer Inhalt', *Deutsche Bauzeitung*, 7 July 1990, pp. 40–45.

Anon, 'Wiederaufbau von Schloss Gottesaue', *Jahrbuch für Architektur*, Deutsches Architekturmuseum, Frankfurt, September 1991, pp. 142–155.

19

One-family House, Lyons
Architects:
Jourda et Perraudin

19.1

General

This self-design, self-build 140 m² one-family house completed in 1989 is to be found peeping over the boundary wall which surrounds the grounds of a detached villa in the Lyons suburb of Vaise. The villa, now home to the 20-strong office of Jourda et Perraudin is located towards one corner of an irregularly shaped site (Figure 19.2). The new house, dividing the site into two roughly equal halves, turns its back on to the shared public approach to the office. The fully glazed south facing elevation leads by stages out to the garden. Full height glazed doors slide away to allow free access onto a veranda which is protected and shaded by the oversailing polyester fabric roof canopy (Figure 19.1).

Structure

The concept of economic self-build was a strong design generator for this building. Simple rectangular bolt-together 7 m span free standing portal frames are bolted down to pad foundations at 3 m spacings (Figure 19.4). Lateral bracing is

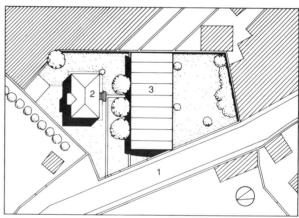

19.2

provided at high level by a complex branching lightweight structure over which is stretched a waterproof fabric to form an independent elevated roof canopy.

Once again the designers concept of substantial base and ethereal canopy is developed on this project (see also School of Architecture, Lyons, Case Study 23). The single storey accommodation is organized along the eight bays into a 5 m wide

19.1
View of garden elevation

19.2
Site plan. 1 Rue Docteur
Horand; 2 office; 3 house

19.3
Plan. 1 Entrance; 2 living
space; 3 kitchen; 4 bedroom;
5 bathroom; 6 utility room;
7 WC; 8 verandah; 9 garden

19.4
Isometric view. 1 Concrete
pad foundations; 2 galvanized
steel portal frames;
3 galvanized steel canopy
structure; 4 steel joists; 5 ply
floor boarding

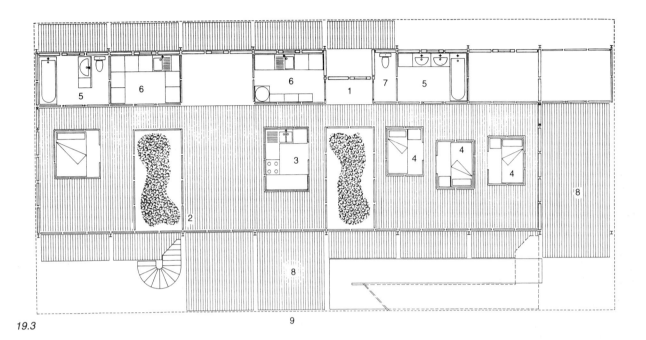

19.3

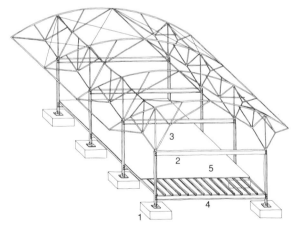

19.4

open plan zone on the garden side (Figure 19.3), with a 2 m wide strip of servant spaces in which bathrooms, utility rooms and toilets are located. The latter form an acoustic/privacy barrier along the north, public elevation of the site. Although built as a single-storey building, the structure has been designed to allow for limited future expansion at first floor level, beneath the canopy should the growing Jourda and Perraudin family require additional space.

The 120 ×120 mm galvanized steel I sections of the main frames and the smaller members of the roof were all erected by the two architects in a week. Each component is simply bolted to the next member. Additional help was draughted in for the installation of the tensile roof covering. In fact the whole building was commenced and made habitable over the span of a 2 month summer vacation.

Cladding

The entire south elevation is made of proprietary sliding glazed doors that fit neatly into each 3 m bay. The mass-produced full height sliding doors are fixed back to timber battens or pressed metal channels that run along the inside of the steel portal frames (Figures 19.5 and 19.6). All the other walls, both internally and externally as well as the floor, ceiling and roof are a crude sandwich construction of insulation between plywood sheets screwed directly to the metal frames (Figure 19.7).

Costs

The cost of building has worked out at 4000FF/m².

19.5
*Vertical section through
sliding doors. 1 Sliding doors;
2 portal frame; 3 canopy
structure base; 4 160 ×
80 mm steel channel; 5 75 ×
75 mm steel angle; 6 50 ×
50 mm timber batten; 7 10 mm
plywood sheeting; 8 5 mm
plywood sheeting; 9 25 mm
composite board; 10 25 mm
timber boarding; 11 100 ×
50 mm steel channel*

19.6
*Horizontal section through
sliding doors. 1 120 ×
120 mm steel column;
2 sliding doors; 3 pressed
metal channel; 4 plywood
skim; 5 silicone seal;
6 plywood wall surface*

19.7
Internal view

19.7

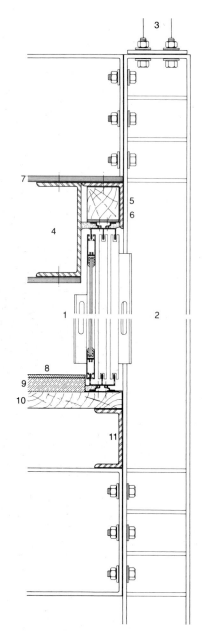

19.5

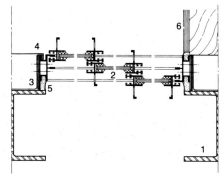

19.6

Credits

Structural engineers: Agibat/Mti Cabinet Martin

References

Pousse, J.F, 'Maison a Vaise'. *Technique et Architecture*, March 1988, No. 376, pp. 82-84.

Pousse, J.F, 'La Dynamique de L ephemere', *Technique et Archiecture*, June/July 1990, No. 390 pp. 58-63.

Carter, B 'Young Lyons: Jourda and Perradin', *Architecture Today*, January 1990, No. 4, pp. 26-32.

Bisi, L., 'Bio-Camouflage Architecture at Vaise', *L'Arca*, June 1991, No. 50, pp. 32-37.

Reina Sofia Museum of Modern Art, Madrid

Architects:
Ian Ritchie Architects in association
with Iñiguez & Vazquez

20.1

23

School of Architecture, Lyons
Architects: Jourda et Perraudin

23.1

General

The new Lyons architecture school, completed in 1989, (Figure 23.1) is situated on the edge of the university campus in the suburb of Vaulx-en-Velin adjacent to the school of engineering. The brief required teaching and studio space, together with the associated administrative staff accommodation for up to 500 students. Some facilities, such as large auditoria, are shared with the neighbouring school of engineering.

The brief is resolved around an efficient Beaux Arts formality. The anthropomorphic building footprint is composed of a main body of teaching accommodation on two levels, split along its entire length by a top-lit central circulation spine, the south end of which culminates in a four storey, semicircular administration block which serves as the literal and metaphorical head of the composition (Figures 23.2 and 23.3).

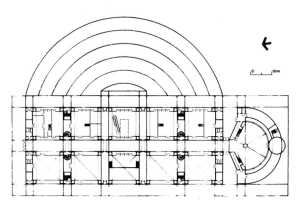

23.2

Working methods

By eschewing the traditional French system of employing a bureau d'études to carry out the detailed design and furthermore by making use of in-house engineering skills (Giles Perraudin is qualified as both architect and engineer), the design

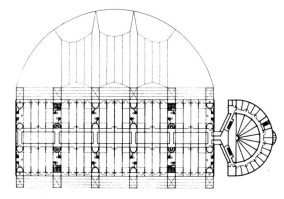

23.3

23.1
General view

23.2
Ground floor plan

23.3
First floor plan

23.4
Working drawing of Y-bracket

23.5
Working drawing of bracket assembly

23.6
Designers sketch of beam to column detail showing down pipes

23.7
Section. 1 Lecture room; 2 services zone; 3 studio; 4 central internal street

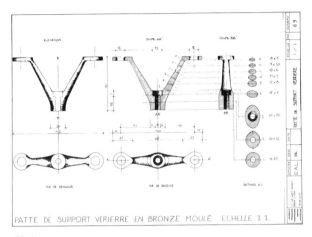

23.4

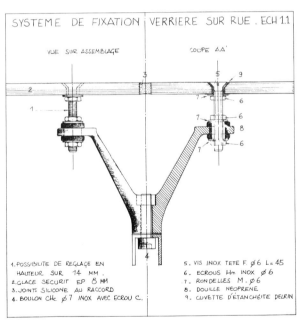

23.5

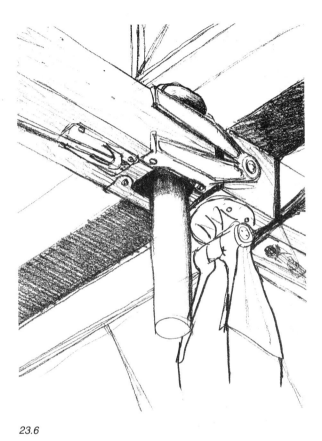

23.6

team were able to create a homologous building. This concern for detail is amply demonstrated by the exquisitely draughted three-dimensional sketches and working drawings (Figures 23.4–23.6) more reminiscent of the technical drawings executed by engineers of a bygone age. The obsession with clarity of expression pervades the drawings and manifests itself in the final form of the junctions within this building.

Structure

The formal teaching areas requiring visual and acoustic isolation are accommodated in the massive load bearing concrete podium (Figure 23.7). Here the structure is organized by a tartan grid that allows services distribution along the secondary bays to the cellular teaching areas and the open plan studios above.

The combination of precast and *in situ* concrete elements of the base demonstrate the fundamental approach to the elemental interfaces between

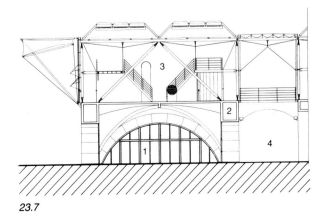

23.7

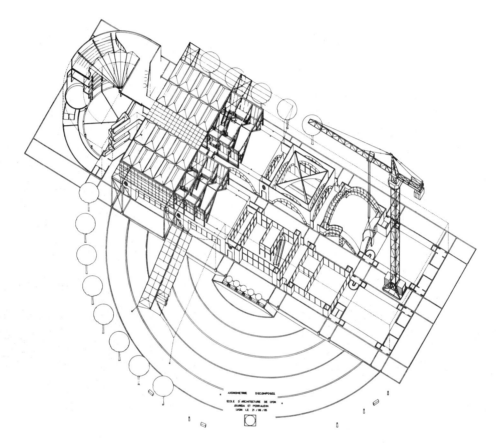

23.8

components and materials. The designers have chosen to concentrate attention and refinement on the 'edges' where precision is required and have 'filled in' the areas between. Hence the precast concrete frame of the administration block and the *in situ* infill panels (Figure 23.8). Similarly in the teaching block the more visible edges of the arches, vaults and stair towers are precast concrete which allows for a far greater measure of quality control than the *in situ* components.

The vaulted lecture rooms provide excellent acoustics. The historical association of the vault crossing is further reinforced by the recessed light fittings reminiscent of the twinkling golden stars stencilled onto the azure celestial vaults of many continental gothic cathedrals.

The flexible studio area is enclosed by a double-height lightweight timber framed structure. Here again castings are used to articulate the joints between unfinished laminated Northern pine columns and beams (Figure 23.9). The roof is made up of a series of prefabricated timber vaults with rooflights incorporated at each apex.

Glazing

The glazed roofs to the internal street and the atrium in the administration block are applications of countersunk fitting glazing (for a detailed account of Planar glazing see Stacey M., 'Maximum Vision', *AJ Focus*, October 1988, pp. 14–15). Delicate metal trusses serve as purlins spanning across timber or concrete beams. To these are fixed Y-shaped cast bronze brackets onto which the glass sheets are bolted (Figures 23.5 and 23.10). The glass sheets are inclined at a 1% slope and drain to gutters along the street edge. Vertical alignment of the glass is achieved by the threaded countersunk bolt that anchors the glass to the support bracket. Tolerance in the dimensions of the glass sheets is taken up by the silicone joint which consequently varies between adjacent panes. The designers suggest that this being a school of architecture, one's attitude towards tolerances could be relaxed, where such details serve to illustrate a point far better than perfection which normally goes unnoticed.

The second glazed feature is the cladding to the

23.9
Column base

23.10
Roof glazing bracket

24.1

General

This group
the depths
seem an u
featured in
objectives
educationa
achieved b

The UK
consumptic
75% by
designer J
local fores
industries
reduced.

Accordir
2500 trees
250 matur
The thinn
roundwoo
thinnings
board an
dispersed
effective

23.9

23.10

long elevations of the studio areas. The architects had originally intended to work on this element with Jean Prouvé but were finally unable. Instead they consulted Martin Francis, who had been instrumental in the development of the glazed envelope of Foster Associates' Willis Faber Dumas office (see Brookes, A.J., *Cladding of Buildings*, Longman, 1983). The transparent glazed walls were achieved to a large extent by the omission of a pressure plate system substituted by a combination of framed structural silicone glazing, for fixed panels and countersunk fittings on the opening panes (Figures 23.11 and 23.12) The omission of a frame to the latter avoided the common problem of doubling up of solid elements which normally occurs with window frames, thus creating a visually lighter assembly. An earlier and cruder version of this detail can be seen at South Poplar Health Centre (see

Brookes, A.J., *Concepts in Cladding*, Construction Press, 1985, pp. 127-130).

At Lyons an ingenious arangement of gas lifts and tension wires allows a bay of four unframed glass panes to be winched open or shut against perimeter gaskets (Figure 23.13).

Conclusion

Jourda and Perraudin's preference for solid-based buildings with lightweight roofs is developed here and should be compared with their own house (Case Study 19). The vocabulary of materials used in this building is unusually diverse and the way in which they are combined and contrasted merits close scrutiny. One would hope that this love for detail will rub off on the students working and looking for inspiration in this building.

23.11
Section
16mm t
fixed-pa
frame; 2
aluminiu
aluminiu
toughen
pane; 5
6 gasket
8 anchor

1

4

5

23.11

1

5

6

23.12

Credi

Client
et des
Cons
Glazi
Proje
Martir
Burea

Refer

Lucar
Lyc
De
Anon
Co
pp

24.6
Roof frame of staff house

24.7
Eaves details. 1 Roof membrane with gravel chips and sprayed with a spore-laden growing medium; 2 60–90 mm spruce thinning on softwood packing; 3 fascia board; 4 membrane welded to flashing; 5 perimeter beam; 6 80 mm Rockwool insulation; 7 vapour barrier; 8 30 mm reinforced rockwool insulation; 9 canvas

One of the major advantages of timber over other building materials was frequently demonstrated during erection: the facility with which members could be eased and trimmed to ensure a neat fit.

Roof and cladding

Steel cables clamped to steel plates at the apex of each A-frame form a curved ridge (Figure 24.5c and 24.6). Rafters are clipped to the ridge, cabled and bolted to the eaves timbers. Sarking boards at 600 mm centres are nailed to the rafters. Insulation built up from 30 mm reinforced rock-fibre quilt on canvas, vapour barrier, and a further 80 mm rock-fibre slab is topped by a single layer roof membrane with holding down fixings to prevent uplift. (Figure 24.7) A polyester membrane was chosen for its ability to expand without deforming and is also covered with a thin layer of stone chippings to protect it against ultraviolet radiation.

The ends of the buildings are clad in 100 mm wide sawn boards. Double glazed window units and full-height joinery units are used on the long sides.

Credits

Client: The School of Woodland Industry
Structural engineer: Buro Happold
Quantity surveyor: Bernard Williams and Associates
Carpentry contractor: Dowding & Udall

References

Burton, R., Moorwood, W., Wilder, A., 'Fruits of the Forest', *Building Design Supplement*, June 1990, pp. 12–13.
Davey, P., 'Forestry Commission', *Architectural Review*, September 1990, pp. 44–48.
Anon., 'Innovation in the Woods', *Architects' Journal*, 20th November 1985, pp. 115–129.

24.6

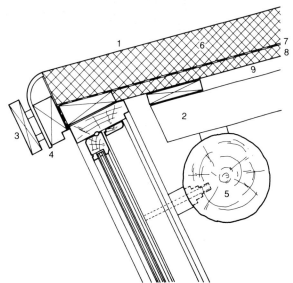

24.7

Sculpture Pavilion, Sonsbeek, The Netherlands
Architects:
Benthem Crouwel Architekten

25.1

General

The international sculpture exhibition at Sonsbeek in Arnhem, has, in the past provided scope for temporary pavilions by such leading lights as Gerrit Rietveld (1955), and Aldo van Eyck (1966). As a response to the theme of the 1986 exhibition, 'The Skin', Benthem Crouwel devised a transparent structure which provided an appropriate setting for the more delicate sculptures and allowed a direct relationship with the surrounding park (Figure 25.1).

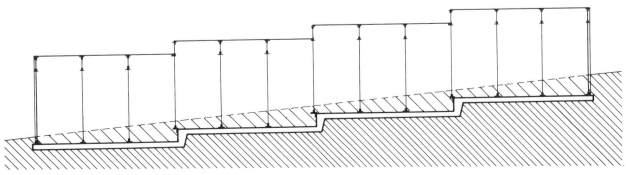

25.2

25.3
Exploded isometric of fin and truss. 1 700 × 250 mm stepped concrete footing; 2 100 × 50 × 4 mm steel angle; 3 M12 bolt; 4 3.65 m × 580 mm, 15 mm thick toughened glass fin; 5 60 × 60 × 4 mm steel angles of bottom boom; 6 60 × 60 × 4 mm steel angles of top boom; 7 20 mm diameter steel bar; 8 M12 bolt; 9 2 m × 3.65 mm, 10 mm toughened glass sheet; 10 140 × 60 × 4 mm patch plate; 11 M2 bolt; 12 120 × 10 mm polyurethane foam; 13 18 mm laminated glass sheet

Structural glazing

This pavilion is a direct development of the earlier relocatable house for Jan Benthem in Almere (see Brookes A.J., Grech C., *The Building Envelope*, Butterworth Architecture, 1990, p.5). By taking the idea of structural glazing even further this pavilion is a totally glazed 24 m long, 6.2 m wide, 3.65 m high transparent box (Figures 25.1 and 25.8).

Two stepped concrete footings march down the sloping site, just below the ground surface. Three M12 bolts clamp each glass fin to two steel angles that are in turn bolted to the concrete footings (Figures 25.3 and 25.5). The 15 mm thick toughened glass fins are 580 mm deep, 3.65 m high. The top of each fin is attached to a steel truss that spans across the pavilion (Figures 25.4, 25.6 and 25.7). These 600 mm deep trusses are made from a top and bottom boom of back to back 60 × 60 × 4 mm steel angles with 20 mm diameter diagonal members in between. At the bearing end of the truss the 20 mm bar is omitted to allow the glass fin to slot between the paired angles. Six M12 bolts pass through the angles clamping the glass in place. The trusses have a shallow pitch to help shed rainwater off the roof. End plates welded to the top and bottom booms provide fixing points from which the 2 m wide, 3.65 m high, 10 mm thick toughened glass side panels are hung. Patch plates on the outside face of the glass distribute the clamping pressure across the glass surface (Figure 25.8). A 2.5 mm thick felt pad separates glass from steel in all of these clamped joints. The roof glazing sits on a 120 mm wide, 10 mm thick pad of polyurethane foam, and is silicone-sealed to the top boom of the steel trusses.

The excavated earth is then replaced to a maximum depth of 800 mm (Figure 25.2), hiding the base fixing detail completely.

Conclusion

The overall minimalism, the way the glass walls plunge straight into the ground, the wood shavings forming a natural carpet at exactly the same level as the surrounding lawn, has prompted some critics to claim that this is not real architecture. This is an arguable point when discussing temporary pavilion structures. The value of this structure lies in its daring application of the structural properties of glass.

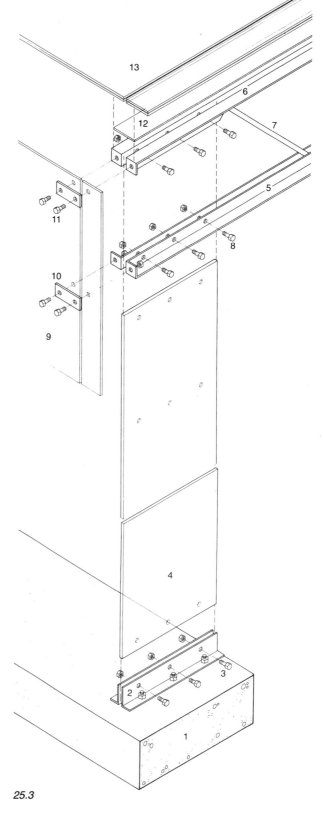

25.3

25.4
Vertical section through top of
fin. 1 15 mm toughened glass
fin; 2 60 × 60 × 4 mm steel
angle; 3 end plate; 4 M12 bolt;
5 2.5 mm thick felt pad; 6 120
× 10 mm polyurethane pad;
7 silicone sealant; 8 18 mm
laminated glass

25.5.
Vertical section through
bottom of fin. 1 15 mm
toughened glass fin; 2 100 ×
50 × 4 mm steel angle;
3 M12 bolt; 4 2.5 mm thick felt
pad; 5 M12 anchor bolt;
6 concrete strip foundation

25.6
Vertical section through side
wall. 1 18 mm laminated
glass; 2 60 × 60 × 4 mm top
boom; 3 60 × 60 × 4 mm
bottom boom; 4 60 × 60 ×
4 mm end plate; 5 10 mm
thick polyurethane pad;
6 10 mm laminated glass;
7 2.5 mm felt pad; 8 140 ×
60 × 4 mm patch plate;
9 M12 bolt

25.7
Horizontal section through
truss end. 1 15 mm toughened
glass fin; 2 60 × 60 × 4 mm
angle; 3 60 × 60 × 4 mm
end-plate; 4 M12 bolt;
5 10 mm polyurethane pad;
6 silicone sealant; 7 10 mm
toughened glass; 8 2.5 mm
felt pad; 9 140 × 60 × 4 mm
patch-plate

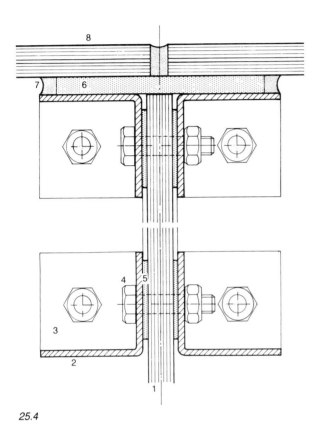

25.4

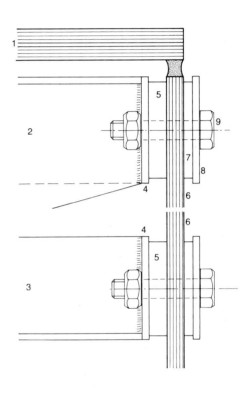

25.6

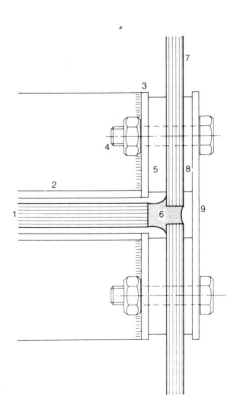

25.5

25.7

25.8
Side elevation of pavilion

25.8

Credits

Client: Stichting Sonsbeek Beelden, Arnhem
Structural engineer: ABT, Arnhem

References

Benthem Crouwel Architekten, 'Sculpture Pavilion, Sonsbeek '86', *Structure and Transparency: Benthem Crouwel Architekten BNA*, Edizioni Tecno 1988.

Buchanan, P., 'Barely There', *Architectural Review*, Vol. 182, No. 1087, September 1987, pp. 81–84.

B.u.C., 'Skulpturen-Pavillon in Arnheim/ Neiderlande', *Glasforum*, Vol. 37 No. 5, October 1987, pp. 35–38.

26

Sterling Hotel, Heathrow Airport
Architects:
Manser Associates

26.1

26.2

General

The Sterling Hotel is located a few minutes walk away from Heathrow Airport's Terminal 4. Sitting in the midst of a miasma of undistinguished airport buildings, this hotel asserts itself by making a bold statement about the British Airport Authority's commitment to commissioning high profile buildings. Manser Associates' hotel follows hard on the heals of Foster Associates' Stansted Airport Terminal Buildings.

The building's morphology is rooted in the aircraft hanger structures dotted around the airport (Figure 26.1). A 20 m wide central atrium space separates the two flanking five-storey blocks of double rooms (Figure 26.3). Raked ends maximise the impact of these elevations by exposing the slim lattice roof structure from which is suspended the full-height glazed end walls (Figure 26.2).

Structure

Almost 400 bedrooms are inserted into the

conventionally reinforced concrete table framed perimeter blocks. The roof over the central atrium space is supported on an independent steel structure. Circular hollow steel section columns (323.9 × 8 mm) support 25 m span steel lattice trusses. The slender columns are braced back to the concrete frame at each floor slab.

Cladding

The sleek external envelope is surprisingly achieved by a basic form of rainscreen cladding. Eternit Glasal panels form a cosmetic external skin to a lightweight wall construction that is rendered weatherproof by an aluminium foil with butyl taped joints (Figure 26.4). The flat fibre cement sheets are predrilled and fixed by monel rivets to vertical aluminium carrier rails. Plastic washers and caps mask the heads of the fixings. The carrier rails are also screwed back to the cement particle board outerskin of the wall. The rounded corner panels are fabricated from aluminium sheets, the colour match

26.1
General view from south

26.2
Internal view of atrium

26.3
(a) Typical floor plan.
1 Atrium; 2 bedrooms; 3 lifts.
(b) Cross-section.
1 Bedrooms; 2 atrium; 3 plant rooms; 4 pedestrian link to terminal 4; 5 vehicular access

26.4
Cut-away detail through external wall. 1 600 × 200 mm reinforced concrete column; 2 acoustic mastic seal; 3 2 no. 12 mm sheets of Pyrok; 4 acoustic resilient fixing; 5 Visqueen vapour barrier; 6 145 mm deep metal stud; 7 24 mm Pyrok outer skin; 8 flow lock high-grade butyl tape; 9 Omega and Zed channels, discontinued at each slab to allow for creep;

10 flow lock tape to joint;
11 Glasal panels; 12 concrete floor slab

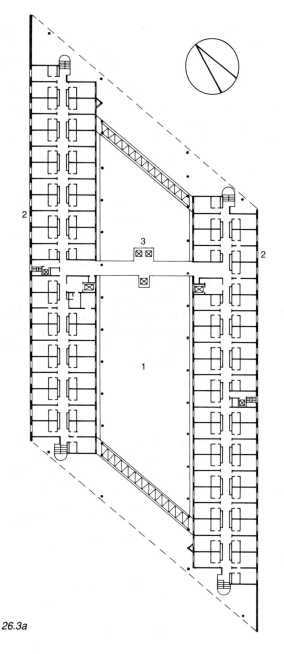

26.3a

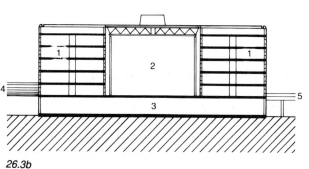

26.3b

26.4

of these powder-coated panels is a near perfect match to the Glasal panels.

The most significant environmental problem to be addressed on this site is the noise from aircraft taking off in the vicinity. The average maximum noise level from aircraft, excluding Concorde is 95 dB(A). The brief set design limits of $L_{10} - 35$ dB(A) and L_{max} (aircraft) -45 dB(A) for the bedrooms and slightly less onerous figures (-45 dB(A) and -55 dB(A) respectively) for the less-sensitive central atrium space. The fast track programme eliminated a traditional wet process in favour of the construction of metal stud panels clad with cement particle boards. The design team designed a wall construction made up of 150 mm deep galvanized steel framing studs with one layer of 24 mm cement particle board on the outer skin and two sheets of

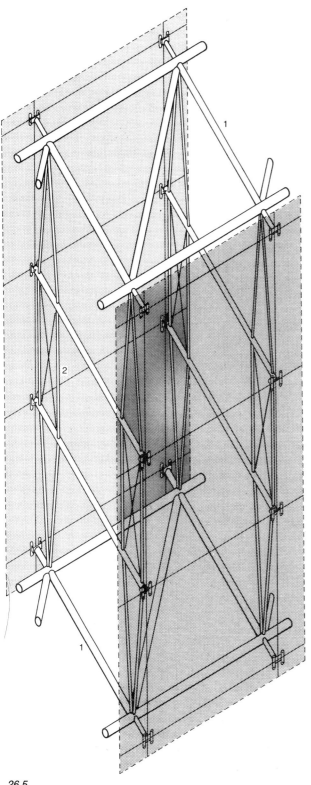

26.5.
Curtain wall arrangement.
1 Horizontal truss; 2 wishbone
structure

12 mm cement particle board on the inner skin. Inserted between the skins of cement particle board is 150 mm of dense rockwool. After acoustic tests the external wall construction was refined to tune its acoustic reduction performance. For example, resilient bars were introduced at the interface between stud and board, these reduce the area of contact between the two materials, thus reducing the proportion of sound transmitted through the fabric of the wall.

On-site assembly time was further reduced by the prefabrication of full-height metal stud panels which were then offered up to the concrete frame. Tolerances were taken up by the use of shims. Gaps were filled with an acoustic sealant to eliminate weak spots in the construction. The windows are formed from two sets of single-glazed aluminium framed units, separated by a 175 mm air space. The sides of this air space are lined with acoustic tiles. The outer window is sealed and uses 10 mm solar control silvered glass. The internal window is top hung with 12 mm clear glass.

Glazing

The requirement to achieve minimally structured glazed end walls and at the same time provide the acoustic reduction of the order already described precluded the use of the Pilkington's double glazed Planar System. The architect achieved the acoustic reduction by using two layers of single glazed Planar glazing set back-to-back. The 2.8 m air gap is determined by one unit of the cladding grid. This air gap is ideal for cleaning as well as environmental control.

Each glazed curtain is suspended from the outer edge of a boxed truss. A series of tubular steel 'wish-bone' structures carry the brackets which provide fixing points for each corner of the glass sheets. Three horizontal trusses transfer windloading back to the main structure (Figure 26.5).

The brackets to which the glass sheets are fixed should be compared to those at La Villette. (see Brookes A.J., Grech C., *The Building Envelope*, Butterworth Architecture, 1990, pp. 74–77). Budgetary constraints prevented the use of highly engineered stainless steel. Instead, painted mild steel flats are welded together in what the architects describe as 'agricultural' details (Figure 26.6 and

26.5

26.6
View of glazing fixing bracket

26.7.
Exploded isometric of glazing fixing. 1 8 mm solid stainless-steel rigging tie; 2 33.7 × 3.2 mm CHS of wishbone structure; 3 60.3 × 4 mm CHS; 4 12 mm thick plate with 9 × 18 mm slotted holes; 5 20 mm diameter stud with M12 thread each end; 6 Pilkington Planar 902 Mk II fixing; 7 M12 chrome-plated self-locking dome nut

26.6

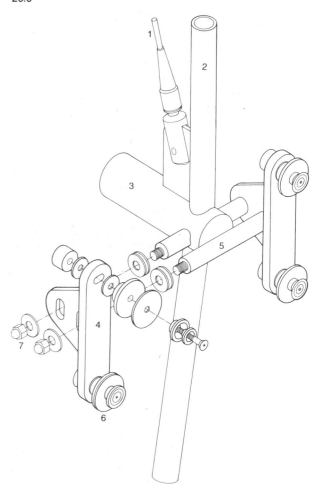

26.7

26.7). The brackets provide far less flexibility than those at La Villette. This is because the supporting steel structure provides greater stiffness due to its greater depth and closer centres. The only movement provided in the long term is at the joint between bracket and structure, where the bracket can rotate about a connecting bolt. The glazing is anchored at its base by a spring-loaded bracket.

The erection of the glazing called for pre-loading of the steel trusses to eliminate excessive deflection during the installation of the glass. Water tanks were suspended from the steel trusses and as each row of glass sheets was installed, the equivalent weight of water was drained from these tanks.

Services

The double glazed wall is also utilized as a buffer zone between internal and external environments, whose primary purpose is to eliminate the deposit of condensation. A variable mixture of fresh and recirculated air is introduced into this space; in winter the humidity in this zone is controlled by ducting cool fresh air which has a low percentage of moisture, along the inside face of the outer pane. The inner pane is kept as warm as possible by blowing warm recycled air up it.

A humidistat located in this zone controls the movement of air automatically. It is important to note that the term 'buffer zone' is in part a misnomer for the winter phase because its function increases the heat loss from the building. In the summer, air is extracted from this zone to prevent a temperature build up due to solar gain. There is no provision for cooling air introduced to this space.

Costs

This building was constructed in two years. It was completed in November 1990 at a total cost of £30 million (£1200/m²).

Credits

Client: BAA Hotels
Structural engineers: YRM Anthony Hunt Associates
Mechanical and electrical consultants: F C Foreman
Acoustic consultants: Hann Tucker
Management contractor: Higgs & Hill
Quantity surveyors: G.D.Walfords and Partners

References

Davies, C., 'Sterling Value', *Architects' Journal*, 13th March 1991, pp. 38–45.

Anon., 'External Walls and Roof', *Architects' Journal*, 13 March 1991, pp. 49–51.

Anon., *Deutsche Bautzeitung*, 4 April 1991, No. 125.

Welsh, J., 'Parallel Planes', *Building Design*, 25 January 1991, pp. 12–13.

Pearman, H., 'Parallelograms Revealed', *World Architecture* No. 11, 1991.

Walker, A., 'Flight Plans', *Designers' Journal*, March 1991.

Sydney Football Stadium
Architects: Phillip Cox, Richardson, Taylor and Partners Pty Ltd

27.1

General

Phillip Cox is well known for his romantic use of structural form to inform his designs. With buildings such as Yulara tourist village, with its canvas shade structures, and the Exhibition Centre at Darling Harbour (see Brookes, A.J., Grech, C., *The Building Envelope*, Butterworth Architecture, 1990, pp. 34–38) carried out with the engineers Ove Arup & Partners, also consultants on the Sydney Football Stadium.

Opened on Australia Day 1988, the Sydney Football Stadium (Figure 27.1), was built to relieve the burden on the adjacent cricket ground which had previously also been used for Australian-rules football games (Figure 27.2).

The client brief required that 38 500 people should be seated, 65% of whom should be under cover. The requirement was for an integrated sports centre with sports training facilities, tennis courts, squash courts, swimming pool and car parking all contained within a formal garden setting in Moore Park just 3 km south of the city centre (Figure 27.3).

Taking as precedent Wembley Stadium in

27.2

London, Santiago Bernabeau in Madrid and the Olympia Stadium in Seoul, this stadium was designed as an 'all round' or bowl form with the roof as a continuous undulating strip around the stadium.

As Cox himself remarked, "we settled for a bold statement of contrast and very careful attention to scale rather than any attempt towards camouflage or submersion within the environment, or any attempt to play it all down".

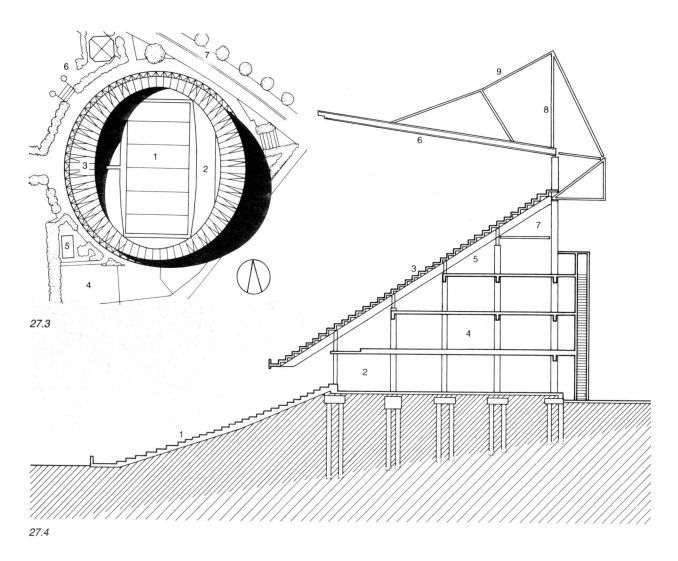

27.1
General view

27.2
Aerial view of football stadium
and cricket ground

27.3
Plan of football stadium.
1 Pitch; 2 seating; 3 canopy;
4 tennis courts; 5 swimming
pool; 6 car park; 7 Moor Park
Road

27.4
Section through stadium.
1 Terrace seating;
2 concourse; 3 grandstands;
4 reinforced concrete
structure; 5 raked beam;
6 suspended rafter beam;
7 space ties; 8 A-frame;
9 bifurcated tension/
compression members

27.3

27.4

Foundations

The site was underlain by two main geological strata with rock varying in depth from zero to 20 m below the surface. As a result of these factors two foundation systems were adopted; the west grandstand has 300 × 300 mm 'Hercules' precast concrete piles to a depth of 20 m and the north and south areas are supported on *in situ* concrete 'Frankipiles' varying from 400–500 mm in diameter, placed singly or in groups.

Concrete structure

The terrace slab of 150 mm thick *in situ* concrete was cast directly onto compacted subsoils and infill material. Seating tiers were later laid on top of this slab (Figure 27.4). Travelling formwork units designed to form eleven levels at a time were used for rapid construction.

The grandstand seating, raked at a 30° angle, consists of precast concrete planks spanning 8.5 m between steel raking beams (Figure 27.5). These beams which allow the grandstand to cantilever up to 10 m over the lower terrace are of steel since the constantly changing geometry makes it a cheaper alternative to the non-standard formwork required for concrete beams. Joints between the planks were waterproofed with a sealant joint with plates welded to each side of the top flange of the raking beam to form a gutter in case of water penetrating the joint. This back-up drainage is a useful principle in jointing assembly.

27.5
Typical structural bay.
1 Grandstand raking beam;
2 space truss; 3 triangulated
tie-down; 4 A-frame;
5 bifurcated tension/
compression members;
6 610 mm deep rafter UB;
7 in-plane roof bracing

27.6
View along terrace showing
cantilevered raking beam

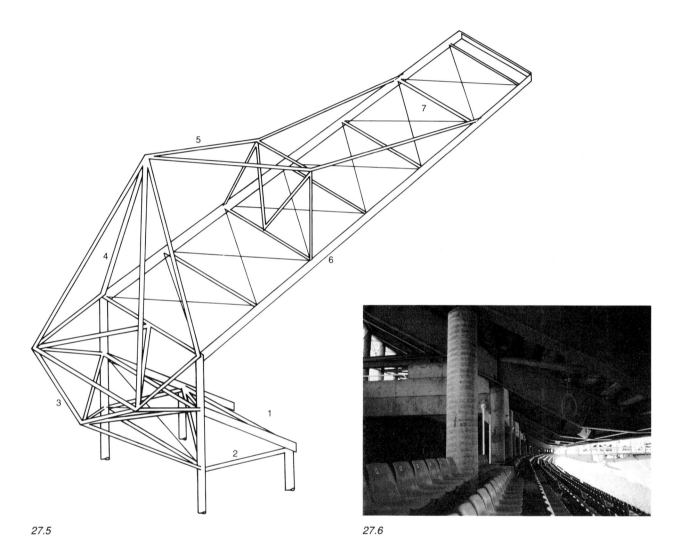

27.5

27.6

The preferred location for watching football is at the halfway line and the more spectators that can be gathered about this location the better. It is also preferable that they should have good sight lines. This was achieved by using tiers of seating which were slightly curved on plan with most of the seating on the east and west sides (Figure 27.3). Front-row seats are level with the players and the highest seats are 30 m above the field.

This gave rise to an undulating perimeter with a continuous 'saddle shape' roof rising high above the grandstand on the east and west and curving down at the two ends. This form had two additional advantages. It reduced the mass of the complex facing the houses on Moore Road to the north and also allowed floodlighting to be positioned along the front edge of the roof so that light spillage, a constant source of local irritation from the existing cricket ground, could be avoided.

To emphasize the dynamic resultant form the playing field was submerged 3 m below the natural ground level, thus increasing the sense of containment.

The steel raked beams are in turn supported by an *in situ* concrete structure which houses all the facilities and amenities for the football stadium.

Canopy structure

The cantilevered metal roof (Figure 27.5), which at its widest part cantilevers 30 m at the halfway line reducing to 10 m behind the goalposts, is supported

27.7

by a steel truss system (Figure 27.7). This transfers the upwards and downwards loads on the roof to the structure below, particularly to the perimeter columns.

As with the Lloyds Building in London, steel sections would have been preferred because they would be simpler to connect, but in order to meet fire proofing requirements they were encased in concrete. At Sydney these columns were encased in concrete before being erected. This precasting along the shafts of the columns was done on site using cardboard spirotube forms. Once erected the areas around the prefabricated connections were also clad in concrete.

The roof structure, (see the *Arup Journal*, Spring 1989) was formally made up of statically determinate independent structural systems in alternative bays with adjacent infill bays (Figure 27.8). These independent forms consist of suspended rafter beams rather reminiscent of the nodding toy bird which ballances on the edge of a glass.

The rafters support purlins which are clad above with profiled aluminium cladding. Perforated aluminium cladding is used to create a smooth soffit to the roof, the perforations act both to increase acoustic absorption and allow wind pressures to pass through and load the structural cladding above.

The elegant form of the roof is reflected in the design of the connections (Figure 27.9). Each connection after structural sizing was modelled by the architect with scale models and three-dimensional computer graphics. To add unusual contrast to the elevation and to minimize wind intrusion, the gap between the grandstands and the roof is partially covered by tensioned fabric using PVC coated polyester tensioned by galvanized steel cables. It is this care for detailing and the decision on scale and massing which has produced such a successful building completed on time and within budget.

Costs

The structure of the stadium cost $Aus 22 million out of a total budget of $Aus 62 million. 1600 tonnes of steel were used in the structure of the stadium, 1100 tonnes of which made up the roof structure.

27.9

27.8.

Credits

Client, project manager and main contractor:
Civil and Civic Pty Ltd
Engineers: Ove Arup and Partners Australia
Steelwork subcontractor: ICAL Ltd
Cladding subcontractor: Chadwick Industries Pty
Ltd

References

Towndrow. J., 'New Australian Functionalisms,'
    RIBA Journal April 1989.
Thompson P., Thomas V, Carfrae T., 'Sydney
    Football Stadium', *The Arup Journal*, Spring
    1990.
Anon., 'Philip Cox's Bicentennial Buildings for
    Sydney, *Architects' Review*, Vol. 184, October
    1988, pp. 66–72.
Anon. 'Sydney Football Stadium', *Constructional
    Review*, May 1988, Vol. 61, No. 2.

28

Tent, Hans Road, London
Engineers:
Whitby & Bird Engineers

28.1

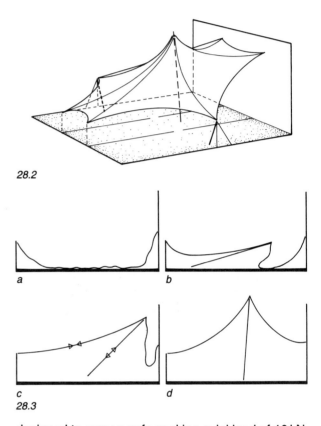

28.2

a

b

c

d

28.3

General

This temporary structure is erected annually over the gardens of three neighbouring Voysey houses to provide shelter for garden parties held there during London's unpredictable summer months. This tent's scale and efficiency of structure make it an interesting case study comparison with the other fabric structures covered in this book.

Structure

Lightweight PVC-coated polyester was identified as a suitable material to provide a canopy over the irregular plan of the combined gardens (Figure 28.1). A 7 m high mast located in the centre of the middle garden props up the fabric to form the main volume (Figure 28.2). The tent is anchored down at six points around its perimeter. At four of these points the tent boundary cables are attached to eye bolts which have been resin anchored to the existing brickwork. At the remaining two points, the fabric is attached to two struts which are themselves anchored to the garden floor.

The mast is prefabricated in three sections and is assembled in location to form a 7 m long element

designed to carry a safe working axial load of 10 kN and yet weighs as little as 7 kg. The triangular-sectioned mast is fabricated from three aircraft aluminium alloy tubes 25 mm in diameter with a wall thickness of 1.3 mm. The simple joints are formed from solid billets welded to one of the tubes which slot into the adjacent hollow tubes. A split pin locks the two halves of the joint in place. The pin is not designed to take any load, the compression forces in the mast are transmitted across the flat ends of the tubes that must bear against one another. Flat strips of aluminium join the three tubes to form a veerendeel mast.

A major factor in the mast design was the desire to keep its weight down to an absolute minimum. Consequently a form was developed which is effective in carrying axial loads, but with only minimal bending resistance. For this reason, Bob Barton the project engineer points out that a careful erection sequence must be followed (Figure 28.3) to maintain axial loads, using the tension forces in the fabric to help erection. As the top end of the mast is raised the tensioned fabric helps to reduce the bending moments induced by the loose fabric.

28.1
Internal view of tent

28.2
Diagrammatic view of tent

28.3
Erection sequence. (a) Fabric
perimeter fastened; (b) mast
head attached to fabric;
(c) tension in fabric relieves
bending moments;
(d) erection completed

28.4
Mast head detail. 1 30 mm
diameter solid aluminium bar;
2 steel sleeve; 3 300 mm
diameter steel ring; 4 webbing
belts; 5 PVC fabric; 6 3 no.
25 mm diameter by 1.3 mm
thick aluminium tubes

28.5
Mast foot detail. 1 3 no.
25 mm diameter by 1.3 mm
thick aluminium tubes;
2 30 mm diameter solid
aluminium bar; 3 60 mm
diameter steel circular hollow
section; 4 bolts fastened to
resin anchor sockets;
5 garden pavement

28.6
Fabric to strut detail

28.6

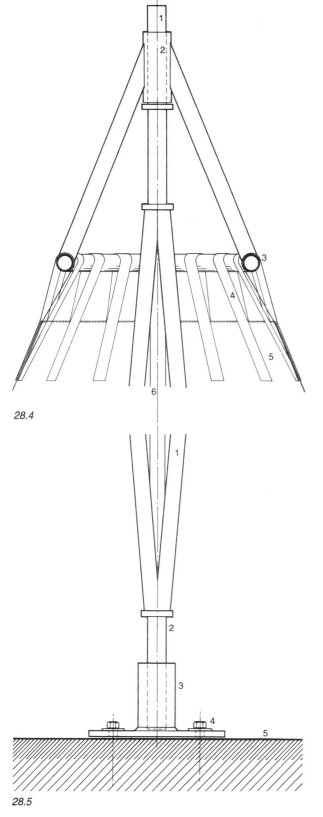

28.4

28.5

Fabric

The interface between mast and fabric is achieved
by an intermediate steel ring whose central
concentric sleeve slips over the end of the mast
(Figure 28.4) Webbing belts stitched to the fabric
wrap around the ring. This central portion, at the
apex of the tent is open to the sky and allows
ventilation. The foot of the mast fits into a sleeve
bolted to the ground (Figure 28.5).

At the fabric's anchor points, webbing belts wrap
around smaller 'dog rings'. Shackles join these rings
to the strut heads (Figure 28.6). Compression is
applied to the strut by means of webbing belts with
buckles borrowed from lorry awning technology.

Boundary cables running along the perimeter of
the fabric, also attached to the 'dog rings' can be
tightened to flatten the perimeter curves and
eliminate small wrinkles in the fabric due to minor
pattern errors.

Costs

The tent covers an approximate plan area of 180
m². The cost of the mast and associated aluminium
works was in the region of £1100. The fabric cost
approximately £11,000 at 1989 prices.

Credits

Client: Dorrington Properties Plc.
Structural engineer: Whitby & Bird Engineers
Fabric material supplier: Serge Ferrari
Fabric contractor: Architen
Aluminium contractor: Original Metal

29.1

254

Tent for the 700th Anniversary of the Swiss Confederation

Architect:
Mario Botta

General

Mario Botta was commissioned to design a demountable structure, capable of travelling around Switzerland, to serve as a 1450-seat auditorium for commemorative events to celebrate the 700th anniversary of the foundation of the Swiss Confederation (Figures 29.1–29.4). The tent will have spent the whole of 1991 touring eight of Switzerland's major cities.

All the parts that make up the tent's structure are prefabricated into elements small enough to be easily transported by road from one site to the next. The whole tent is packed away for transportation into approximately thirty army trucks.

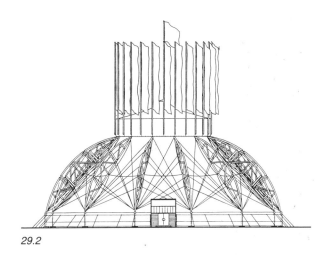

29.2

Structure

Viewed from a technological standpoint, this tent does not employ the most efficient means of enclosing the space required. However Mario Botta, who usually designs in more massive and substantial materials has chosen to confront contemporary media with a symbolic gravity influenced by the culture and architecture of the past. Such a philosophy, which refuses to isolate technology or to identify it as a purely 20th Century phenomenon, gives the tent a pedigree of historical precedent.

To this architect, structural pyrotechnics take a second place to the cultural significance of events which leave a deep impression on the popular memory. In a similar way, the installation of the obelisk in St Peter's Square, Rome, instigated by Pope Sixtus V under the supervision of the architect Domenico Fontana seemed to involve, not only an army of 800 workers, but the entire population of Rome (Figure 29.5). Consequently it is the dome-like silhouette of the thirteen trusses (one for each of the original cantons to sign the 'Eternal Pact' of 1291) supporting the steel crown with its 26 flagpoles (one for each of the current cantons), that is more important than the slimming down of elements and the refinement of joints.

Each of the thirteen radial trusses is split into three hinged sections. At the perimeter the trusses are pinned to steel columns which are supported on specially prepared, precast concrete pad

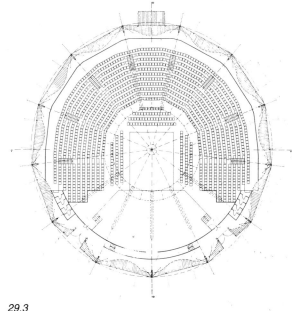

29.3

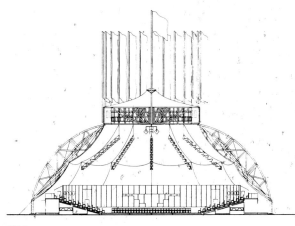

29.4

29.1
General view

29.2
Front elevation

29.3
Plan

29.4
Section

29.5
Erection of obelisk in St Peter's Square

29.6
Assembly of crown

29.7
Folded trusses attached to crown

29.8
Crown being raised

29.9
Crown raised to its full extent and trusses fully extended

29.5

29.6

29.7

29.8

29.9

29.10
Exploded isometric of hinged
joint at top boom of truss.
1 60 mm diameter, 280 mm
long steel pin; 2 121 mm
diameter threaded cap with
fastening lugs for steel
cables; 3 60 mm thick steel
stiffener plate welded to;
4 30 mm thick elliptical steel
end plate; 5 193.7 mm
diameter, 6.3 mm thick

circular hollow section top
boom; 6 88 mm thick pierced
plate

29.11
1 50 mm diameter, 300 mm
long steel pin; 2 193.7 mm
diameter, 6.3 mm thick
circular hollow section top
boom; 3 193.7 mm diameter,
10 mm thick circular hollow
section bottom boom;
4 60 mm thick steel plate;
5 50 mm diameter, 217 mm
long steel pin; 6 top of
adjustable steel column

foundations. These columns are telesoopic and can be adjusted to the level differences of the site. The other end of each truss is pinned to a substantial circular steel truss which when in its final position, forms the tent's crown. This crown is assembled at ground level (Figure 29.6) connected to the thirteen truss ends and raised by three hydraulic rams. It is at this moment that the importance of the hinged trusses is apparent. The radius distance between centre of the tent to supporting perimeter column remains constant, but as the crown is raised, the vertical dimension, and therefore the hypotenuse of the triangle increases. The rotation of the truss sections and the resulting straightening out provides this increase in length (Figures 29.7–29.9). At full extension the hinges lock the trusses in a flat plane. Taken in isolation from the totality of the structure, some of the joints may seem clumsy. However, on analysis this criticism is mitigated by the highly specialized requirements of these members. These details merit close examination because they demonstrate a clear structural logic and an explicit articulation of junctions in a building whose component members must cope with a greater degree of movement even than most demountable buildings.

Figure 29.10 shows the hinge detail between each section of the truss. The hinges are located at the top and bottom boom of each section. A 60 mm diameter steel pin provides the pivot. At one end of each pin are welded two lugs to which steel ties can be anchored. The central section of each hinge has a protruding tongue which acts as a stop to prevent the truss from rotating further than 180°. The forces in the hinge are transferred back to the steel tubes by means of a 30 mm thick elliptical steel plate welded to the circular hollow sections at the mitred joint. The total weight of the steel structure is 120 tons.

Figure 29.11 shows the junctions between the lower end of a truss and the supporting column. An intermediate component, pierced by two 50 mm diameter pins permits rotation in horizontal and vertical planes. The additional flanges on the truss-end accommodate more steel pins to which a multitude of steel ties can be anchored. Horizontal steel plates at the top of each column provide a connection for the circular sectioned spars that form a ring beam around the tent at 'eaves' level.

One major advantage of this method of erection

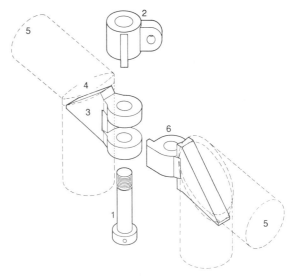

29.10

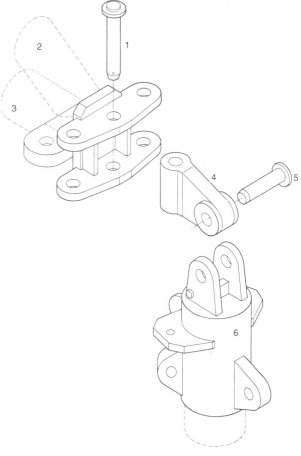

29.11

29.12
Mario Botta sketches

means that the size of components remains small, thus facilitating transportation to and around each of the constricted sites. In addition, all tension forces are resolved at the foot of each steel column so that there are no anchor ties more than 2.5 m outside the footprint of the building enclosure. The tent was first erected in the restricted courtyard of Bellinzona Castle (Figure 29.1).

Tent fabric

A silver grey Trevira-Polyester PVC fabric is suspended from the external structure to give the impression of soft drapes enclosing the internal space. A total of 2600 m^2 of fabric weighing 3300 kg is used to enclose the auditorium.

The roof fabric is a single membrane without any additional insulation. Self contained mobile units provide heating for the tent.

An independent ground supported tiered structure provides a platform for the specially designed seating.

Working method

That the finished building is so little changed from the architect's initial sketches (Figure 29.12) is testimony of the power and clarity of the initial design concept.

The detail design of this unfamiliar building type could not be dealt with in the usual way where Mario Botta considers every last detail. A shortage of in-house experience of complex steel structures lead to the use of a performance-type specification whereby the architect issued sketches and outline 1:50 drawings to the engineer who, in conjunction with the steelwork fabricator, resolved the structure and developed all the details. The steelwork shop drawings were finally submitted to the architects for inspection prior to fabrication. Although this form of procedure is rare on the continent, it is standard practice in the UK.

Cost

The estimated cost of this demountable building is approximately one million Swiss Francs. However, this does not include for erection which was carried out by the Swiss army. The architect donated his services free of charge.

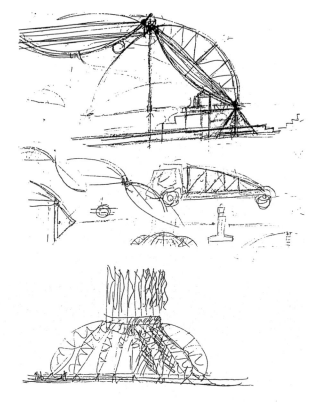

29.12

Credits

Client: Eidg. Department des Innern. Eidg. Volks-wirtschaftsdepartement.
Structural engineer: R. Passera & M. Pedretti, Lugano.
Steelwork fabricator: Officine Franzi Sa, Lugano.
Tent fabric supplier: Bieri Blachen AG, Grosswanden.

References

Carloni T., Pilet J., Szeeman H., *La Tenda*, Edizioni Casagrande Sa, Bellinzona, 1991.
Gazzaniga L., Mario Botta, 'Tenda per il 700°b della Confederazione Elvetica,' *Domus*, March 1991, No. 725, pp. 1–3.
Anon, 'Tent's Movement' *Architects' Journal*, 13 February 1991, p. 13.

Visitors' Centre, Cardiff Bay
Architects:
Alsop Störmer

30.1

General

In March 1990 the Cardiff Bay Development Corporation held a competition for a Visitors' Centre intending to focus attention on the redevelopment of the largely derelict docklands. The competition results were announced in March, Alsop, Lyall and Störmer had been selected to carry out their scheme on an optimistic programme that required the building to be completed and ready for use by the end of May that year. The building was eventually completed October 1991.

Although the building was required to comply with all current planning and building control requirements, its temporary nature meant that a relaxed attitude could be taken regarding the customary concerns of longevity and liability, freeing the architects to make a bold and dramatic statement (Figure 30.1). Although the end result may seem crude it is worth examining some of the details because they demonstrate a simplicity that is wholly appropriate to this type of structure.

Structure

The tubular body of the visitors' centre is divided into 21 2.4 m wide bays. Each bay of structure is assembled on the ground and lifted onto a four-legged support structure (Figures 30.2 and 30.3). Of the three concrete strip foundations, the central one provides a footing for the galvanized steel support legs and the two outside strips provide an anchor for the ties that, when attached to the ends of the support legs stabilize the structure (Figure 30.4).

Each structural bay is made up from four prefabricated ladders which are bolted together to form the oval frame. These ladders are welded up from perimeter steel angles, 2.4 m apart linked by steel battens at 1.2 m centres. The spacing of the bays and the battens is critical to avoid any cutting of the standard 2.4x1.2 m sheets of Douglas fir plywood (Figure 30.3). Two different thicknesses of plywood are used to allow bending of the sheets to the varying curvature of the frame. A 19 mm plywood is used on the shallower top and bottom

30.1
General view

30.2
One structural bay being
lowered into position, with
ladder frame sections in
foreground

30.3
Diagram of frame assembly.
1 Concrete strip foundations;
2 ladder frame structure;
3 support structure; 4 plywood
sheets with slits; 5 membrane
covering

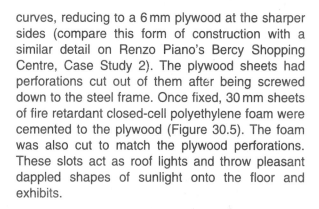

30.2

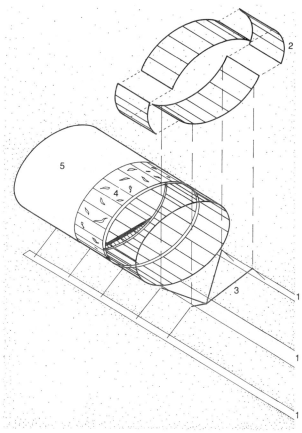

30.3

curves, reducing to a 6 mm plywood at the sharper sides (compare this form of construction with a similar detail on Renzo Piano's Bercy Shopping Centre, Case Study 2). The plywood sheets had perforations cut out of them after being screwed down to the steel frame. Once fixed, 30 mm sheets of fire retardant closed-cell polyethylene foam were cemented to the plywood (Figure 30.5). The foam was also cut to match the plywood perforations. These slots act as roof lights and throw pleasant dappled shapes of sunlight onto the floor and exhibits.

Membrane skin

The Hostaflon membrane is a PVC-coated polyester fabric stretched around three-quarters of the building. The membrane is anchored down to the plywood sheets by means of screws which have their own plastic covers to maintain the weathertightness of the membrane. Nylon belts stitched to the perimeter of the fabric membrane at 2.4 m intervals are threaded through ratchet buckles borrowed from lorry awning technology (Figure 30.6). The buckle is fixed directly to steel D-rings welded to the elliptical steel frame. The ratchet allows a permanent tension to be applied to the fabric.

Costs

The total building cost, including fitting out came to £420 000, giving an area cost of £850/m². The 1000 m² of fabric accounted for £22 000 of that sum. The total cost may seem higher than would be expected for a temporary building; this is mainly due to the costs associated with an accelerated programme.

30.4
View of support structure, stabilizing rods and membrane fastenings

30.5
Section through external skin. 1 Steel angles forming sides of ladder frame; 2 20 mm spacer; 3 19 mm wbp Douglas fir plywood to achieve Class 0 surface spread of flame; 4 30 mm fire retardant closed cell polyethylene foam; 5 PVC-coated fabric; 6 membrane fixing screw with plastic cover

30.6
Exploded isometric of junction between support structure and membrane fastenings. 1 Steel angles forming side of ladder frame; 2 ends of support legs; 3 fork end of stabilizing rod; 4 D-lugs welded to steel angles; 5 ratchet buckle

30.4

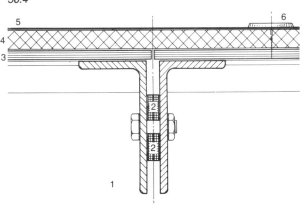

30.5

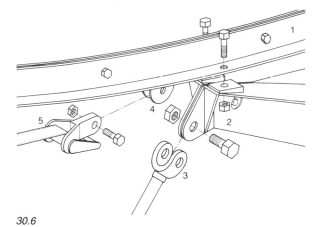

30.6

Credits

Client: Cardiff Bay Development Corporation.
Structural engineer: Atelier 1
Quantity surveyor: Roger Farrow
Mechanical consultant: Rybka, Smith, Ginsler & Battle
Main contractor: Constructors Tern
Steelwork subcontractors: Sheetfabs (Nott'm) Ltd
Fabric subcontractors: Landrell Fabric Engineering

References

Murray, C., 'On the Dock of the Bay', *Architects' Journal*, 24 April 1991, pp. 26–29.

Anon, 'Visitors' Centre, Alsop, Lyall & Störmer', *Architects Journal*, 24 April 1991, pp. 42–45.

Welsh, J., 'Star Roll', *Building Design*, 2 November 1991, pp. 32–33.

Welsh, J., 'Will Power', *Building Design*, 12 October 1991, p. 15.

Brookes, A.J., Stacey, M., 'Product Review', *AJ Focus*, July 1991, p. 38.

Acknowledgements

We are indebted to numerous colleagues for their help, advice and encouragement, especially partners Mike Stacey, Nik Randall and Andy Fursdon of Brookes Stacey Randall Fursdon for hosting and tolerating our activities, Richard Hind our research assistant and Jane Anderson for assistance in all forms of word processing.

We were especially encouraged in our work by the widespread generosity of the practices featured in affording us time and resources. Although we cannot list all those involved we would like to mention the following: Bob Barton, Pierre Botschi, Simon Conolly, Bill Dunster, Mick Eekhout, Ron Herron, Shunji Ishida, Françoise-Hélène Jourda, Mark Lovell, John Lowe, Jonathan Manser, Prof. Volkwin Marg, Pankaj Pandya, Bernard Plattner, and John Pringle. We are also indebted to the following for assistance in sourcing our illustrations: Pauline Shirley of Ove Arup and Partners, Carla Garbatto and Francois Bertolero of Renzo Piano Building Workshop, Britt Baffert and Isabelle Maisoneuve of Jourda and Perraudin and Claudia Hoge and Harriet Watson of the Richard Rogers Partnership. Our thanks also to Karin Möllfors, Marian Farraday, Adriana Barnhard, Paula Pellandini, Katy Harris, Michael Jones and Fiona Millar.

Photographic credits

Reasonable care has been taken by the authors to ascertain copyright sources, however in the case of error they offer their apologies and would welcome correction.

Alsop Störmer, 30.1, 30.2, 30.4
Ambler, G., 27.2
Arup Associates, 22.1, 22.6, 22.7
Baines, R., intro 6
Barton, B., 28.6
Benthem Crouwel Architekten, 25.1, 25.8
Berengo Gardin, G., 1.6, 1.7, 1.12, 2.6
Bertin, F., 16.1, 16.3
Botta, M., 29.12
Brookes, A. J., 2.3, 27.9
Charles, M., 7.1, 7.7, 14.1, 23.13, 24.1
Cook, P., 24.6
Courtauld Institute of Art, 29.5
Couturier, S./Archipress, 13.1, 13.6, 19.7
Davies, R., 6.1, 6.9
Donat, J., 24.2
Fessy, G./Editions du Demi-Cercle, 19.1
Foster, N., intro 3
Fotodesign Esch, 17.1, 17.2
Gabb, C., 9.2
Gibbons, B., 20.2
Grech, C., 2.2, 2.10, 5.1, 8.7, 15.6, 15.7, 15.8, 22.5, 23.1, 23.9, 23.10, 26.1, 26.2, 26.6
Ian Ritchie Architects (Jocelyne van den Bossche), 20.1
Kinold, K., 18.1, 18.2, 18.5, 18.6, 18.7, 18.8
Lämsa, 11.1
Lehesmaa, E., 11.2, 11.3, 11.4, 11.9, 11.10
Mandelmann, E., 16.2
Musi, P., 29.1, 29.6, 29.7, 29.8, 29.9
O'Mahoney, E., 3.1, 3.5, 3.9
Ove Arup Partnership, intro 5, 1.8, 1.9, 1.11, 27.1, 27.6, 27.7, 27.8
Pacciorini, M., 5.4
Peck, J. and Reid, J., 10.1, 10.3, 10.6, 10.8
Randle, J., 14.9
RPBW, 1.2, 1.3, 1.6, 1.7, 1.12, 2.6
Savioli, A., 15.1, 15.4
Sekiya, M., 1.1, 21.2
Stacey, M., 8.5, 8.8
Threlfall, H., 8.4
van der Vlugt & Claus, 12.1, 12.7, 12.8
Weinreb, M., 9.1
YRM/AHA, 8.2